Voices of Taiwanese Women

Three Contemporary Plays

Voices of Taiwanese Women

Three Contemporary Plays

JOHN B. WEINSTEIN, EDITOR

East Asia Program
Cornell University
Ithaca, New York 14853

The Cornell East Asia Series is published by the Cornell University East Asia Program (distinct from Cornell University Press). We publish books on a variety of scholarly topics relating to East Asia as a service to the academic community and the general public. Address submission inquiries to CEAS Editorial Board, East Asia Program, Cornell University, 140 Uris Hall, Ithaca, New York 14853-7601.

國立台灣文學館贊助出版
Publication of this volume is supported by the
National Museum of Taiwan Literature.
Cover Image: Production photo of *One Year, Three Seasons*.

Number 177 in the Cornell East Asia Series
Copyright © 2015 Cornell University East Asia Program. All rights reserved.
ISSN 1050-2955
ISBN: 978-1-939161-57-4 hc
ISBN: 978-1-939161-77-2 pb
ISBN: 978-1-942242-77-2 ebook
Library of Congress Control Number: 2015945074
Printed in the United States of America

*For my parents, Ronald and Mary
and my husband, Brian*

Contents

Acknowledgments

L ike any successful theater production, this volume is the result of the collective work of many, and I find myself, as editor, feeling the same kind of gratitude I feel when directing a play. I would like to begin by thanking my direct collaborators, the playwrights and translators whose talents were fundamental to my even undertaking this project: Hsu Rey-Fang, Yawtsong Lee, Peng Ya-Ling, Wang Chi-Mei, and Wang Wan-Jung. Through translating their words from Chinese, and editing their words in English, I have gotten to know each of them more deeply as artists and as people. Thank you as well to their staffs at the Tainaner Ensemble and the Uhan Shii Theatre Group.

I also received much administrative support from the team. Hsu Rey-Fang took charge of the arrangements for many of my visits to Tainan, and she made sure that I experienced the warmth and beauty of her home-town. Wang Wan-Jung spearheaded our subvention application, and she has been a vital support to me every step of the way. Wang Chi-Mei, as the senior scholar of our group and a teacher to many of us, spurred all of us onward, always modeling the highest artistic and scholarly standards in her own work as both playwright and translator. This group has truly become my Taiwanese family.

The publication of this volume would not have been possible without a generous subvention from the National Museum of Taiwan Literature in Tainan. Thank you to the museum for encouraging translation of Taiwanese literature into English, and for including drama translation within the scope of their subvention grants. Nor would publication have been possible without the Cornell East Asia Series and their willingness to take on this project.

Thank you in particular to Managing Editor Mai Shaikhanuar-Cota for shepherding this first-time editor through the multiyear publication process.

For my interest in Taiwan that forms the root of this work, I thank my doctoral advisor, David Der-wei Wang. When I first entered his classroom at Columbia University, I was quite committed to studying mainland literature, so much so that I had rather resented having to learn traditional characters at Harvard College, given that I would never be traveling to Taiwan anyway. When Professor Wang introduced me to Taiwanese literature, he changed my world. By the time I sought traveling fellowships for my dissertation research—which was nearly all focused on mainland theater—I wanted to go nowhere more than Taiwan.

A Fulbright grant to Taiwan, for 1997–1998, gave me that opportunity, and I thank the Foundation for Scholarly Exchange for the support and opportunities they provided me that year. Thank you in particular to Director Wu Jing-jyi, Julie Hu, and the entire staff of the FSE office. During that year, I saw the 1997 production of *The Phoenix Trees Are in Blossom*, among many other fine plays. On a second trip to Taiwan in 2000, funded by a grant from the China and Inner Asia Council of the Association for Asian Studies, I saw the original production of *One Year, Three Seasons*. In 2005, I traveled to Taiwan to present on both plays at a conference sponsored by the International Center for Tainan Area Humanities and Social Sciences Research and the Tainan County Government, who later published my paper in a conference volume. Thank you to Fiorella Allio and Lin Yu-ju for including me in the conference and publication, and to the Tainan City Government for permission to republish portions of my paper in the introduction to this volume.

The bulk of the collaborative translating occurred during my 2007 sabbatical as a visiting professor in the Department of Drama Creation and Application at the National University of Tainan. In addition to collaborators Rey-Fang and Wan-Jung, both of whom are on the faculty of that department, I would like to thank Department Chair Lin Mei-chun and Lu Chi Hua for hosting me so warmly. The draft of this volume received a needed boost with two intensive weeks of collaborative work in Tainan in 2011, when I received a Taiwan Scholars Grant from the Ministry of Education, R.O.C., administered by the Boston TECO Office. Thank you to Director Chou, Shan-nan Chang, and Angela Yao for offering me that opportunity at a pivotal moment in this project. Timed with the 2015 book release, *Wen Hsun Magazine* is including articles about this book in the December issue; thank you to Editor-in-Chief De-ping Feng and writer Ya-xian Xu for their contributions.

The time spent on this project, from start to finish, has encompassed three jobs for me, each of which has played a role. Most recently, as Principal and Dean of the Early College at Bard High School Early College–Newark, I have had the good fortune to have faculty, staff, and students who made it possible for me to lead a campus while still completing scholarly projects important to me. Prior to that, I taught on the faculty of Bard College at Simon's Rock for nearly a decade. In that time, my administrators, colleagues, and students gave me an intellectual and artistic home without which this project would never have arisen, as well as repeated financial support from the Simon's Rock Faculty Development Fund.

Interestingly, my first job, as Faculty in Chinese and theater at what is now Bard High School Early College–Manhattan has the most direct linkage to this project. I staged an earlier version of the translation of *One Year, Three Seasons* there in 2002, and that production's success planted the seed that bears fruit now, many years later. I would like to give special thanks to the students who participated in that workshop and performance: Nikita Anikeev, Bahiyyah Asante, Reyna Bonaparte, Giovanni Cruz, Janiquwa Dais, Jillian Gritz, Dwight Hodgson, Kenyetta Jefferson, Veronica Marquez, Ally Morales, Jessica Perez, Nyla Rock, Jolene Rodriguez, Nicole Rodriguez , LaToya Smith, and Jonathan Williams. Even now, when I read through this final translation, theirs are the voices I hear.

I have also benefited from the support of colleagues in my field, both inside and outside my institutions. Thank you to those who always answered my late-night questions about how to translate a certain word or term: Claire Conceison, Scott Simon, Chuan-Chih Chiara Wang, Biyuan Yang, and Carsey Yee. Thanks as well to Sung-Peng Hsu and Zooey Salazar for reviewing portions of the manuscript and sharing their thoughts with me. Organizationally, thank you to the Association for Asian Performance for providing me with so many opportunities to present portions of this work at conferences and to receive helpful feedback. When it came time to include Hakka romanization, I was fortunate to find Karen Cheung and her Hakka Mauritians website, www.hakkamauritians.org. Beyond learning that Hakka have emigrated to Mauritius, I also learned about the *Hakka pinyin* system. Karen offered to provide *Hakka pinyin* for all of the words I needed, and I thank her deeply for her contribution.

In this volume, we have aspired to create translations that are as performable as they are readable, with the hope that English-speaking theaters will share these women's stories with their audiences. To that end, all three plays had readings with professional actors, to check for elements confusing to those culturally unfamiliar with the subject matter, or word choices that, while accurate to the original, could not flow, as Hamlet might say, "trippingly on the tongue." I would to thank Jim Frangione of the Berkshire Playwrights Lab in Great Barrington, Massachusetts, for his generosity in organizing these readings. And thank you to the actors who gave their time and insights: Annie Considine, Joan Coombs, Deann Halper, Stephanie Hedges, Hana Kenny, Jake Ireland, Summer Plouffe Vogel, Tod Randolph, Johnny Segalla, and Alexander Sovronsky, as well as stage manager Zoe Hu.

This volume on Taiwanese women would not have come into being without the steadfast support of an American man, my husband Brian Mikesell. Like Xiang-lian's beloved Wen-tai, Brian has, for nearly two decades, supported my need to fly across the ocean, spending weeks or even months at a time in Taiwan, in order to pursue my research and complete this project. Thankfully, unlike Xiang-lian and Wen-tai, we did not put off our marriage, but instead have enjoyed our married life together for the past ten years.

The final thanks must go to my parents, Mary and Ronald Weinstein. When their six-year-old son declared out of the blue that he wanted to learn Chinese, they could easily have brushed that wish aside, taking it as a momentary whim that would be quickly forgotten. Instead, they found a way for me to study the language, at a time when Chinese language learning options for a six-year-old without Chinese heritage were nearly nonexistent. Over the decades-long journey from that initial wish to the publication of this volume, they have always been there for me, whenever I needed them. They have waited many years to see my first book in print—I hope it fulfills their dreams for their loving and grateful son.

Note on Romanization

Romanization is a complex matter in Taiwan. The *Hanyu pinyin* system, official on the mainland since the late 1950s and increasingly standard internationally, was only recently officially adopted in Taiwan. Though now official, its usage is far from consistent. Romanized place names in Taiwan were originally derived from the Wade-Giles system, and to minimize confusion I use the spellings still most commonly found on maps, such as Taipei and Kaohsiung. The majority of people in Taiwan romanize their names with a variant of Wade-Giles, often altering the less intuitive letters, adding capitals, and/or omitting apostrophes. All three playwrights within this collection are examples of these practices: Hsu Rey-Fang instead of the "correct" Hsu Jui-fang, Peng Ya-Ling instead of P'eng Ya-ling, and Wang Chi-Mei instead of Wang Ch'i-mei. For the real people named in this volume, I use their preferred spellings when known. For most of the fictional characters, and for people whose preferred spellings I do not know, I use *pinyin*, even though some in Taiwan may find that inauthentic. As a nod to an evolving Taiwanese custom, I have added the hyphen between the two syllables of the given name, a hyphen used by many in Taiwan who do choose to write their name in *pinyin*.

Romanization systems for the Taiwanese language have been evolving, as that language gains increasingly widespread and official status. The romanization system currently promoted by the government is *Taiwan Minnanyu luomazi pinyin fang'an* (*Tai-uan Ban-lam-gu lo-ma-ji phing-im hong-an*), literally "romanized *pinyin* system for Minnan language in Taiwan," and often abbreviated as *Tai-lo* or *TL*. In the bilingual play *The Phoenix Trees Are in Blossom*, within the translation itself *Tai-lo* is used for most names of people and places in the scenes performed in Taiwanese, though to diminish confusion, certain words appear in *pinyin* (such as Li Xianglan, predominantly associated with the scenes performed in Mandarin) or in frequent English renderings (such as Taipei). For both *The Phoenix Trees Are in Blossom* and *One Year, Three Seasons*, I include Conversion Charts showing the corresponding Chinese characters, *pinyin*, *Tai-lo* and, where relevant, Japanese for proper names and other words I thought might be of interest to readers. Similarly, *We Are Here* has Conversion Charts for Chinese characters, *pinyin*, and the Hakka romanization system called *Hakka pinyin (HagFa PinYim)*. In all three plays, Chinese and Japanese names appear in their traditional order, with surnames preceding given names.

List of Illustrations

List of Tables

Glossary

Most items are alphabetical by *pinyin*; preferred spellings of personal names are used when known.

benshengren	本省人
Biaoyan gongzuofang	表演工作坊
Dai wo qu kan yu	帶我去看魚
Dangdai Taiwan shequ juchang	當代台灣社區劇場
Danjiang daxue	淡江大學
Ding Nai-chu	丁乃竺
Fenghuanghua kaile	鳳凰花開了
Fuzhi xinniang	複製新娘
Guoli Chenggong daxue	國立成功大學
Guoli Taibei yishu daxue	國立台北藝術大學
Guoli yishu xueyuan	國立藝術學院
Guotuo juchang	果陀劇場
Guoyu	國語
Heluo	河洛
Hsu Rey-Fang	許瑞芳
Huadeng jutuan	華燈劇團
huaju	話劇
Huanxi banxituan	歡喜扮戲團
Jide Xiang Gang	記得香港
Kejiaren	客家人
Lai Sheng-chuan	賴聲川
Lanling jufang	蘭陵劇坊
Lee Kuo-shiu	李國修
Li Xianglan	李香蘭

Lin Keh-hua	林克華
Lin Weiyu	林偉瑜
Linjiedian juxianglu	臨界點劇象錄
Liu Mei-Yin	劉梅英
Minnan	閩南
Peng Ya-Ling	彭雅玲
Pingfeng biaoyanban	屏風表演班
shequ juchang	社區劇場
Shequ jutuan huodong tuizhan jihua	社區劇團活動推展計劃
shiyanju	實驗劇
Taidong jutuan	台東劇團
Tainanren jutuan	台南人劇團
Taiwan chaburen de gushi	台灣查埔人的故事
Taiwan gaobai	台灣告白
Taiyu	台語
Tiantang lüguan	天堂旅館
waishengren	外省人
Wang Chi-Mei	汪其楣
Wang Yüeh	王月
Wenhua jianshe weiyuanhui	文化建設委員會
Wenjianhui	文建會
Women zai zheli	我們在這裡
wutaiju	舞台劇
Xiang-lian	香蓮
xiao juchang	小劇場
Yinian sanji	一年三季
zhuanye juchang	專業劇場

Introduction[1]

Community Theater in the Taiwanese Context

JOHN B. WEINSTEIN

This anthology introduces three new translations representing an aspect of modern Asian drama largely unavailable in English to readers and theatergoers: the community-based theaters of Taiwan, working in Chinese languages beyond Mandarin. Community theater (*shequ juchang*) contrasts with the more mainstream theater that has emerged in Taiwan from the 1980s onward—a theater dominated by male playwrights, centered in the capital city of Taipei, and, despite its roots as an experimental "Little Theater Movement" inspired by oppositional politics and alternative aesthetics, increasingly commercial and professionalized.[2] Community theater, conversely, has maintained the more fluid line between professional and amateur that initially characterized contemporary Taiwan theater; it exists primarily outside of the capital, in regional cities like Tainan; and the driving forces, artistically and administratively, have historically been women. Taiwan's community theaters have become a key site for the expression of women's creative voices on the contemporary Taiwan stage.

---

[1] Portions of this introduction were previously published in John B. Weinstein, "The Streets of Tainan: A Local Path for Taiwanese Theater," in *Nanyi de lishi, shehui yu wenhua lunwenji*, eds. Lin Yu-ju and Fiorella Allio (Tainan: Tainan County Government, 2008), 431–44.

[2] For a history of the Little Theater Movement, including the evolution of the relevant terminologies, see Chung Mingder, "The Little Theater Movement of Taiwan (1980–89): in search of alternative aesthetics and politics" (PhD diss., New York University, 1992).

The plays presented here highlight two major groups in Taiwan who, while ethnically Chinese, are not Mandarin speakers. Taiwan is a multilingual society, but for many years the government suppressed that multilingualism as an act of political hegemony. Mandarin, the Beijing-based Chinese language, was brought over when China reclaimed Taiwan from Japanese occupation in 1945 and became the official tongue. It acquired the name *Guoyu*, meaning "national language," despite being anything but that, for it is not the native language of the majority. The majority language is the *Minnan* dialect of southern Fujian Province, the language brought by immigrants who came to Taiwan from Fujian beginning in the seventeenth century. In Taiwan today, their language is now called either "Taiwanese" (*Taiyu*) or, for those eager not to inscribe yet another "national language" discourse, "Hok-lo" or "Ho-lo" (*Heluo*), after the name for the people of Fujian as pronounced in their own language. After decades of being officially forbidden in school, the language is now a school subject, with government-developed textbooks.

The first and third plays in this volume, Hsu Rey-Fang's *The Phoenix Trees Are in Blossom* (*Fenghuanghua kaile*, 1994, revised 1997) and Wang Chi-Mei's *One Year, Three Seasons* (*Yinian sanji*, 2000) use scenes in the Taiwanese language to portray members of the ethnic group descended from those immigrants from Fujian Province. When these two plays were written in the late twentieth century, this group was often referred to in English as "native Taiwanese," and in Chinese as *benshengren*, literally "people of this province." The term "native Taiwanese" can be slightly confusing, given that Taiwan does have an equivalent of "native Americans," the Austronesian peoples—called "Aborigines" in Taiwan—who already inhabited the island when the Fujianese immigrants arrived. The same word used to name the language, "Hok-lo" or "Ho-lo," has been gaining traction in lieu of "native Taiwanese." Given the likely continued evolution of these identity terms, I continue to use "native Taiwanese" in this collection, to reflect the time period of the plays' creation.

The second play in this collection, Peng Ya-Ling's *We Are Here* (*Women zai zheli*, 1999), presents stories of another ethnic and linguistic group, the Hakka. A minority within both mainland China and Taiwan, the Hakka originated in central China and made their way over time to southern

China, including Guangdong Province. From Guangdong, some later emigrated to Taiwan beginning in the seventeenth century, a timeframe similar to the early native Taiwanese settlers. The Hakka group's name in Chinese, *Kejiaren,* literally means "guest families." That name reflects the group's diasporic status within the Chinese world, and later beyond the bounds of China and even Asia, with significant populations reaching Africa and North America. As the stories in *We Are Here* demonstrate, the Hakka have historically maintained their own communities. While intermarriage has occurred in Taiwan, also seen within the play, it was not favored within the Hakka communities there. The Hakka language remains a minority tongue in Taiwan, but it does have some official recognition. On the subways in modern-day Taipei, all announcements are made in Mandarin, Taiwanese, and Hakka, as well as English.

Though not given major roles in any of the plays, there is a group in Taiwan that are more accustomed to speaking Mandarin in their daily life. These are the "mainlanders." The most recent immigrant group to come to Taiwan, the mainlanders came in large numbers in the late 1940s, when the Nationalist (KMT) party followers of Chiang Kai-Shek fled to Taiwan as Chiang's army was losing the civil war against Mao Zedong's Communist (CCP) forces. Those who fled to Taiwan in this tumultuous period spanned the social gamut. Some were elite families, often former Nationalist generals and other high officials; others were teachers, merchants, or rank-and-file soldiers in the Nationalist army. Whether elite or humble, the members of this group are most often called *waishengren,* literally, "people from outside provinces." Within this anthology, mainlanders make their most significant appearance in *We Are Here,* primarily as the men that the Hakka women portrayed either strongly do, or do not, wish to marry.

Whether highlighting the stories of the native Taiwanese or the Hakka, the content of the plays in this anthology reflects the historically female gendering of Taiwan's community theater. In *One Year, Three Seasons* and *We Are Here,* stories of women dominate. *The Phoenix Trees Are in Blossom* also has significant female roles, both fictional and historical. Another essential feature is that these stories come from within local communities. To connect with those communities, the playwrights seek out local stories, often through text-based or interview-based research, and then contextualize those stories within the larger historical narratives of Taiwan, itself already a "local" element within the broader Chinese culture. The community theater troupes that present these plays draw performers from local areas, with women forming the majority of the participants. Through the dual foci of gender and locality, the stories of the women of Taiwan emerge as meaningful elements in Taiwan's modern history. These plays go beyond the walls of the theater spaces, to educate the local, national, and—through translation—international communities about those significant, but often hidden, stories.

Plays and Playwrights

Hsu Rey-Fang (b. 1961) is a pioneer of theater performance in the southern city of Tainan, a former capital city and continued center of traditional Taiwanese culture. She was an inaugural member of the Hwa Deng Theatre Troupe (*Huadeng jutuan*), founded in 1987 under the direction of American priest Father Don Glover. Hsu took the helm as artistic director in 1994, and the troupe was rechristened in 1997 as the Tainaner Ensemble (*Tainanren jutuan*), though the name was translated as "Tainan Jen Theatre Troupe" during the years Hsu ran the troupe. Hsu continued as artistic director through 2002, and in those years this community theater focused its energies on explorations of Taiwanese identity, often through historical subject matter. The 1997 version of *The Phoenix Trees Are in Blossom*, a revision of Hsu's 1994 MFA thesis and published play,[3] was the Tainaner Ensemble's inaugural production. The play traces a native Taiwanese family's experiences in the city of Tainan from the 1940s through the 1990s. The play begins during World War II, when Taiwan, already occupied by the Japanese for half a century, experienced conflicting loyalties that challenged their sense of identity. The further challenges of Taiwan's return to China follow, culminating in the horrors of the February 28 Incident in 1947, when the mainlander-dominated Nationalist government cracked down on the local Taiwanese population. Economic devel-

---

[3] Hsu Rey-Fang, *Fenghuanghua kaile* (Taipei: Council for Cultural Affairs, 1995).

opment and the changes it brought form a coda for the narrative of the family, who, while fictional in their details, are based on Hsu's own family, and reside on the same street where she grew up.

Hsu weaves a second, research-driven narrative into the play, a narrative that brings to light the true story of a woman significant on both sides of the Taiwan Strait, 1940s film actress Li Xianglan. Born in China to Japanese parents, she made films in three languages under three names. As Li Xianglan, a Chinese name given to her by a family friend, she made the wartime-era Chinese films referenced in *The Phoenix Trees Are in Blossom*. After the war's end, she settled in Japan and made Japanese films using her birth name of Yamaguchi Yoshiko. She also had a film and stage career in the United States, performing as Shirley Yamaguchi in Hollywood and on Broadway. Within *The Phoenix Trees Are in Blossom*, this star of collaborationist films in Japanese-occupied Shanghai serves as a counterpoint to the identity struggles of the Taiwanese family. Li's duality as a person sometimes identified as Japanese and sometimes as Chinese reflects the identity struggles of a Taiwanese family first forced to be Japanese, then forced to be Chinese, and only later allowed to explore what it means to be truly Taiwanese. Beyond serving this metaphorical role, Li was also historically significant in Taiwan on a more literal level, as evidenced within the play by the passion that the fictional Taiwanese family's women demonstrate for Li's films and songs.

Peng Ya-Ling (b. 1962) founded the Uhan Shii Theatre Group (*Huanxi banxituan*) in 1995.[4] The first incarnation of Peng's career in theater was as a successful actor and director in Taiwan's experimental theater scene of the 1980s, where much of her work focused on adaptations of Western drama and literature.[5] Her sense of being drained by so much Western-based work led to the seemingly ironic choice to go to the United Kingdom to study. That experience, including several appearances at the Edinburgh Festival, brought Peng Ya-Ling to the self-realization that "the most moving kind of performance to me is always something very small, subtle,

---

[4] Peng Ya-Ling, *Women zai zheli*, in *Guomin wenxuan, xiju juan II*, ed. Wang Chi-Mei (Taipei: Yushanshe, 2004), 235–91.

[5] Wan-Jung Wang, "Reminiscence Theatre: Devising and Performing" (PhD diss., Royal Holloway College, University of London, 2006), 15.

and ethnic in human nature rather than something grandiose or spectacular."[6] This prompted her to interview elders in Taiwan, which in turn led to founding a theater troupe centered on telling the stories of Taiwan's senior citizens, with those seniors as the main performers. Uhan Shii Theatre Group presented the first installment of the *Echoes of Taiwan* (*Taiwan gaobai*) series in 1995. That series, with ten parts from 1995 through 2003, presents stories of elders from many of the groups within Taiwan, including the native Taiwanese portrayed in Hsu's and Wang's plays, as well as the mainlander soldiers who retreated to Taiwan with Chiang Kai-Shek's army and ended up stranded in Taiwan for the rest of their lives.

Echoes of Taiwan VI: We Are Here, the original full name of the selection in this anthology, presents the story of the Hakka, particularly Hakka women. Developed through oral histories, and originally performed by the actual women and men whose stories are told, *We Are Here* weaves specific stories of individual, everyday Hakka women together with folk songs common among the Hakka people. Peng incorporates customs specifically Hakka, such as the use of blue bundles to carry the family's possessions when migrating, together with theatrical conventions she uses throughout her *Echoes of Taiwan* series, particularly the "reminiscence boxes" that metaphorically house the characters' memories. *We Are Here* serves to empower Hakka women, a group marginalized on multiple levels: as minorities, as women, and, as is the case for most of the real-life characters in the play, as the impoverished. The act of creation becomes an integral part of the project, and the opportunity to perform in the play serves as an additional mode of empowerment for the participants. Throughout her series, Peng finds the historic in the everyday, and her plays are organized not by a chronology of political events, but by the personal stories of individuals who collectively create history and culture within their communities.

Wang Chi-Mei (b. 1946) had a long career as a playwright and director in her hometown Taipei, prior to her work in Tainan with the Tainaner Ensemble. She also served as a professor and Dean of Academic Affairs at the National Institute of the Arts (*Guoli yishu xueyuan*), or NIA, now

---

[6] Peng Ya-Ling, interviews with Wan-Jung Wang, Sept. 2002–Jan. 2003.

called Taipei National University of the Arts (*Guoli Taibei yishu daxue*), or TNUA. Wang has made women's stories the focus of much of her playwriting career. In her preface to *One Year, Three Seasons*, she writes, "Ever since writing [my 1987 play] *Paradise Found* [*Tiantang lüguan*], my feelings have been continuously aroused by the possibilities of depicting every kind of Taiwan woman through theater."[7] In the ensuing years she has depicted a wide range of female characters in plays like *Remember Hong Kong* (*Jide Xiang Gang*) and *The Bride and Her Double* (*Fuzhi xinniang*). Hsu Rey-Fang, aiming to raise the quality of the Tainaner Ensemble's productions, had sought to collaborate with the more experienced Wang Chi-Mei as early as 1998. In 1999, Wang moved to Tainan to teach at National Cheng Kung University (*Guoli Chenggong daxue*),[8] a fortuitous circumstance that catalyzed the collaboration. The following year, the Tainaner Ensemble produced the second play in this anthology, Wang's *One Year, Three Seasons*.[9]

One Year, Three Seasons fuses history and economics, with women at the center. Starting in the 1970s and extending into the 1990s, this lyrical play is a tale of Taiwan's economic miracle: the rapid economic development that transformed Taiwan from a poor agrarian society in the 1950s into a developed industrialized economy by the 1980s. For Americans, this transformation is most familiar from the "Made in Taiwan" labels on seemingly just about everything in the 1980s. For the Taiwanese, this so-called miracle was really a lot of hard work, much of it done by women. Xiang-lian, the heroine of *One Year, Three Seasons*, starts as a seamstress working in one shop while doing piecework for another. She then becomes proprietor of her own tailor shop, and crescendos as a successful business-woman in the world of international fashion. She is supported throughout her endeavors by other women in the developing workforce. The older women are limited to repetitive tasks like assembling plastic flowers and Christmas lights, but their daughters and granddaughters can go on to run their own business enterprises. The indomitable spirit of Taiwanese women shines through, in all time periods. However, the play is not a fairy

---

[7] Wang Chi-Mei, *Yinian sanji* (Taipei: Yuanliu, 2000), 11.

[8] Wang, email message to author, Sept. 15, 2005.

[9] Wang, *Yinian sanji*, 15.

tale of happily ever after. Sacrifices are made in personal lives, and the streets of the city of Tainan suffer from peaks and valleys of economic development.

Community-Based Languages

All three plays in this anthology place the community experience at the center, and all three playwright/directors use the languages of the local communities to connect more strongly with their audiences. Tainaner Ensemble uses language as a primary means of local engagement when performing in or near its home base of Tainan, a stronghold of the Taiwanese language. Using Taiwanese is essential for bringing in audiences who do not understand Mandarin well, and, perhaps even more so, for those who understand Mandarin but prefer to be entertained in their truly native tongue. Hsu Rey-Fang herself began to make use of Taiwanese in her 1991 play *Take Me to See the Fish* (*Dai wo qu kan yu*) and has used it in all of her subsequent major plays.[10] In Peng Ya-Ling's *Echoes of Taiwan* series, the characters on stage speak whatever language they would speak in real life, which given the range of identities presented throughout that series, varies from play to play. For example, in the 1997 play *Echoes of Taiwan III—The Story of Taiwanese Men* (*Taiwan chaburen de gushi*), the characters speak Taiwanese. In *We Are Here*, the play in this anthology, the characters all speak Hakka. Wang Chi-Mei similarly uses the language that makes sense for her characters. Much of her previous work was in Mandarin, but for the Tainan-centered story of *One Year, Three Seasons*, Taiwanese was the natural choice.

Tainaner Ensemble and Uhan Shii Theatre Group are not the only two troupes in Taiwan to use Taiwanese or Hakka, but their approach has some distinctive aspects. They generally do not subtitle the Taiwanese or Hakka lines with Mandarin, as is done by the Ping-Fong Acting Troupe (*Pingfeng biaoyanban*), a major promoter of multilingualism among the larger the-

---

[10] Hsu Rey-Fang, email message to author, 15 Nov. 1999.

ater companies based in the capital city of Taipei.[11] In Tainaner and Uhan Shii productions, viewers who do not understand Taiwanese or Hakka are rarely given any verbal cues (the Mandarin-subtitled Taipei performance of *We Are Here* being an exception). These theatergoing experiences reflect the day-to-day reality of life on the streets of Tainan, or of the Hakka regions of Taiwan, where those who do not understand Taiwanese or Hakka on the street are not provided with Mandarin subtitles or simultaneous translation. Though all three of the playwright/directors represented in this volume state that using Taiwanese or Hakka is simply a natural choice, there is more at stake. Given the politicization of language use in Taiwan, to write and perform plays in Taiwanese or Hakka has elements of a political statement.

The two theater troupes represented in this anthology diverge on the matter of publishing scripts in the non-Mandarin languages. A distinctive aspect of Tainaner Ensemble's approach is writing and publishing scripts directly in Taiwanese. Writing directly in Taiwanese is a challenge, given its relatively short history as a language of written literature. What constitutes "correct" Taiwanese is ever-evolving, as the language becomes more established as a subject in schools and as a literary language. Contrary to the popular myth about Chinese "dialects," they are not all identical in written form, and a reader of Mandarin can only garner the gist of written Taiwanese. As Wang Chi-Mei explains in a brief statement in the published version of *One Year, Three Seasons*, she made use of rehearsal time to adjust and alter her script to best capture the specifics of language in Tainan, and friends with particular expertise in Taiwanese assisted her in the endeavor.[12] The choices she ultimately made are recorded in the written script, published in a series that she edits. Hsu, as a playwright, and Wang, as both a playwright and an editor, preserve and promote Taiwanese as a literary language. Peng Ya-Ling, herself of Hakka descent but not a native speaker of the Hakka language, takes a different approach in her script writing. Though *We Are Here* was created in Hakka through the oral

---

[11] For further discussion of the multilingual qualities of Taiwan theater, including *The Phoenix Trees Are in Blossom*, see John B. Weinstein, "Multilingual Theatre in Contemporary Taiwan," *Asian Theatre Journal* 17.2 (2000): 269–83.

[12] Wang, *Yinian sanji*, 13.

histories, and every character except the Narrator speaks his or her lines in Hakka, the published script is written entirely in Mandarin. The significant multilingual aspects are, alas, not elements well-conveyed in translation. For the two plays that are largely monolingual within themselves—Taiwanese in the case of *One Year, Three Seasons* and Hakka for *We Are Here*—this is not a major issue. To translate such a play entirely into English is not substantially different than doing so for a play in any language. *The Phoenix Trees Are in Blossom* is a different matter. It is a multilingual play, roughly alternating between scenes in Taiwanese telling the family's story, and scenes in Mandarin plus a bit of Japanese (subtitled in performance, and not written in Japanese in the published script), for Li Xianglan's story. That poses more of a challenge to the translator. There is no way in English to distinguish between the two in a manner that truly reflects the experience of viewing a play performed in two mutually unintelligible languages. There is a particular complexity to translating Scene 11, in which different characters speak different languages within a single conversation—a comic effect not easy to convey in translation. For that scene alone, this translation indicates Mandarin lines in italics, but in a production that would not be visible. A director of an English-language production of *The Phoenix Trees Are in Blossom* can decide how, if at all, to reflect the contrast of Mandarin and Taiwanese, and that choice will no doubt depend on the nature of the specific production. Such challenges aside, these translations were done with performance in mind, and all the songs that pervade the plays have been translated to be singable to the original melodies.

What's in a Name: "Community Theater" in Taiwan

All three plays in this anthology can be categorized under "community theater," but while those words capture the denotation of *shequ juchang*, the connotation of the words is quite different in American and Taiwanese contexts. The term "community theater," and indeed most modern theater terminology in Taiwan, merits some explanation. The broadest category for the kinds of plays in this translation is "stage play" (*wutaiju*). "Stage play" may seem bland and undescriptive, but the mainland term "spoken drama" (*huaju*) was rejected by those who gave Taiwan's spoken theater its new life in the late 1970s and early 1980s. Now known as "little theater" (*xiao juchang*), these artists' work was actually called "experimental theater" (*shiyanju*) at the time.[13] Much of that early theater was truly little, but during the 1990s a number of these little theater companies developed into big theater companies with largely professional staffs. The most notable of the 1990s were Ping-Fong Acting Troupe, Performance Workshop (*Biaoyan gongzuofang*), and Godot Theatre (*Guotuo juchang*). Ping-Fong tended to focus on Taiwan's cultural uniqueness, Performance Workshop situated Taiwan within broader Chinese contexts, and Godot celebrated Taiwan's internationalized culture, though each of these prolific companies included all three approaches within their repertoires. Together, these Taipei-based troupes formed the core of the mainstream national theater of Taiwan, a place simultaneously Taiwanese, Chinese, and international.

To call them a "national theater" is my doing, however, not theirs. Instead they operate under the label "professional theater" (*zhuanye juchang*). For readers accustomed to American theater terminology, "professional" can be misleading, due to the differing conceptions of professional theater in Taiwan and in the United States. Theater professionals in Taiwan are those paid to do work in the theater, with great latitude in terms of the percentage of their income that comes from such work. Many Taiwan theater professionals earn income from other sources, sometimes from teaching theater, sometimes from work entirely outside of the arts. American theater professionals may also teach, but theater professors in the United States are more likely than their Taiwanese counterparts to consider their work in academia distinct from their "professional" work. Even if everyone in one of Taiwan's "professional theaters" is paid, they are not necessarily earning all, or most, of their income from such work. This is not a mark against the quality of the productions, which can be very high. The experience, training, and credentials within the professional troupes are often quite considerable. Nevertheless, a lit-

---

[13] Chung, "Little Theater Movement," 7.

eral translation of "professional theater" may not fully convey all aspects of their actual circumstances.

While a large-scale professional troupe might continue to call itself a "little theater" out of homage to its past, the term seems more valid for its other users: the many small, often student-run troupes that appear and disappear with great regularity and in great numbers. In its initial incarnation in the 1980s, the little theater was closely linked to the Western avant-garde, featuring troupes whose work was as likely to baffle the audience as it was to entertain them. The troupes used an aesthetic based on political opposition, the breakdown of formal theatrical spaces, and, in many cases, minimal human and financial resources. Visual impact often took precedence over textual detail, and linear narrative and realistic dialogue were largely eschewed. By the end of the 1990s, the early groundbreaking little theater troupes, such as Lan-ling Theatre Workshop (*Lanling jufang*) and Critical Point Theater Phenomenon (*Linjiedian juxianglu*), had mostly run their course. The numerous successors to the movement—a plethora of troupes too long to list, and generally unstable from one year to the next—were still performing in informal spaces with minimal resources. Their political consciousness, however, was less apparent and often diluted considerably by a love of the hip and trendy. The ethos of the little theater was not dead, but it had certainly been transformed.

This division into "professional theater" and "little theater" is generally adequate for troupes in Taipei, but the Tainaner Ensemble and the Uhan Shii Theatre Group fall neatly into neither category. In some ways, they fall right in the middle. In terms of training, the professional theater troupes have numerous participants with specific theater training. Performance Workshop's artistic director, Lai Sheng-chuan, has a doctorate in theater from the University of California at Berkeley, and many of his staff have degrees from prestigious institutions in Taiwan. A little theater troupe, in contrast, might have only students of theater, students of other subjects, or people from various walks of life who enjoy doing theater on the side. Tainaner and Uhan Shii fit neither mold entirely. Hsu Rey-Fang herself earned a master's degree in dramatic writing from NIA,[14] but the diverse

---

[14] Hsu Rey-Fang, *Fenghuanghua kaile*, program (Tainan: Tainanren jutuan, 1997), 14.

staff of *The Phoenix Trees Are in Blossom* brought more enthusiasm than formal theater training. Wang Chi-Mei, herself holding an American master's degree, brought some more professional staff with her for *One Year, Three Seasons*, including Yale School of Drama–educated scenic and lighting designer Lin Keh-hua, but the bulk of the staff and cast were similar in training to those of *The Phoenix Trees Are in Blossom*. Peng Ya-Ling began her education in the English department at Tamkang University (*Danjiang daxue*) in Taipei County, and later went abroad to study at the London School of Mime and Movement.[15] Her cast is the least trained of all, by design, as she primarily uses ordinary senior citizens, who are generally acting for the first time when in her productions.

Performance venues fall somewhere in the middle as well for the community theaters. When Ping-Fong's founding Artistic Director Lee Kuo-shiu created a new play for his troupe, he could expect to tour the island with perhaps thirty performances; one production played a record-setting seventy times.[16] In Taipei, Ping-Fong performed on the main stage of the National Theatre or one of the other large-scale theater spaces. Outside Taipei the troupe used formal theater spaces in the cultural centers in each city. The little theater troupes, in contrast, would play for a weekend or two in a converted room, with little hope of a tour. Tainaner Ensemble's productions have toured to major venues, but usually for just one performance in each location. *The Phoenix Trees Are in Blossom* had four performances in four cities; *One Year, Three Seasons* had eight, two in the National Tainan Education Hall and one in each of six other cities.[17] *The Phoenix Trees Are in Blossom* had a Taipei performance in Novel Hall, a venue for the likes of Performance Workshop; *One Year, Three Seasons* stayed out of Taipei's theater spaces, playing instead in a variety of municipal cultural centers and university theaters. The premieres of each play in Peng Ya-Ling's *Echoes of Taiwan* series tended to be runs of two to four performances, with the most frequent venue the National Experimental

---

[15] Wang, "Reminiscence Theater," 15.

[16] Li Li-heng, *OH? Li Guoxiu!* (Taipei: Shibao wenhua, 1998), 235.

[17] Hsu, *Fenghuanghua kaile*, program, 1; Wang Chi-Mei, *Yinian sanji*, program (Tainan: Tainanren jutuan, 2000), inside cover.

Theatre in Taipei, the smaller space within the National Theatre building.[18] Unusual for Uhan Shii, *We Are Here* actually premiered at an international festival in Germany before playing in Taipei and then touring Hakka communities back home in Taiwan.[19]

The growth of community theater arose from an intersection of artistic interest on the part of theater artists like Hsu Rey-Fang and Peng Ya-Ling and government support targeted at developing theater more broadly throughout Taiwan. Tainaner Ensemble, Uhan Shii Theatre Group, and other troupes in cities outside Taipei were given a big push in the early 1990s. As Lin Weiyu recounts in *Contemporary Taiwan Community Theater* (*Dangdai Taiwan shequ juchang*), from 1991 to 1994 the Council for Cultural Affairs (CCA; *Wenhua jianshe weiyuanhui* or *Wenjianhui*), implemented a "Plan for Promoting Community Theater Activities" (*Shequ jutuan huodong tuizhan jihua*).[20] This government directive categorized its beneficiaries under the new label of "community theater." The CCA's goal for the plan was to encourage local people to create theater out of stories and issues they considered relevant and familiar; these activities were to enhance their understanding of the unique aspects of their local areas and communities.[21]

In an essay she published at the time of the CCA's plan, Hsu Rey-Fang seeks to offer an ethos for the term "community theater," a term that had suddenly become the subject of much attention. Hsu defines community theater as "a call for an area's residents to organize a theater troupe together and rehearse plays in accordance with their common interests, [and] to perform from time to time in their own neighborhoods."[22] Hsu goes on to emphasize performing at local festivals on holidays, just like the local festival performances of an earlier era in Taiwan's past. While Tainaner Ensemble does make use of holidays—*The Phoenix Trees Are in Blossom* opened in Tainan on Retrocession Day in 1997[23]—the reality of

---

[18] Wang, "Reminiscence Theater," 358–98.

[19] Wang, "Reminiscence Theater," 374.

[20] Lin Weiyu, *Dangdai Taiwan shequ juchang* (Taipei: Yangzhi, 2000), ix.

[21] Cai Qizhang, "Alternative Theatre in Modern Taiwan" (manuscript, n.d.), 6–7.

[22] Hsu Rey-Fang, "Shequ jutuan zai Taiwan," *Tainan shili wenhua zhongxin qikan* (1991), 44.

[23] Hsu, *Fenghuanghua kaile*, program, 1.

the group's touring schedule is rather different from the festival performances of yesteryear. Hsu also offers a less lofty but probably more accurate definition of community theater: "outside of Taipei."[24] Challenging to define even in Chinese, "community theater" becomes problematic when translated into American English, given that American "community theater" rarely creates new work, tours anywhere, or has significant artistic impact at the national level. Taiwan's community theaters remain uniquely tied to their own local contexts.

They are also run predominantly by women. A distinctive element of Taiwan's community theaters is the significant role of women in the artistic side of leadership. Hsu Rey-Fang, Wang Chi-Mei, and Peng Ya-Ling are by no means the only women in Taiwan to work as playwright/directors, but on the national level such work is largely the domain of men. The two most famous playwright/directors in the time period under consideration were both male, namely Performance Workshop's Lai Sheng-chuan and Ping-Fong's Lee Kuo-shiu. Both of those troupes grew from the work of husband-wife teams—Lai Sheng-chuan and Ding Nai-chu, and Lee Kuo-shiu and Wang Yüeh—with each husband serving as the artistic director and primary playwright/director of the troupe and each wife working as the principal producer. Both wives have had moments as playwright/director; moreover, producing the most eminent theater companies in Taiwan is a significant achievement. Still, contemporary fame and theatrical history favor the "creative" side. The plays of Lai and Li—the two men—are what (and who) will be remembered. By taking the helm of theaters outside of the Taipei mainstream, Hsu Rey-Fang, Peng Ya-Ling, and Wang Chi-Mei create a space for themselves, and for the many women whose lives they portray, to be remembered.

Celebrating the Past, Looking to the Future

All three of these plays come from the last decade of the twentieth century, which was in retrospect an apex for theater exploring history and identity

---

[24] Hsu, "Shequ jutuan zai Taiwan," 44.

in Taiwan. After the lifting of martial law in 1987, artists in a variety of media began openly probing Taiwan's suppressed histories. There was, for the first time, open discussion of events like the February 28 Incident—portrayed in *The Phoenix Trees Are in Blossom*—and the ensuing White Terror, when elite Taiwanese were taken by the police, sometimes disappearing forever. The Taiwanese language, after years of suppression in schools and other official settings, began to make a comeback. No longer identifying solely as the rightful heirs and faithful guardians of traditional Chinese culture, the Taiwan government began to rebrand the island as a multiethnic, multilingual society. The ideals of a multiparty society began to be realized when the former opposition party, the Democratic Progressive Party (DPP), started to win major political offices, including the office of the President in the year 2000 with the election of Chen Shui-bian. All of these events offstage led to a flourishing of identity-focused theater onstage, including all three of the plays in this anthology. For the arts scene as a whole, the first post–martial law decade was an inspired time.

It was not to last forever. The Asian financial crisis, beginning in 1997, hit Taiwan's economy hard, and the shifting of Taiwanese-run business enterprises to mainland China (referenced in *One Year, Three Seasons*), was a further negative economic trend. For a theater scene that needed government and other subsidies even in the best of times, the economic downturn was damaging. Political optimism was fading as well, as DPP high officials' corruption and scandals made them look a lot like their KMT predecessors. The Taiwanese people had to face the reality that even if a two-party system was better than a one-party one, politics was still politics. With a variety of languages—Mandarin, Taiwanese, and Hakka—now heard every day on the streets, in the media, and on the subways, the theater productions in those languages, while still relevant, were not as watershed as they once were. This collection of plays, each of which centers on memory—sometimes individual, sometimes collective—serves as a form of collective memory of a theatrical era so rich in its explorations of the lives of ordinary women and men, speaking in their true voices, in the communities in which they lived.

Looking toward the future, it is hoped that this anthology is the first of many to bring the voices of Taiwanese women, and men, to wider audiences in the English-speaking world. Even the most significant of the large, professional theaters have little of their work available in English as of yet. In selecting these three plays, a tight focus was maintained on plays written by women, staged in community theaters, and performed primarily in languages beyond the hegemonic "national language" of Mandarin. The collection reflects a range of ethnic groups—native Taiwanese, Hakka, and mainlander—but unfortunately does not represent any of the Aboriginal cultures. That lacuna might have been lessened by including a play by Liu Mei-Yin and her Taitung Theatre (*Taidong jutuan*), a community theater whose work in Taitung often incorporates elements of the Aboriginal groups who live in that region on Taiwan's eastern coast. However, her plays use Mandarin as their predominant language, falling outside the linguistic criteria used here. That being said, Liu is one of many whose voices should be heard in future anthologies. In *One Year, Three Seasons*, the entrepreneurial Xiang-lian remarks, "There's no lack of local talent here."[25] She is speaking of women who create clothing, but she could just as well be speaking of women who create theater. Hsu Rey-Fang, Peng Ya-Ling, and Wang Chi-Mei are three of the many women who bring theater to life in their local communities, celebrating significant, yet previously untold, stories of the women and men of Taiwan.

Bibliography

Cai, Qizhang. "Alternative Theatre in Modern Taiwan." Manuscript, n.d.

Chung, Mingder. "The Little Theater Movement of Taiwan (1980–89): In search of alternative aesthetics and politics." PhD diss., New York University, 1992.

Hsu, Rey-Fang. *Fenghuanghua kaile*. Taipei: Council for Cultural Affairs, 1995.

Hsu, Rey-Fang. *Fenghuanghua kaile* program. Tainan: Tainanren jutuan, 1997.

Hsu, Rey-Fang. "Shequ jutuan zai Taiwan." *Tainan shili wenhua zhongxin qikan* (June 1991).

Li, Li-heng. *OH? Li Guoxiu!* Taipei: Shibao wenhua, 1998.

Lin, Weiyu. *Dangdai Taiwan shequ juchang*. Taipei: Yangzhi, 2000.

---

[25] Wang, *Yinian sanji*, 80.

Peng, Ya-Ling. *Women zai zheli.* In *Guomin wenxuan, xiju juan II,* ed. Wang Chi-Mei, 235–91. Taipei: Yushanshe, 2004.

Wang, Chi-Mei. *Yinian sanji.* Taipei: Yuanliu, 2000.

Wang, Chi-Mei, *Yinian sanji* program. Tainan: Tainanren jutuan, 2000.

Wang, Wan-Jung. "Reminiscence Theatre: Devising and Performing." PhD diss., Royal Holloway College, University of London, 2006.

Weinstein, John B. "Multilingual Theatre in Contemporary Taiwan." *Asian Theatre Journal* 17.2 (2000): 269–83.

Weinstein, John B. "The Streets of Tainan: A Local Path for Taiwanese Theater." *Nanyi de lishi, shehui yu wenhua lunwenji.* Eds. Lin Yu-ju and Fiorella Allio. Tainan: Tainan County Government, 2008. 431–44.

The Phoenix Trees Are in Blossom

HSU REY-FANG
(1994, revised 1997)

translation by
John B. Weinstein

The Tainaner Ensemble, formerly the Hwa Deng Theatre Troupe, premiered this version of *The Phoenix Trees Are in Blossom* on October 25, 1997, in the Tainan Municipal Cultural Center in Tainan, Taiwan, followed by a tour to theaters in Taipei, Taichung, Chiayi, and Kaohsiung.

Director	Hsu Rey-Fang
Producer	Lin Ming-Hsia
Technical Director	Li Wei-mu
Stage Design	Zhao Hua-yu
Lighting Design	Chao Rui-guang
Costume Design	Lin Ming-Hsia
Sound Design	Huang Shi-yuan
Multimedia Design	Hong Jia-dai
Stage Manager	Chen Hui-huang
Properties Manager	Guo Nai-hua
Costume Manager	Wang Mei-zhu
House Managers	Chen Shu-hui, Wu Ya-qing
Photography	Liu Wei-ning, Chen Wei

Actors

THIAM-GUAN	Ye Deng-yuan
SIOK-HUN	Deng Li-Chi
THIAM-HOK	Hong Qi-zhi
BI-LING	Wu Qing-hong
THIAM-GI	Liao Qing-quan
A-BUAN	Guo Xiang-yin
TSONG-TIK	Shen Hui-xiong
AKIKO	Hong Jia-dai
TSONG-BING	Cai Jie-wen
HUI-ING	Du Qiong-yi
GRANDSON	Cai Mei-juan
KONG GUOXIANG	Cai Xin-chang
LI XIANGLAN	Wu Hui-yan
SACHIKO	Guo Rong-hua
LI XIANGLAN'S MOTHER	Hong Jia-dai

CHEN YUNSHANG	Chen Li-rong
HASEGAWA KAZUO	Wu Huan-wen
KAWAKITA NAGAMASA	Wu Huan-wen
RADIO ANNOUNCER	Lu Xuan-ya
FILM DIRECTOR	Lu Xuan-ya
FILM PRODUCER	Wu Qing-hong
TRANSLATOR	Hong Qi-zhi
YOUTH A, B, C	Chen Yu-hui, Wang Mei-zhu, Du Rong-zhong

Figure 1.1　Program cover from the original production of the 1997 version of *The Phoenix Trees Are in Blossom*, performed by the Tainaner Ensemble.

Dramaturgical Notes for *The Phoenix Trees Are in Blossom*

JOHN B. WEINSTEIN

The Phoenix Trees Are in Blossom weaves together two narratives, one from each side of the Taiwan Strait. One plot line focuses on the lives of a fictional Taiwanese-speaking family who lives in the city of Tainan, a center of traditional Taiwanese culture in southern Taiwan. Told partially in flashbacks, the action begins with a scene in 1997, jumps back briefly to 1961, and then goes further back to 1941, where the bulk of the action begins. At that time, Taiwan is under Japanese occupation, as it has been since its 1895 cession to Japan, when Japan defeated China in the First Sino-Japanese War and received Taiwan as part of the ensuing treaty. By 1941, the Second Sino-Japanese War (soon to merge into the worldwide conflict called World War II) is raging, and the Taiwanese family finds themselves on the Japanese side of the war, in opposition to the Chinese, with whom they both do and do not identify as cultural brethren. In Taiwan, a movement called Kominka is in full swing. This movement, whose name means "becoming the Emperor's subjects," aims to fully Japanize Taiwanese society. The Taiwanese are being encouraged to speak Japanese, wear Japanese clothing, live in Japanese-style houses, follow Japanese customs and the Shinto religion, and even adopt Japanese names.

In the first scene set during the Japanese occupation period, the Taiwanese family is decorating its home for the New Year's holiday in accordance with Japanese, not Chinese, customs. Even the date itself is now different for them, as the Japanese had begun, during the reign of the Meiji emperor (1868–1912), to celebrate the New Year according to the Western calendar, not the lunar one. The years themselves are marked by the emperor's reign, making 1941 the sixteenth year of the Showa Emperor, Hirohito. At the start of the scene, the family is putting up Japanese-style New Year's decorations called *shide*. These hanging paper decorations, made by folding strips of plain white paper in a zigzag pattern, contrast with the traditional Chinese *duilian*, paired vertical strips of bright red paper with traditional sayings, often written in shiny gold characters and sometimes accompanied by elaborate designs. The color change is a strikingly visual representation of the culture clash. In Chinese culture, white is traditionally associated with death, making the Japanese New Year's celebration look a whole lot like a Chinese funeral. Later in the scene, the family seeks out materials for another common Japanese New Year's decoration, the bundles of bamboo and pine sprigs, and sometimes plum blossom twigs, called *kadomatsu*.

Though the family portrayed here does not follow the occupying government's wish that they speak Japanese, the Japanese language is present in their daily conversation. At one point, the daughter Hui-ing tells her mother she needs a plum to make a *hinomaru bento*, a Japanese lunchbox (*bento*) including a plum in the center of the white rice, to resemble the Japanese flag. Hui-ing, and many other young people in Japanese-occupied Taiwan, had to bring this lunch to school on the first day of each month. The Taiwanese-speaking characters sometimes use the Japanese word *hai*, meaning "yes," and the Japanese word for "radio," conveniently the easily comprehensible *radio*. To give the feel of the Japanese-occupation period, this translation uses the Japanese word for teacher, *sensei*, even though Taiwanese speaking people at the time may have pronounced that word in their own language. This linguistic influence of Japanese persists long after the Japanese have left, which they did in 1945, when Japan was defeated in World War II and Taiwan's retrocession to China occurred. In the final 1997 scene, a young Taiwanese sightseer, born decades after the Japanese occupation, calls Hui-ing *obasan*, which appears in the original script in Chinese characters transliterated from Japanese. Originally meaning "grandmother," *obasan* was, and continues to be, used in Taiwanese speaking areas of Taiwan to refer to an older woman.

Despite the Japanese influence of the era, traditional Taiwanese culture and local history are readily seen and heard. Toward the end of the prologue, *nanguan* music wafts in. *Nanguan* is a type of traditional Chinese music that originated in Fujian Province, the ancestral home of most of the Taiwanese-language speaking population of Taiwan, a group that immigrated to Taiwan beginning in the seventeenth century. The patriarch Thiam-guan speaks of the decline of the "Three Companies," a local trade organization established in the Tainan region during the Qing dynasty (1644–1912). Throughout the play, many of the famous temples, monuments, and historic sites that pepper the city of Tainan are referenced. The matriarch Siok-hun references cultural practices in the domestic sphere, including the Taiwanese practice of mixing sweet potato in with the rice, a practice done to make the rarer, more expensive rice last longer. Taiwanese wedding customs, which includes a bridal veil in the auspicious red color not seen during the time of the Kominka movement, appear as well. The wedding's timing reveals another cultural practice. When someone in a family was ill or had suffered a misfortune, a family wedding was considered a way to "wash in happiness." Though not readily apparent in an English-language production, the family's scenes were originally spoken in the Taiwanese language, not the Mandarin that is called the "national language" in Taiwan.

The cultural clashes of Taiwan's return to Chinese rule in 1945 are presented both comically and tragically. The Mandarin-speaking teacher Kong Guoxiang comes over from the mainland to help the Taiwanese-speaking local population learn their new "national language." In the original production, Scene 11 was a bilingual one, with Thiam-guan and Kong Guoxiang trying to understand one another despite sharing no mutually intelligible language. The political situation turns tragic for both men in 1947, when the February 28 Incident occurs. Thiam-guan, like many other Taiwanese prominent in their communities, is arrested and imprisoned during this government crackdown on the local population. Though the local Taiwanese bore the brunt of the violence, the mainlander population suffered misfortune as well, and Kong Guoxiang briefly hides in the family's home to escape the backlash. The February 28 Incident is now openly discussed in Taiwan, but even speaking of the event was taboo in Taiwan for decades. Official public acknowledgment did not come until 1995, when President Lee Teng-hui formally apologized to the victims of the families during a ceremony unveiling a monument to the incident. By this time, the first version of this play had already been written, though the prologue and epilogue were not added until 1997. In Taiwan, years are still officially counted from the founding of the Republic of China in 1911, so 1997 is considered the eighty-sixth year of the Republic.

The events and customs described here would be readily familiar to audiences in Taiwan, and hence the play often references them only obliquely. Less well known, and therefore explained more fully within the play, is the nonfictional story of movie star Li Xianglan, presented here through scenes originally in Mandarin. Born as Yamaguchi Yoshiko in 1920 to Japanese parents living in China's Manchuria region, she began making films under the stage name Li Xianglan. That name was given to her by one of her Chinese godfathers, her father's close friend Li Jichun (a second family friend and godfather, Pan Yugui, gave her another Chinese name, Pan Shuhua). This play recounts Li's career from 1941 to 1946, when she made the films *China Nights*, *A Good Name for Generations*, and *Sayon's Bell*. Her breakthrough film, *China Nights*, was made in Japanese but shown to Chinese markets. The title used a Japanese word for China, a pair of characters pronounced as "Shina" ("Shee-na") in Japanese. The foreign-sounding "Shina" characters, pronounced as "Zhina" in Mandarin, were generally disliked by Chinese people and carried a derogatory connotation. To convey this derogatory sense, while still being clear to English audiences that China is being referenced, the word is written as "Chee-na" in the spoken lines in this translation. The word appears in the title of the film and of the eponymous song from that film that made Li Xianglan so famous at the time.

Another signature song of hers was the "Candy-Peddling Song" from *A Good Name for Generations*, a Chinese collaborationist film sometimes titled *Eternity* in English. The lyrics of the song are challenging to understand without some explanation. The song begins with describing the beauty of the opium implements and fragrant smell of the opium itself, but then quickly moves to describing how smoking opium destroys a person's physical appearance, before suggesting that opium addicts should turn to candy instead. The Japanese film *Sayon's Bell* is notable for being set and filmed in Taiwan. Based on real incidents, the film portrays a love affair between a Japanese man and a woman from one of Taiwan's aboriginal groups, the Austronesian peoples who came to the island millennia before the first ethnic Chinese settlers. The Taiwanese women in the play unflatteringly refer to Li's character of Sayon as a "Barbarian," reflecting local prejudices against these peoples. Li Xianglan had a fascinating life, only the surface of which is scratched in this play. After the war ended, she made films in Japan as Yamaguchi Yoshiko, in Hollywood as Shirley Yamaguchi, and in Hong Kong as Li Xianglan. She was briefly married to eminent Japanese architect Isamu Noguchi, and she served for many years in the Japanese parliament, using the name Otaka Yoshiko, her married name from her marriage to Japanese diplomat Otaka Hiroshi. Her dramatic, eventful life came to an end in 2014, when she died at the age of ninety-four.

In addition to the Chinese and Japanese films, an American film, *Casablanca*, makes an appearance, in a way distinctive to the region. In Scene 12, the action of the climactic final scene of the film is explained by the "Translator." "Translator" is an imperfect rendering of *pian-su* (*benshi* in Japanese). The *pian-su* did not translate the film word for word, but instead explained what was happening more generally, and then concluded with a moral lesson, which may or may not have matched the actual morals of the film in its original language. The names of the characters were not necessarily matches either, and in this case they are not at all. The leading man, Rick Blaine, famously played by Humphrey Bogart, is renamed "Tom," transliterated here as "Tom-mu." Ingrid Bergman's signature role of Ilsa Lund now has the more familiar English name of "Mary," transliterated as "May-lee." Her husband, Victor Laszlo, played by Paul Henreid, is now "George," transliterated as "Jyo-jee," and a bodyguard is called "Brown," transliterated as "Bu-lang." Though more an interpretation than a translation, the Taiwanese film-viewing convention of the *pian-su* facilitated Taiwanese audiences' comprehension of U.S. and other foreign films, which were not available with either subtitles or dubbing in Taiwanese. Emerging from a crossroads of cultural intersections—Chinese, Japanese, and Western—the Taiwanese have developed their own unique culture. They continue to define their ever-evolving identity as a people.

Characters[1]

Thiam-guan

Siok-hun	Thiam-guan's wife
Thiam-hok	Thiam-guan's middle brother
Bi-ling	Thiam-hok's wife
Thiam-gi	Thiam-guan's youngest brother
A-buan	Thiam-gi's wife
Tsong-tik	Thiam-guan's older son
Akiko	Hui-ing's classmate, later Tsong-tik's wife
Tsong-bing	Thiam-guan's younger son
Hui-ing	Thiam-guan's daughter
Grandson	Thiam-guan's grandson

Kong Guoxiang Tsong-tik's friend, came from Hebei Province to Taiwan to teach Mandarin

Li Xianglan (Yamaguchi Yoshiko) Japanese, lived in China for a long time, active in music and film circles during the Second Sino-Japanese War

Sachiko Japanese, Li Xianglan's assistant, had already lived in China for a long time

Li Xianglan's mother

Chen Yunshang Chinese movie star of the wartime era, in 1939 came from Hong Kong to Shanghai to act in *Hua Mulan*, and became famous overnight

Hasegawa Kazuo like Li Xianglan, a Japanese person active in Chinese film circles

Kawakita Nagamasa Japanese, dispatched to Shanghai after the war broke out in the Pacific to bring together the local film circles and take charge of film production; produced a signifi cant number of Chinese-Japanese joint productions

Radio Announcer

---

[1] To distinguish between Taiwanese-speaking and Mandarin-speaking characters, the names of the Taiwanese-speaking characters are written in Taiwanese *Tai-lo* romanization. Mandarin-speaking characters' names are written in *pinyin* romanization.

Film Director
Film Producer
Translator
Youth A, B, C

Explanation of the Scenes and Settings

The Phoenix Trees Are in Blossom has eighteen scenes, plus a Prologue and an Epilogue, so in effect it is a play of twenty scenes.

Within these twenty scenes, the Prologue, Scene 1, Scene 17, Scene 18, and the Epilogue have outdoor settings. In performance, to facilitate smooth flow from one scene to another, there need only be one blackout, after Scene 9. The blackout will bring a sense of conclusion to that section of the play, and will make a distinction between the times before and after retrocession.

The differences between before and after retrocession can be shown by a change in the settings, or perhaps more easily by changes in props and decorations. Before retrocession, the stage needs an image of the Japanese goddess Amaterasu; after retrocession, the image of Amaterasu needs to change into those of Taiwanese gods, such as Ma-tsoo (Mazu), Kuan-kong (Guan Gong), or Kuan-im (Guanyin).

The primary setting of *The Phoenix Trees Are in Blossom* takes the city of Tainan's Pak-si Street (now called Sin-long Street) as its backdrop. The set design can reference the structure of an old two-story house on Pak-si Street. At that time, practically every house had three generations living together, with grandparents, grandchildren, aunts, uncles, and cousins all huddled under the eaves of these two-story buildings.

Prologue

TIME: 1997, the eighty-sixth year of the Republic

The three siblings, Tsong-tik, Tsong-bing, and Hui-ing, reach the Weather Observatory to stop and rest. Tsong-tik walks onto the stage first.

TSONG-TIK: *(Shouting offstage.)* Hui-ing, are your feet sore? There's a place to sit over here.

Hui-ing and Tsong-bing walk onto the stage.

HUI-ING: It's a good thing we took a taxi to the Emperor's Temple. If we'd walked around on so many roads, it would be too much. After all, we're old people now.

TSONG-BING: Ever since I was little, the thing I loved most was wandering around these lanes.

HUI-ING: Brother, you really did like walking around here.

TSONG-BING: Do you remember? Back then, when I went to the Amitabha Buddhist Temple to read Chinese texts, I went right along these lanes. First, I'd come out by the Water Spirits Temple, then I'd pass the Buddhist Ancestor Temple. I'd walk along Tua-tiann Street, then along the street with the Heavenly Temple. I'd cross the big road again, and then I'd go from the Thai-Peng-Keng Church to the Clear Water Temple. I'd walk on Iu-hang-bue Street, which led right to the Great Person Temple. I'd cross the train tracks, and then I'd be right there at the Amitabha Temple.

HUI-ING: Those lanes you're talking about—there are a lot that I don't know.

TSONG-TIK: In these past few years, they've gotten rid of a number of them.

HUI-ING: When there are many places you haven't been for a while, if you suddenly want to go, you can't find the roads.

TSONG-TIK: True, true. For a while, they were saying they were going to tear down this Weather Observatory. They said they wanted to build a big office building. *(Pause.)* This place has a hundred years of history. How could you even talk about tearing it down?

TSONG-BING: I remember when we were little we all called this place "the pepper pot," because of its shape.

TSONG-TIK: Right. Do you remember the Tainan Assembly Hall, that later became the Social Education Hall? It was supposed to get torn down. They were saying they wanted to build a big office building.

HUI-ING: What they want to build better not look like that "Chinatown" building, so ugly ...

TSONG-TIK: Now, all of the new buildings, they're those big glass buildings, "Chinatown" was out of date so fast.

TSONG-BING: "Chinatown"?

HUI-ING: That big shopping center at the end of Chiang Kai-Shek Road, it was built more than ten years ago.

TSONG-BING: So, then, the wharf by the canal ...

TSONG-TIK: It's long gone.

HUI-ING: There haven't been boats there for years.

TSONG-TIK: Where do we want to go eat?

TSONG-BING: Let's go to Sakariba.

HUI-ING: There's hardly anything to eat at Sakariba anymore, there's only three or four stalls.

TSONG-TIK: Nowadays, most of the food stalls have moved to the end of Hu-tsian Road. It's called "New Sakariba."

TSONG-BING: So then, let's go to Hai-an Road.

HUI-ING: It's all torn down. If you had come back two years ago, you could still have seen Hai-an Road.

TSONG-BING: I really don't recognize anything!

HUI-ING: Of course. You haven't come back for forty years. *(Pause.)* Now that you did come back, why didn't you bring your children with you?

TSONG-BING: They each have their own things to do.

HUI-ING: My husband died a long, long time ago. Each of the kids has their own work to do. I just let them be.

Silence.

TSONG-BING: Tsong-tik, Sister-in-Law passed away a long time ago, right?

TSONG-TIK: It's been eight years.

HUI-ING: I never thought that Akiko would be my Sister-in-Law. When we were girls, we often went to the movies together. *(Stops.)* The trees here are nice and shady.

Tsong-tik: I don't know how long it's been since I've seen a movie!

Hui-ing: Now I can watch TV and there's the cable channels, too. I could never finish watching all of those programs. How would I have time for movies? Everyday, when I've got nothing else to do, it's fine if I can just watch TV.

Tsong-bing: *(Asking Tsong-tik.)* Tsong-tik, after you became the principal, you never changed schools?

Tsong-tik: I was there until I retired. Just one day after another.

Tsong-bing: When Dad died, and Mom died, I couldn't come back. It was that way for forty years. Who would have thought that?

Hui-ing: When I went to America a few years ago, I saw that your children could really speak Taiwanese.

Tsong-bing: I taught them here and there. With the grandchildren, there's no way to do it, they're too naughty. They're basically foreigners.

Hui-ing: If they came back, they might not be able to get used to it here. *(Pauses and sighs.)* Kids today have it so good.

Tsong-tik: These past forty years, Taiwan has changed so fast. If you were to come back a few years later, it would be totally different again.

Hui-ing: Who knows, in the future we won't even be able to see these alleys. It'll be big roads and big buildings everywhere.

Tsong-bing: So it will be just like Taipei, Hong Kong, and Singapore.

Hui-ing: *(A little sad.)* Ah, yes, just like that.

Silence.

Tsong-bing: I'd like to come back and stay for a year or two.

Hui-ing: But your life in America ...

Tsong-bing: This year I'll get everything wrapped up, so that I won't have anything to worry about.

Tsong-tik: If you want to come back here and do anything, and at your age, you'd be starting everything from scratch.

Tsong-bing: Let's wait and see. Anyway, everything around here is already so different from before. If I don't come back now, I won't have the chance later.

Silence.

Hui-ing: This way, the whole family could finally get together.

TSONG-BING: Our old house ... I've been thinking about fixing it up.

HUI-ING: Isn't it rented out to someone else now?

TSONG-TIK: After our own family moved out of the first floor, some of the relatives fought to use it as a storefront. All that shouting, and now they don't even live there anymore. The house is rented out, and the relatives manage the rent. I don't want to deal with any of that. Now, I only go worship at the temple next door on the birthdays of Kuan-te-ia and Ong-ia. Most of the time, I rarely go there.

HUI-ING: Didn't you say before, that our uncle's family kept shouting about building some big building there?

TSONG-TIK: It's not that simple, the land is part of the temple property, you can't just change things around at will.

TSONG-BING: What if I don't want to tear down the house, I want to fix it all up, and maintain the character of that street? Is that allowed?

TSONG-TIK: You could talk it over, but it might take a lot of energy. *(Pause.)* Can't say for sure, but maybe one day the city plan might change again. Who knows?

TSONG-BING: Do you remember? A long time ago, Dad told us the story of the five canals?

TSONG-TIK: Right, and he heard it from Grandpa, and from Great-grandpa before him.

TSONG-BING: That was during the time of the old canals. The Lam-si Canal and Water Spirits Temple by our house were so full of activity. Back then, everything happening on our own Pak-si Street was work related to the port.

TSONG-TIK: A big traveling theater troupe came from the mainland, and performed there for quite some time.

Slow nanguan *opera music starts to play.*

HUI-ING: Grandpa often went to the temple to sing *nanguan* music.

Thiam-guan leads a bicycle onto the stage, accompanied by his Grandson.

TSONG-TIK: Dad did that, too.

TSONG-BING: This stuff is all from such a long, long time ago!

The lights change to Scene 1.

Tsong-tik, Tsong-bing, and Hui-ing exit.

Scene 1

TIME: 1961, the fiftieth year of the Republic

This scene is accompanied by projections of early photographs of Tainan. It has a dreamlike atmosphere.

GRANDSON: Grandpa, my teacher said, the reason we call Tainan the "Phoenix City" has nothing to do with the phoenix tree. It's because Tainan was originally an actual phoenix. Is that really true?

THIAM-GUAN: The people in the olden days said Tainan was a vulture.

GRANDSON: A vulture?

THIAM-GUAN: A vulture is a bird that really looks a lot like a phoenix, when people go telling their stories, a vulture can easily turn into a phoenix. Anyway, they say all of this because of the geography. Tainan really was shaped like a bird. The nostrils on the bird's beak are at Phoo-tse Hall, the eyes are right at Chihkan Tower. One of the two wings goes off toward Tainan Hospital and Jade Emperor Palace. The other goes to the Provincial Girls' Middle School and the Temple of the Five Concubines. The tail is at that Circle at East Gate. The Emperor's Temple is at the very heart of the phoenix. *(Pause.)* This feng shui is really good. It's just right how it comes out from the center at Phoo-tse Hall and makes an eight trigram web. Because of this feng shui, this shape, our city of Tainan was made the capital of the whole prefecture of Taiwan. This trigram web musn't ever be destroyed, or things will be really bad for us!

GRANDSON: So then, if my teacher says it's a phoenix, then that's OK.

THIAM-GUAN: Sure. In the olden days, some called Tainan the coral tree city, which just meant there were lots of coral tree flowers. When the flowers bloomed, it was like the whole tree was red, red, red!

GRANDSON: *(Picking up a phoenix tree flower from the ground.)* Grandpa, look, does this phoenix tree flower really look like a phoenix?

THIAM-GUAN: Actually, it looks more like a butterfly. These phoenix trees were planted by the Japanese. When Grandpa was little, the whole city was filled with phoenix trees. In the summer, the streets were all red flowers, so beautiful, really so beautiful.

Thiam-guan and his Grandson slowly walk away, exiting.

The nanguan *music ends.*

The projected images conclude.

The lights change to Scene 2.

Scene 2

TIME: 1941, the sixteenth year of Showa

PLACE: Thiam-guan's old family home on Pak-si Street

Hui-ing is pasting up strips of paper as New Year's decorations. Because of the Kominka Movement, these New Year's decorations are white.

HUI-ING: Mom, look—is the way I've hung them up OK?

Siok-hun enters.

SIOK-HUN: *(Pointing at the decorations.)* Make the one on the right a little higher ... still a little higher ... OK, it's fine.

Hui-ing moves a chair over to the other side, Siok-hun hands her daughter another paper strip.

Tsong-tik enters.

TSONG-TIK: *(Looks at the New Year's decorations.)* Mom, you're not hanging them up right. At the top of the strip you're supposed to tie a fancy knot.

SIOK-HUN: *(Angrily.)* Tear it all down, hanging this stuff makes it look like we're having a funeral.

Tsong-tik and Hui-ing look at one another and don't dare say a word.

Siok-hun sees that no one is going to tear down the decorations, so she grabs the chair herself, steps up onto it, and tears down both strips.

TSONG-TIK: Mom, if you just tied a knot at the top, then it'd be fine.

SIOK-HUN: *(Jumping down from the chair.)* Where did you run off to? I didn't see anyone this morning. You know how busy we are at New Year, and you don't help out at all. And celebrating Japanese New Year, I can't figure out these customs.

TSONG-TIK: *(Takes a cake out of his pocket.)* Do you want to try this cake? *(Pause.)* Matsumoto *Sensei* gave it to me. I went to his house this morning to help him clean.

SIOK-HUN: *(Glancing at the cake.)* I'm busy!

HUI-ING: Brother, just give me a piece.

Tsong-tik breaks the cake in half and gives one of the halves to his little sister Hui-ing. A-buan enters, carrying a blue grocery bag.

A-BUAN: My, oh, my, I just can't stand it! The market was totally crazy, everyone pushing and shoving. It was like they were just giving the stuff away.

SIOK-HUN: A-buan, did you manage to buy the pork?

A-BUAN: Fortunately, I ordered it yesterday, and the butcher saved me a piece.

HUI-ING: Auntie, you bought a lot besides that.

A-BUAN: I can't help myself at New Year. Even if we're celebrating Japanese New Year now, I still want it to be fun and festive!

Hui-ing helps A-buan bring in the groceries.

SIOK-HUN: In just a moment, we'll offer our prayers.

A-BUAN: Do we also have to pray to "Amaterasu, Great Spirit"?

HUI-ING: Will the Japanese gods eat our sacrificial foods, too?

TSONG-TIK: Our teacher says, the Japanese race doesn't offer sacrificial foods, they offer flowers and four kinds of fruit.

SIOK-HUN: We haven't made offerings to the ancestors in a long time, so we should use this chance to do it. How will they know?

A-BUAN: Sister-in-Law, I think we shouldn't. If the Big People[2] come by later, what a disaster ...

SIOK-HUN: Well ...

Tsong-tik takes out a Japanese flag.

TSONG-TIK: Mom, these decorations still need the national flag. Can I hang it up?

A-BUAN: Along the street I saw people hanging up these white paper things, and putting up bamboo sticks and pine branches. In the middle of the doorway, they were hanging up two Japanese flags, crisscrossed, just like this. *(Makes a gesture with her arms to show the diagonal cross.)* It was festive, really festive.

Siok-hun takes another look at the decorations on the wall.

SIOK-HUN: With all this white, how can it feel like New Year?

A-BUAN: We should still hang it all up. *(To Tsong-tik.)* Your *sensei* taught you this, right? Go hang it up, just like your *sensei* said.

---

[2] "Big People" was a way of referring to the Japanese police at that time.

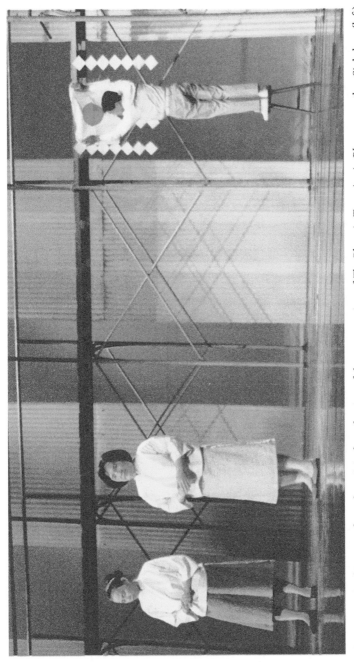

Figure 1.2 In this scene from the original production of the 1997 version of *The Phoenix Trees Are in Blossom*, mother Siok-hun (left) and aunt A-buan watch son Tsong-tik (right) hang up the flag of Japan, as part of the Japanese New Year decorations required of Taiwanese families by the Kominka ("becoming the Emperor's subjects") Movement.

Tsong-tik holds up one Japanese flag at the top of the door, trying it out in different places to get it just right.

TSONG-TIK: Hmm, we don't have any bamboo or pine branches in the house. I'll go buy some.

A-buan takes money out of her pocket to give to Tsong-tik.

SIOK-HUN: *(Takes some money from her pocket to give to Tsong-tik.)* A-tik, here, take this and go buy them. On the way, look for your little brother, and bring him back. I haven't seen him all morning.

A-BUAN: *(Toward the inside.)* A-ing, take the greens out and snap off the leaves.

TSONG-TIK: *(Taking the money.)* I'm going. *(Exits.)*

Hui-ing enters, holding a bunch of greens.

HUI-ING: Tsong-bing went to the Amitabha Temple.

SIOK-HUN: To the Amitabha Temple?

HUI-ING: He went to study Chinese.

SIOK-HUN: He never studies, and then he picks New Year, of all times, to go do it.

A-BUAN: I never noticed that your Tsong-bing was that studious.

SIOK-HUN: I wonder if he's really studying, or if he's just horsing around all day.

A-BUAN: Boys are all like that.

SIOK-HUN: Now that we're celebrating this Japanese New Year, I don't know if we're allowed to celebrate our old Lunar New Year any more.

HUI-ING: We definitely can't. Now they've imposed Kominka, "becoming the emperor's subjects." Everything has to follow their Japanese rules. This year, we won't even have school vacation at New Year. It's really annoying.

SIOK-HUN: Don't worry. Mommy will steam cakes just like she always has, cakes aren't illegal!

A-BUAN: If we don't eat New Year's cakes, it won't seem like New Year.

HUI-ING: If I still have to go to school, it won't seem like New Year.

SIOK-HUN: On New Year's Eve, I'll still prepare special things for us to eat while we sit around the hot pot.

HUI-ING: But yesterday my *sensei* said the school is having a "Student Recital" on New Year's Eve, so we have to prepare a performance. Our families also have to attend.

SIOK-HUN: If the cakes aren't steamed yet, where will I find the time to attend that?

A-BUAN: A-ing, what are you performing?

HUI-ING: Our group wants to sing and dance. Another group says they want to imitate Li Xianglan. Their group has a girl who's really pretty, with big, big eyes, who sings like this. *(Imitates Li Xianglan singing.)* She really looks just like Li Xianglan!

A-BUAN: You've never seen Li Xianglan sing. How do you know she looks just like her?

HUI-ING: Hey! I've seen pictures of her, and I've heard her sing. I know it in my imagination!

A-BUAN: Let me see you imitate her.

HUI-ING: I can't ...

SIOK-HUN: Of course she can't. OK, if you're done with these vegetables, take them in.

Hui-ing takes the vegetables from the table, and exits.

A-BUAN: Sister-in-Law, how are we cooking the chicken?

SIOK-HUN: Boiling half of it for soup, and steaming and slicing the other half. We'll arrange it all pretty on a platter.

A-BUAN: Oh. *(Prepares to go inside.)*

SIOK-HUN: Oh, and save the chicken's blood. It'll be good for making rice blood cakes.

A-BUAN: If there's glutinous rice left over from the steamed cakes, you can use it for the rice blood cakes. OK, I'm going inside to kill the chicken.

SIOK-HUN: I'll come in as soon as I finish mending these pants.

Siok-hun looks at the hanging decorations. The more she looks at them, the less they please her.

She pulls down the unfinished decorations.

The music for "When Will My Lord Come Again?" begins.

Siok-hun sits at her sewing maching, mending the pants.

The lights change to Scene 3.

Scene 3

Li Xianglan, wearing a long qipao, *stands in front of a microphone singing "When Will My Lord Come Again?"*

LI XIANGLAN: *(Sings.)*
Splendid flowers seldom bloom, splendid views are seldom seen,
Worry weighs on smiling brows, tears soak longing, lovesick eyes,
When we've bid farewell tonight, when will my lord come again?
Drink up the last cup, eat up the last bites,
Rare to find life's intoxication,
No joy to wait for him once more,
Spoken line in the song.
Come, come, come, drink up the last cup, say it again,
Singing.
When we've bid farewell tonight, when will my lord come again?
Speaks, in Beijing dialect.
Thank you, thank you. This song was originally sung by Zhou Xuan. I really like singing this song, and I hope that you enjoy hearing me sing it.
Sings.
Splendid flowers seldom bloom, splendid views are seldom seen,
Worry weighs on smiling brows, tears soak longing, lovesick eyes ...
Sachiko, Li Xianglan's assistant, walks toward her.

SACHIKO: Xianglan, Xianglan, the police just came backstage. They said "When Will My Lord Come Again?" is a banned song, and you aren't allowed to sing it again.

LI XIANGLAN: Why?

SACHIKO: Now it's wartime. They said singing this kind of song is too decadent.

LI XIANGLAN: But each time I go to the front lines to sing for the troops, many of them request this song.

SACHIKO: But if they make this rule, then we can't sing it any more.

LI XIANGLAN: Is it only banned in Manchuria?

SACHIKO: I don't know. You probably can't sing it in any Japanese-controlled area!

LI XIANGLAN: There are more and more soldiers coming here from Japan. When they leave their hometowns to come to China to fight, if the songs I sing can give them a little comfort, then isn't that a good thing?

SACHIKO: There's nothing wrong with what you're saying, but if the military stipulates that you can't sing this song, then we don't want to break the law. There are still a lot of songs you can sing, right? Don't make trouble for yourself. We're depending on this work for our food!

LI XIANGLAN: But this kind of rule is completely unreasonable.

SACHIKO: But you're finally making it big. Better not to make trouble ...

LI XIANGLAN: I know, I know. You don't have to say it again!

The lights change to Scene 4.

Li Xianglan and Sachiko exit.

Scene 4

TIME: 1941, sixteenth year of Showa

Siok-hun is working at her sewing machine. The two brothers Thiam-guan and Thiam-gi have been at the Tainan Assembly Hall, watching the proceedings of the dissolving of the "Three Companies." When they return home, Thiam-guan is still furious.

THIAM-GUAN: Fucking idiots![3]

THIAM-GI: They really are fucking idiots! Those people are really traitors. Two hundred years of the Three Companies' history in their hands, and they throw it all away.

Siok-hun hears them return, and stops the sewing machine.

SIOK-HUN: Why were you gone so long?

THIAM-GUAN: Bring some tea.

Siok-hun goes inside right away to make tea.

THIAM-GUAN: From early on, our own grandfather managed the accounts at Three Benefits Hall.

THIAM-GI: What's Three Benefits Hall?

THIAM-GUAN: You mean you don't know? It was the assembly hall for the Three Companies. Everyone went there to volunteer.

THIAM-GI: I really didn't know that.

THIAM-GUAN: *(Pause.)* Now, Three Benefits Hall is full of mice, and there's little happening there. No wonder you don't know what it is.

THIAM-GI: Right. Since I was little, I've never heard of much of anything going on there.

THIAM-GUAN: The Three Companies' headquarters was set up at the Water Spirits Temple. Grandpa often said when he was small the Water Spirits Temple was full of activity. There used to be a river behind our house, and it went right up to the Water Spirits Temple. Back then, the Three Companies' businesses were really active, number one in all of Taiwan. The shops all around had connections to the Water Spirits

---

[3] Written in Japanese in the original script.

Temple. Even our family's Golden Temple was first built as a warehouse for the Three Companies.

Siok-hun brings in tea.

THIAM-GI: It's fortunate that we bought it, so it didn't get sold to the Japanese.

THIAM-GUAN: Never! Our ancestors bought the Golden Temple from the Three Companies for three hundred yuan. If not for that, how else would we still be able to worship our Kuan-te-ia? Our ancestors labored bitterly for every last dollar and cent needed to build the temple to protect us. From early on, it had no connection to the Three Companies.

THIAM-GI: That's really a good thing.

THIAM-GUAN: Such a loss of face. The Three Companies have even sold off the Ma-tsoo Temple and the Water Spirits Temple to the Japanese.

THIAM-GI: *(Quietly.)* The Japanese pushed them to stamp the contract, there was really no way out.

THIAM-GUAN: What does that mean ... no way out.

SIOK-HUN: *(To Thiam-guan.)* A little quieter.

THIAM-GUAN: This is my house. If I want to be loud, I'll be loud! *(Gets up out of his seat.)*

THIAM-GI: Big brother, really, a quieter voice attracts fewer mosquitoes.

SIOK-HUN: *(Quietly.)* Did they really sell the Ma-tsoo Temple and the Water Spirits Temple?

THIAM-GI: At that time, when they were about to sign the contract, a Japanese official from the Cultural Bureau, doing religious research, said it was a historic site, and you couldn't just sell it off, you should protect it well.

SIOK-HUN: Thank heavens, *Amitahba*, the Bodhisattva protected us.

THIAM-GI: So, are you saying that our house is connected to the Three Companies?

THIAM-GUAN: The land this house is on belongs to the Golden Temple. It hasn't been part of the Three Companies for a long time. If you want to sell it, you need twenty people to stamp the contract, it's not so simple.

The two brothers Tsong-tik and Tsong-bing run onstage, carrying their school bags.

THIAM-GI: *(Pulling Thiam-guan back to his seat.)* Come on, sit down, why get so upset? Things are all this way. They say things come together, then they come apart. Didn't you say that the Three Companies' organization had more than two hundred years of history? If it comes apart, that's only natural. Why get so angry about it?

THIAM-GUAN: It's exactly because of those two hundred years that I'm angry. The younger generation knows nothing, all they care about is making it big. They don't think about how their ancestors labored and toiled for this land, to piece together everything that's here. We should all think of a way to work together to fight for it. How can we just casually take the Three Companies and throw it all away?

THIAM-GI: Times are different now, let it go. … *(Pause.)* Well, today at the Tainan Assembly Hall, when we saw them selling those buildings, I was worried that we wouldn't have a place to live, and we'd have to go live in front of the temple.

SIOK-HUN: *(To Tsong-tik and Tsong-bing.)* How did you two come home together today?

TSONG-BING: We ran into each other at the airport. Today we all went to do volunteer labor.

THIAM-GI: You went to do that again?

TSONG-BING: We still have to go next week.

TSONG-TIK: Next week we're going to Jin-tik.

TSONG-BING: This is exactly how we're being used by the Japanese. When we should be studying, we have to go help them by laboring.

THIAM-GI: As long as you don't have to go be a soldier, it's fine.

THIAM-GUAN: It's also good to get some exercise.

TSONG-TIK: Dad, six students from our class volunteered to be soldiers.

THIAM-GUAN: Don't go be a mother fucking soldier yourself.

TSONG-BING: My *sensei* says, the Greater East Asia War has already begun, and sooner or later he'll have to join the army.

THIAM-GI: Well, the Japanese all have to go fight, but we Taiwanese should avoid it if we can. The Japanese still wouldn't trust us.

TSONG-BING: Are they afraid we'd grab the guns and fight back?

TSONG-TIK: I hear that if you go volunteer, you get decent money each month, plus you get a lot of stuff from the government.

THIAM-GUAN: Phantom stuff! You can't tell a taro root from a sweet potato! Don't go if you don't have to. We don't have to give up our lives for other people.

TSONG-TIK: But *sensei* says ...

THIAM-GUAN: Did you not hear me?

Siok-hun gestures to Tsong-tik not to say anything more.

SIOK-HUN: Children should hold their tongues. *(To Tsong-tik and Tsong-bing.)* Go change your clothes, you two.

Tsong-tik and Tsong-bing exit the stage, and Siok-hun exists with them.

THIAM-GUAN: I should write a letter to Thiam-hok in Amoy. I don't know what it's like for him over there. A-gi, go get paper and a brush.

THIAM-GI: Last time, didn't Brother say he planned to go to Shanghai?

THIAM-GUAN: China and Japan are already at war, the interior is such a mess. Don't you think it's safer if we ask him to come back?

THIAM-GI: I think Brother has his plan. Going to Shanghai is relatively safe.

THIAM-GUAN: It's a mess now. Going everywhere is about the same. Tell him to come back.

THIAM-GI: Fine, I'll tell him again. *(Pause.)* Brother, our boss wants to send me to Japan to get more merchandise. He wants me to go for a week.

THIAM-GUAN: Are you crazy? We just said there's about to be war, and then you say you want to go there.

THIAM-GI: The war is being fought on the mainland. It won't spread to Japan. I'll go for a bit, and then come back really fast!

A-BUAN: *(Offstage.)* A-gi, A-gi, come here for a moment.

THIAM-GI: What do you want?

THIAM-GUAN: I can tell you're still thinking about it. Don't make your wife worry.

THIAM-GI: What do you want from me? This is an opportunity!

A-buan enters.

A-BUAN: *(To Thiam-gi.)* I just heard your voice, and I called for you, but you didn't answer me. Are you deaf?

THIAM-GI: Can't you see that I'm talking with my elder brother?

A-BUAN: *(Gestures with respect to Thiam-guan; then, to Thiam-gi.)* The water is stopped up! Go take a look at it right now. I want to go borrow some salt from Sister-in-Law. *(Exits.)*

THIAM-GUAN: This business of going to Japan—you should still think it over more.

THIAM-GI: I know!

The music of the song "Suzhou Nocturne," from the film China Nights, *begins.*

The lights change to Scene 5.

Thiam-gi and Thiam-guan exit.

Scene 5

The film China Nights *is being projected on a screen. On the screen, the male lead Hase Tetsuo waits for the female lead Guilan to come out of the bath; later on, he will be seen slapping Guilan. A Radio Announcer holding a microphone introduces the story of* China Nights. *On stage, imitating the action from part of the film, Hasegawa Kazuo, playing the male lead Hase Tetsuo, enters. He sits and waits for the female lead Guilan, being played by Li Xianglan, to enter.*

ANNOUNCER: *(In Beijing dialect.)* The film *Chee-na Nights* stars Hasegawa Kazuo and Li Xianglan, and it takes Shanghai as its setting. Li Xianglan plays the young Chinese girl Guilan. She loses both parents in the war, and her home is burned down by Japanese soldiers. She deeply despises the Japanese. One day, on a street in Shanghai, she is harassed by a Japanese drunk, and just at the critical moment, the Japanese youth Hase Tetsuo saves her. Hase knows that this girl has no family in Shanghai, so he takes her to a hotel and asks for someone to take good care of her.

After that, Li Xianglan, dressed as Guilan, wearing a bathrobe, enters into the scene.

ANNOUNCER: When she finishes her bath, her face scrubbed clean, the Guilan who emerges from the bathroom seems to have become a different person entirely. As soon as she sees Hase Tetsuo, she can't keep herself from screaming at him, shouting that it was the Japanese who murdered her family and destroyed her life. In the end, Hase reaches the point where he can no longer bear it ...

Hasegawa Kazuo and Li Xianglan imitate the frame from the film when Hase Tetsuo slaps Guilan across the face. The music "Suzhou Nocturne" stops. The movie frame freezes.

HASEGAWA: *(Playing Hase Tetsuo, speaking in Japanese.)* Wake up! Will you be this stubborn forever! *(Slaps Li Xianglan, who is playing Guilan.)*

Li Xianglan, playing Guilan, faints.

ANNOUNCER: He wants Li Xianglan to wake up. He wants her to stop being stubborn. *(Announcer exits.)*

The movie frame disappears.

In the next part of the play, the conversation between Li Xianglan, Hasegawa Kazuo, and the Director is in Japanese. At the side of the stage, projected subtitles provide translation. But Li Xianglan and Sachiko's conversation is still in Beijing dialect.

DIRECTOR: *(Clapping his hands, speaking in Japanese.)* Your performance was excellent.

HASEGAWA: *(To Li Xianglan, in Japanese.)* My apologies, I hit you too hard just now.

DIRECTOR: Not at all, the scene is only true to life if you do it forcefully.

LI XIANGLAN: It's no big deal.

DIRECTOR: Right, right, this is only acting.

HASEGAWA: *(To Li Xianglan, in Japanese.)* But I'm still very sorry.

DIRECTOR: This slap is very important. Tomorrow we're filming the scene where Guilan develops a high fever after getting slapped, and Hase takes care of her. That is the start of the first sprouts of love for each other, so this slap is the crux. After that, their relationship gets closer and closer, and Guilan starts to be willing to speak a few sentences of Japanese, and to be intimate with Hase.

HASEGAWA: I'm sorry, but isn't this film *Chee-na Nights* going to be shown in China?

DIRECTOR: I'll select a few places there to show it, but what's important is that it can also be shown in Japan. This film uses Japanese much of the time … it isn't necessarily suitable for showing in China. Ah, yes, Taiwan, it can definitely go to Taiwan. I hear the title song of *Chee-na Nights* is already causing a sensation there.

HASEGAWA: That part we just shot, I feel like it's not very natural. The two of us seem wooden, like puppets, not like real people. *(To Xianglan.)* Xianglan, what do you think?

XIANGLAN: It's a bit unnatural. I feel like Chinese people aren't like this.

DIRECTOR: Don't think too much. Your acting is good. You can't see that yourselves, so you have all these doubts. I think this film will definitely cause a sensation domestically in Japan. For the premiere, I'm planning to arrange for you to go back to Japan to give a concert, and you can do publicity at the same time.

HASEGAWA: If this film is likely to be shown in China, I think it's best to

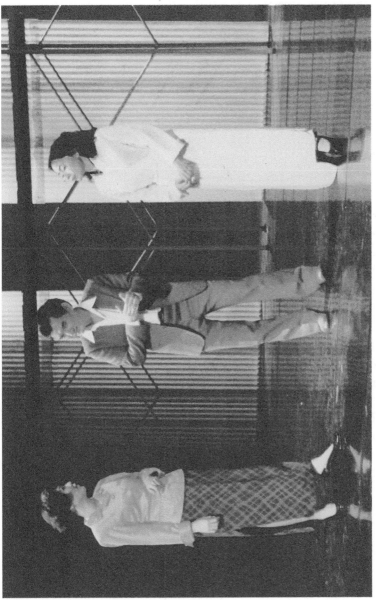

Figure 1.3 The Director (left) of *China Nights* takes a break during filming to discuss the infamous scene where Hasegawa Kazuo (center), playing the Japanese youth Hase Tetsuo, slaps Li Xianglan, who portrays Guilan, a Chinese orphan. Guilan became the breakout role for rising star Li Xianglan.

change the name. The Chinese, it seems, don't like having their country called by our word "Chee-na."

Sachiko, holding a make-up box and a few letters, comes off the set.

DIRECTOR: That's something I'll definitely give careful thought. Thanks for your suggestion. I'll talk it over with the producer.

SACHIKO: *(To the Director.)* Director, you have an urgent phone call. The producer wants you to come right away.

DIRECTOR: *(To Hasegawa and Li Xianglan.)* I'm going now. Tomorrow will be the announcement, don't forget.

Director exits.

HASEGAWA: I'm worried that this film will disgust the Chinese people.

XIANGLAN: Why?

HASEGAWA: The war has already started. Right now, anti-Japanese feelings are high among the Chinese.

XIANGLAN: This is just a romantic picture. It shouldn't be all that serious.

HASEGAWA: But Guilan's love for a Japanese is unforgiveable.

XIANGLAN: I never thought about that.

HASEGAWA: I believe this film is completely inappropriate for screening in China. *(Stops.)* You didn't hear me say it—maybe I think too much. I'm heading back now. *(Exits.)*

XIANGLAN: See you tomorrow.

SACHIKO: *(Hands the letters to Xianglan.)* Was everything good today?

XIANGLAN: I was just slapped by Hase. It still hurts.

SACHIKO: Which scene?

XIANGLAN: It's that one where Guilan is saved, the scene where she sees Hase Tetsuo after coming out of the hotel bathroom.

SACHIKO: You're progressing really fast, if you've already filmed to there.

XIANGLAN: Hasegawa is worried that Chinese people will be disgusted by this film.

SACHIKO: Right ... today there was a letter from the interior. It only said a few words. The contents were a bit strange. *(Takes out a letter and gives it to Li Xianglan.)* Take a look.

Xianglan takes the letter and reads it.

XIANGLAN: *(Reading the letter, in Japanese.)* Please value yourself. Don't be a tool of Japanese government propaganda. Take care of your pure, shining heart. Please value yourself as best you can. *(Folds the letter up.)*

SACHIKO: What does it mean?

XIANGLAN: *(Using Beijing dialect, reads it once again.)* Please value yourself. Don't be a tool of Japanese government propaganda. Take care of your pure, shining heart. Please value yourself as best you can. *(Pause.)* Don't be a tool of Japanese government propaganda?

SACHIKO: Who is this? Who would write such a letter?

XIANGLAN: Maybe Hasegawa Kazuo was right. The war has already started. While *Chee-na Nights* is being filmed, China and Japan are becoming all intertwined. It's just too sensitive.

SACHIKO: No one is going to take it that way. The movie is just a made-up story. It's simple entertainment.

XIANGLAN: But do you think Guilan falling in love with Hase Tetsuo is far-fetched?

SACHIKO: Without a love story, a film wouldn't be good to watch. OK, let's move a little faster, it will soon be time to get on the set.

Sachiko helps Li Xianglan get out of the bathrobe and into a pretty, two piece "phoenix-fairy" outfit,[4] then carefully straightens up her clothing for her.

XIANGLAN: How long do you think this war will go on?

SACHIKO: What war?

XIANGLAN: China and Japan.

SACHIKO: Who knows?

XIANGLAN: After we finish shooting this film, come home with me to Manchuria. It's already been more than a year since I've been back. How I miss home!

SACHIKO: Will you go see your godfather?

XIANGLAN: Yes. My godfather loves me most dearly. You know, it was he who chose the name "Li Xianglan" for me.

SACHIKO: Li Xianglan is a pretty name. When you make films in China, it will be easy to use that name for publicity. There probably aren't too many people who know your real name is Yamaguchi Yoshiko. Oh,

---

[4] A traditional Chinese outfit consisting of a top that buttons along an angle, and a long skirt.

hurry, or we won't make it in time. Quick, touch up your make-up a little. *(Touches up Xianglan's make-up.)*

The music from China Nights plays.

Sachiko exits.

Hui-ing quickly runs onto the stage.

HUI-ING: *(Shouting loudly toward backstage.)* Mom, Auntie, hurry up, the front of the theater is full of people.

Hui-ing looks straight in the direction of the theater. Hui-ing's classmate Akiko hurriedly runs onto the stage, as if she's looking for someone.

HUI-ING: Akiko, you also want to go see Li Xianglan!

AKIKO: I don't know where my mom and grandma got squeezed in. I can't find them.

Siok-hun and A-buan, in their best clothing, rush out.

HUI-ING: *(Shouting.)* Mom, hurry up.

SIOK-HUN: What on earth are you up to, child?

HUI-ING: *(Pointing in the direction of the theater.)* Look, the World Hall is full of people everywhere.

AKIKO: *(To Siok-hun.)* Obasan, it's so crowded that you can't get in, you came too late.

HUI-ING: *(Introduces Akiko to her mother.)* This is my classmate Akiko. *(Indicates Siok-hun, A-buan.)* This is my mother and third aunt.

AKIKO: *(Bowing.)* Hello.

SIOK-HUN: *(As a way of greeting Akiko.)* Ah, it's really so full that we can't go in?

A-BUAN: Who cares, Sister-in-Law, never mind, we're going in. If Li Xianglan is on the stage, we're definitely going to go see her.

SIOK-HUN: OK, OK, hurry in. *(Pulling Hui-ing's hand.)*

Li Xianglan stands on a high place singing China Nights' main theme song, "China Nights."

"China Nights" lyrics

 Chee-na at nighttime,
 Chee-na at nighttime, oh,
 Glowing of the harbor lights,

Purple color of the night,
Dreams emanate off the sails,
Nighttime ship of dreams.
How can I forget,
Sounds of the *huqin*?
Chee-na at nighttime,
Dreaming at nighttime.

The lights change to Scene 6.

Li Xianglan exits.

Scene 6

TIME: 1943, eighteenth year of Showa

Tsong-bing is practicing brush writing. Tsong-tik is correcting his students' homework.

TSONG-BING: Brother, loan me some of your ink. This piece of inkstick isn't any good.

TSONG-TIK: *(Pointing to the inkstone on the table.)* It's right there.

TSONG-BING: *(Taking the inkstone.)* The ink that you teachers use is really good.

TSONG-TIK: This inkstick was given to me by Sato.

TSONG-BING: Who?

TSONG-TIK: Our coworker.

TSONG-BING: A Japanese?

TSONG-TIK: He's really a good guy. Yesterday he got his draft notice, so he went off to be a soldier. He gave us all of his stuff.

TSONG-BING: A good number of our classmates and teachers also went in that group.

TSONG-TIK: Yesterday, when Sato was about to go, on the blackboard in his classroom it said *(In Japanese.)* "We exist together and flourish together."

TSONG-BING: A few days ago, two students in our class were fighting, and finally one shouted "Chee-na" at the other. Our *sensei* slapped him across the face. *(Stops.)* Our *sensei* said, "Chee-na" is what the Japanese call our China. It means you're really looking down on someone.

TSONG-TIK: Is that Mr. Tan, the teacher who took you to the Amitabha Temple to read Chinese with the monks?

TSONG-BING: That's him.

TSONG-TIK: You should be more careful. Don't criticize things so casually around other people.

TSONG-BING: Why do we want to "exist together and flourish together" with the Japanese? We aren't Japanese. I'll read a line of song for you to hear, I studied it before, "Liu the Official had lots of plans but didn't do anything, flies change into honeybees, earthworms change into centipedes, big houses change into thin air, Taiwan turns into barbarians, the Japanese have no hair."—ha, ha, ha!

TSONG-TIK: Don't stick your nose where it doesn't belong. Remember that we're now the subjects of the emperor. You can't just say whatever you're thinking.

TSONG-BING: Don't you forget we are Han people. *(Pause.)* Someday, I'm going to the mainland to look for Second Uncle.

TSONG-TIK: Watch what you say. You didn't know that when Second Uncle got to Shanghai, he was immediately apprehended and questioned by the Japanese military police. Fortunately, in the end it wasn't anything.

TSONG-BING: Teacher Chen said if he had the opportunity, he would take us to travel on the mainland.

TSONG-TIK: *(Pause.)* It's best if you don't go to the Amitabha Temple anymore.

TSONG-BING: Brother, what are you afraid of? You think that going to read Chinese will also cause trouble?

TSONG-TIK: Over these past two years, Kominka has been attained. You can be arrested and punished severely for doing just about anything. You young people don't know life from death.

TSONG-BING: That's what we call courage. *(Pause.)* Why does Dad want to be the neighborhood head? So he can bow his head to the Japanese? To me, he seems useless.

TSONG-TIK: How can you speak about Dad that way? We, who are now ruled by the Japanese, are also Japanese. We should listen to them in each and every matter. Besides, the neighborhood head's aim is to collectively maintain order in the area around our home. Dad is the one who has that ability, so people asked him to do it.

TSONG-BING: One with true ability refuses to be a slave to the colonizers.

TSONG-TIK: This isn't for you to decide.

TSONG-BING: I don't want to talk to you anymore. The way I see it, out of our whole family, only Second Uncle and I think alike.

Silence.

TSONG-TIK: Today at school we were talking. Perhaps, at the end of the year, schools might suspend classes. It won't matter if you're Japanese or Taiwanese, all high school students will have to go be soldiers. When the time comes, you'll have no choice.

Hui-ing enters the stage holding an iron. Air raid siren sounds. The two brothers and sister hide on account of the air raid siren. Tsong-tik and Tsong-bing exit. Hui-ing comes out from the corner.

The lights change to Scene 7.

Scene 7

Music from the film "Cassia Tree of Love" slowly emerges. Hui-ing carefully irons her skirt.

Siok-hun and A-buan enter the stage, A-buan holding a cake in her hands.

SIOK-HUN: That song from the movie, why does it feel so familiar?

A-BUAN: The song "Cassia Tree of Love" is often played on the *radio*.

Siok-hun, A-buan sit down.

HUI-ING: Mom, you're back! When they did the air raid drill just now, where did you hide?

SIOK-HUN: In the movie theater.

A-BUAN: This time, why didn't they tell us there would be a drill?

SIOK-HUN: They wanted to scare us on purpose. *(To Hui-ing.)* Daughter, have some cake.

HUI-ING: *(Going over to her mother.)* Where did you get the cake?

SIOK-HUN: I bumped into your uncle. He gave it to me.

A-BUAN: During the air raid, they only played half of the movie.

HUI-ING: You just sat right there?

SIOK-HUN: No, we all hid under the chairs, it was all very serious. Unexpectedly, your father came into the theater, acting as the air raid warden. At his side was one of the Big People. I was so scared, so uncomfortable, that I didn't even go say hello to your father.

A-BUAN: It's a good thing the Miyako Theater makes you take off your shoes when you go in. Hiding under the seats wasn't too dirty.

HUI-ING: Father acted as the air raid warden?

SIOK-HUN: It looked like he was practicing, being taught. Right now he's just the "neighborhood head," he needs to study some more. Later your father will show us how to flee from air raids. *(Pause.)* Your brothers haven't come back yet?

HUI-ING: I haven't seen anyone.

Hui-ing returns to the ironing board and continues to iron her skirt.

SIOK-HUN: Hui-ing, just now, during the alarm, you weren't afraid to be all alone?

Figure 1.4 In the midst of war and hardship, sisters-in-law Siok-hun and A-buan share a joyous moment after seeing the film *Cassia Tree of Love.*

HUI-ING: I knew it was fake.

A-BUAN: *(To Hui-ing.)* You're still very brave. My A-ing is all grown up.

HUI-ING: I really hate that high school students can't go watch movies at the theater.

SIOK-HUN: I talked about this with you several times. Girls shouldn't say "hate." Saying "hate" sounds uncouth.

A-BUAN: *(Walking toward Hui-ing.)* A-ing, that's the rule for you high school students. *(Seriously.)* You should respect it.

HUI-ING: Hai! *(Pause.)* Auntie, was the movie good?

A-BUAN: Oh yes, only it wasn't suitable for you girls.

A-buan goes toward the stairs in the back, and prepares to go up to the second floor.

SIOK-HUN: *(To Hui-ing.)* Did you finish ironing your skirt?

Siok-hun walks toward Hui-ing.

HUI-ING: Not yet.

SIOK-HUN: You have to tug on the pleats when you iron it, or it won't ever get flat. *(Teaches Hui-ing how to iron the skirt.)* *(To A-buan.)* A-buan, if this movie didn't have Tanaka Kinuyo and Uehara Ken acting together, it definitely wouldn't have been any good.

A-BUAN: *(Turning around, and walking toward Siok-hun.)* True, but the story was written really well. The doctor loves the nurse, every day they run into each other.

HUI-ING: Is Tanaka Kinuyo prettier than Li Xianglan?

A-BUAN: They're both pretty.

SIOK-HUN: No, no, they're different types. Li Xianglan doesn't have that sort of Japanese girl "Hai, hai" ... that soft little look. She looks much livelier.

A-BUAN: She's definitely not Japanese ...

HUI-ING: She is so! Everyone at school says so.

SIOK-HUN: After the sirens were done, we watched the other half of the movie. Anyway, it was pretty good.

A-BUAN: Right, when it continued, how perfect that his parents were beginning to accept that nurse ...

HUI-ING: Did they get married?

A-BUAN: After they got married, they moved back to Kyoto.

SIOK-HUN, A-BUAN: *(The two speaking together.)* Happy ever after!

Siok-hun and A-buan, the two sisters-in-law, laugh at their unexpected identical responses.

SIOK-HUN: A-buan, when we have time, we should go watch another.

A-BUAN: Sounds good. *(Walks in the direction of the second floor.)*

SIOK-HUN: A-buan, wait a minute, *(Takes something out from under the table.)* this is for you to cook.

A-BUAN: What is it?

HUI-ING: Mom, *(Taking the skirt off of the ironing board.)* I think it looks about right.

SIOK-HUN: *(To Hui-ing.)* When you're done, bring it inside. *(To A-buan.)* It's nothing much, *(Quietly.)* a piece of pork, my side of the family gave it to me. *(Hui-ing takes her skirt and slowly walks toward the back of the stage.)*

A-BUAN: *(Opens the paper package, happily.)* Thank you, thank you. I'm always eating your food.

SIOK-HUN: We're so close, don't say that ...

A-BUAN: If only my A-gi could be as responsible as his older brother, that would be good.

SIOK-HUN: A-gi helps a lot at the store. Thiam-guan says his boss really praises him. Does he still talk about going to Japan?

A-BUAN: I've forbidden him to go. I said he couldn't go two years ago. Now, it's impossible.

SIOK-HUN: True. If, by some chance, the bombs fell, it would be really bad.

A-BUAN: That's just what I said. *(Picking up the pork.)* Sister-in-Law, thank you. I'm going upstairs!

SIOK-HUN: I've already salted that piece of meat. If you don't want to cook it right away, it's best to hide it.

A-BUAN: OK, thank you! *(Goes up the stairs, exiting the stage.)*

SIOK-HUN: *(Sees that Hui-ing is about to take the skirt inside.)* Daughter, remember to put the skirt under the tatami, and place it correctly, pleat by pleat.

HUI-ING: I know!

SIOK-HUN: You should use newspaper between the pleats.

HUI-ING: I know! *(Exits.)*

Siok-hun holds the pork and tries hiding it in various places. Thiam-guan enters and stands at the side, watching what Siok-hun is doing. Siok-hun doesn't realize he has returned.

THIAM-GUAN: *(To Siok-hun.)* What are you doing?

SIOK-HUN: I'm hiding pork.

THIAM-GUAN: What?

SIOK-HUN: A few days ago there were people selling pork on the black market, it was much cheaper. I've already salted it. I also gave a piece to A-buan. I lied and said my family gave it to me. I have to hide it well so that the Big People won't snatch it.

THIAM-GUAN: *(Pause.)* Oh, hide it carefully. *(Sits down, takes the documents that were in his hand and looks them over.)*

Siok-hun finally finds a satisfactory place, and she visibly hides the pork in there. Thiam-guan gives her a look.

SIOK-HUN: How come you ran down to the Miyako Theater today? When I saw you I was so startled.

THIAM-GUAN: The Big People came to the store to get me. There was nothing I could do. In these difficult times, you're still going to the movies.

SIOK-HUN: A-buan invited me. *(Pause.)* How come you and A-gi didn't come back together?

THIAM-GUAN: He said he wanted to go see his friends!

SIOK-HUN: If he's always going to see his friends, he won't even need to have one child.

THIAM-GUAN: You care about who has kids, who doesn't have kids. It's none of your business.

Hui-ing enters again.

SIOK-HUN: I'm just saying ... I just see that A-buan doesn't have anybody.

HUI-ING: Mom, I'll clean the rice.

SIOK-HUN: Hey, remember to slice in the sweet potato.

HUI-ING: How much should I slice?

SIOK-HUN: Starting now, we'll have to put in more sweet potato with the rice. The amount will depend on our situation.

HUI-ING: Oh, mom, it seems like we don't have any plums in the house. Tomorrow we have to eat a *hinomaru bento*.

SIOK-HUN: So fast, it's the first of the month already.

HUI-ING: It's fine, I'll go buy it in a bit.

SIOK-HUN: You go buy it, I'll slice the sweet potato.

HUI-ING: I'll slice it really fast, just a few strokes of the hand, that's all. *(Exits.)*

THIAM-GUAN: Our A-ing is graduating soon, right?

SIOK-HUN: Still another year.

THIAM-GUAN: When she graduates, I want to find her a good job.

SIOK-HUN: It's more important to find her a good husband.

THIAM-GUAN: You'll kill that child. She's still young, and you want to marry her off right away.

SIOK-HUN: It's always been that way.

THIAM-GUAN: Today, that A-tsai down at the store said he's gotten a suitcase all ready, all of the important things, rings, necklaces, all put inside. If they really sound the air raid siren, he'll just grab it and go …

The air raid siren sounds. Thiam-guan and Siok-hun hurriedly gather things. Hui-ing comes out, and gathers things together with her parents. A-buan, also wrapping things up, runs down the stairs, panic-stricken.

THIAM-GUAN: Everyone, quickly hide.

HUI-ING: Ah, my skirt! *(About to go upstairs, is grabbed by her father.)*

SIOK-HUN: You can't get it!

The four of them—Thiam-guan, Siok-hun, A-buan, and Hui-ing—hastily run off stage.

The lights change to Scene 8.

Scene 8

Air raid siren sound continues. Slides are projected with images from Li Xianglan's performance in A Good Name for Generations.

RADIO ANNOUNCER: Nineteen forty-two marks the hundredth anniversary of the Opium War, when China conceded to England by signing the humiliating Treaty of Nanking. In special commemoration, three film companies in Shanghai have made a costume drama about the story of Lin Zexu going to war with England to put a stop to the opium trade. A famous, splendid line from a historical play, "Lin Zexu's righteousness leaves a good name for generations," has inspired the film's title, *A Good Name for Generations*. In the eyes of the Japanese, this film schemes to resist the British; but as the Chinese see it, a phony England is standing in for Japan. It's an out-and-out film for resisting the Japanese. *A Good Name for Generations* takes "Stand up, China!" as its motto. Ever since its premiere, it's been earning great praise.

The air raid siren stops. The melody of the "Candy-Peddling Song," the theme song from the film A Good Name for Generations, *begins.*

ANNOUNCER: Whether in the areas that are occupied by the Japanese, or in the areas that aren't, as long as they've got a movie theater, they're all showing this film. In the film, Li Xianglan plays a girl who peddles candy. In the blink of an eye, her "Candy-Peddling Song" has become popular all over China.

Li Xianglan, dressed as the candy peddler from A Good Name for Generations, *sings the "Candy-Peddling Song." The whole stage becomes a teahouse, as she sells candy while she sings.*

"Candy-Peddling Song"

Smoke fragrant, cases elegant,
Pipes so exquisite, bubbles of gold.
How many good times ruined, destroyed?
How many good looks transformed, declined?
Lacquered teeth, misshaped mouth,
Back like a bow, shoulders so hunched,
Eyes tear, nose runs, all day long.

Ah ...
Selling candy, ah, candy.
Selling candy, ah, candy.

Li Xianglan, playing the candy peddler, sings and dances for a period of time. Chen Yunshang and the Producer enter the stage, one after the other, with Chen Yunshang in front and the Producer behind her. Li Xianglan continues singing and dancing, but the music diminishes in volume.

The projection of images from A Good Name for Generations *stops.*

PRODUCER: Chen Yunshang, you've absolutely got to help out with this. The captain of the Japanese warship mentioned you by name. He wants you to go present bouquets to the sailors. If you don't go, it'll have great repercussions for the studio.

CHEN YUNSHANG: You just go yourself. That'll be fine. You're the producer. This is your job, not mine.

PRODUCER: They mentioned you by name. You're the big star. Please, I'm begging you, just do it this once.

CHEN YUNSHANG: You should know full well that I despise Japanese soldiers. Because of my involvement in *A Good Name for Generations*, I'm already vilified as a traitor to the nation. They're saying I shouldn't participate in Chinese-Japanese joint productions. Now, to run off to some Japanese ship to present bouquets to the Japanese—who knows what will be said about me later on?

PRODUCER: Those people, I think, haven't seen the movie yet. *A Good Name for Generations* is a completely patriotic film. If they only see the film, I know they'll stop wagging their tongues. Even more, they'll praise you, Chen Yunshang, for being part of a film so filled with patriotism.

CHEN YUNSHANG: I can't go do this. You'd better look for someone else. Why haven't you tried to get Li Xianglan? Everyone says she's Japanese. Having a Japanese go give flowers to the Japanese—that would be the right thing to do.

PRODUCER: Don't say that kind of thing so recklessly. Did you ask her yourself?

CHEN YUNSHANG: No, but ... she comes from Manchuria.

PRODUCER: Hurry. The ship will be docking just an hour from now. Come on, help me out. *A Good Name for Generations* is now playing. I don't want to bring on any trouble. Really, just think of it as helping me out.

Producer looks at Chen Yunshang imploringly.

CHEN YUNSHANG: You really can't find someone else?

PRODUCER: They've mentioned you by name. How can some random person take the place of Chen Yunshang? Please, I rarely beg like this. Just go this once!

CHEN YUNSHANG: *(Silence.)* Well ... you have got to keep this story out of the news. I don't want it in the papers.

PRODUCER: *(Letting a bit of his happiness show through.)* Not a problem. I absolutely won't allow them to put it in the papers. There isn't much time. Go do your make-up. I'll wait and go with you.

CHEN YUNSHANG: I'll only go if you can look me in the eye and tell me. It absolutely, positively cannot appear in the papers ...

PRODUCER: It absolutely won't, don't worry ...

Chen Yunshang and the Producer leave the stage together. The music of the "Candy-Peddling Song" gradually increases in volume. Li Xianglan continues to sing and dance on stage. Kawakita Nagamasa and Sachiko come onstage together.

KAWAKITA: *(Rushes toward Li Xianglan and grasps her hand.)* Congratulations, congratulations! You're already famous all over China. To have this kind of success your first time acting in a Chinese movie—it's really amazing.

SACHIKO: Xianglan, look, so many fans have written you letters. You seem to have fans everywhere. *(Gives Li Xianglan the letters.)*

KAWAKITA: I'm planning to promote this film in Yan'an and Chongqing. As long as the place has a movie theater, I'm showing this film there. *(To Li Xianglan.)* Maybe you can come on stage after the screenings.

SACHIKO: Are you also going to non-occupied areas?

KAWAKITA: Of course. This first Chinese-Japanese joint film production is causing such a sensation. I want to seize this opportunity. We'll definitely go to the non-occupied areas. Besides, we've already earned the confidence and backing of the Chinese film industry in Shanghai. In the future, there will be more and more opportunities to collaborate.

SACHIKO: Right. Now, when you walk around on the streets, you can hear the "Candy-Peddling Song" everywhere. Many people are comparing you with Zhou Xuan. Before, only Manchurians recognized you. Now, it's totally different. I think all of China knows you're a star now.

KAWAKITA: From the beginning, I've insisted on not going the way of the Manchukuo Film Association, and on not making political propaganda films like their *Chee-na Nights*. You see how quickly Xianglan has gained a different place in the hearts of the Chinese people.

LI XIANGLAN: Kawakita, have you heard about what happened at yesterday's press conference?

KAWAKITA: No, I haven't. It was surely a great success.

LI XIANGLAN: It was very successful, fifty-plus reporters came, but, suddenly, a reporter stood up and asked me why I wanted to make *Chee-na Nights*. He said, why would you, as a Chinese person, want to make a film so disrespectful and so humiliating for your race?

Sachiko and Kawakita exchange glances.

LI XIANGLAN: It came out of nowhere. I was completely unprepared. Right, why would I want to make *Chee-na Nights*? All I'd been thinking was that I wanted to act in movies! *(Pause.)* I stood up, lowered my head, and apologized to everyone. I asked everyone to forgive me. I said, at the time, I was just starting out, I wasn't good enough yet at judging the situation ...

KAWAKITA: You did very well.

LI XIANGLAN: Yes, the reporters all stood up and applauded. But I'm completely at a loss. I'm Japanese. Why didn't I just tell them that directly, that I'm Japanese?

SACHIKO: It's the producer who doesn't want you to say it. He said if you acknowledge that at the press conference, you'll likely bring yourself a lot of trouble.

LI XINAGLAN: So, am I to continue pretending? Pretending I'm Chinese?

KAWAKITA: Xianglan, just wait until the war is over, and then these problems will no longer exist! Even though the Japanese military itself arranged for me to come make films in Shanghai, the Japanese government sees that I'm with Chinese people every day, and the Chinese-

Japanese joint films I've made don't conform to the content the military was expecting. So they've started to suspect me. Did you know? I've been followed by the government for a long time now. They probably believe I'm going to do all sorts of traitorous things. *(Pause.)* More than thirty years ago, because my father loved China, he lived in China for a long stretch of time, and even served as Yuan Shikai's military advisor. But he was assassinated, and it was the Japanese government that did it. Like my father before me, I only hope for friendship between China and Japan, and all the more so, because I grew up in China and have so many Chinese friends, just as you do. Xianglan, all the problems we're confronting are from errors of the era, not of ourselves.

LI XIANGLAN: But I'm a public personality. I'm unwilling to deceive my audience, and let them mistakenly think I'm a Chinese movie star. If the Chinese people knew I was Japanese, they might not like me anymore.

SACHIKO: That couldn't happen. They like hearing your songs, they like watching you perform.

LI XIANGLAN: Yesterday, Chen Yunshang got written about in some little newspaper because she presented flowers, and she cried the whole day. She asked me, if it were me instead, would I have gone to present flowers to the Japanese? Would I have gone? I myself don't know. Right now, all I want to do is give up this work with the Manchukuo Film Association, throw away the name "Li Xianglan," and go back to Manchuria to just rest and relax.

The sounds of a Japanese folk ballad, filled with a melancholy nostalgia. The lights change.

Sachiko and Kawakita exit. In front of the rear scrim, white snow slowly flutters in.

Li Xianglan's mother, holding a bowl of borscht, comes out. In the scene below, Li Xianglan and her mother speak Japanese; Chinese subtitles appear at the side of the stage.

LI'S MOTHER: Yoshiko, it's cold outside, hurry in.

Li Xianglan walks toward her mother.

LI XIANGLAN: There's so much snow falling outside.

Figure 1.5   Li Xianglan (left), now playing the Candy Peddler in the film *A Good Name for Generations*, questions why she continues to pretend to the world that she is Chinese when she is actually Japanese. She shares her thoughts with her friend Sachiko (center) and film impresario Kawakita.

LI's MOTHER: *(Holding up the bowl.)* Come on, this is your favorite Russian borscht. Hurry up and drink it while it's hot. Don't let it get cold.

LI XIANGLAN: *(Takes the soup from her mother's hands.)* Borscht. *(Holds up the bowl and takes a gulp.)* Mother, thank you!

LI's MOTHER: I've made a lot of the borscht, have all you want.

LI XIANGLAN: When I make it myself, it's never this good.

Li's Mother takes out a piece of Japanese-style clothing.

LI's MOTHER: *(Holds up the Japanese-style clothing for Li Xianglan to look at.)* I only finished making this a few days ago. I've made it for you to wear when you get married. I know you're busy, and probably won't have time to prepare your own wedding clothes. Originally, I wanted to go back to Japan to pick out fabric, but now, with the war causing such chaos, I fear I wouldn't be able to return. Here, try it on.

Li Xianglan gives the bowl to her mother, and puts on the Japanese-style clothing over her "phoenix-fairy" clothing.

LI's MOTHER: You look truly beautiful in Japanese clothing. My daughter is truly beautiful!

The lights change to Scene 9.

Li Xianglan and Li's Mother exit.

Scene 9

Thiam-guan reads the letter his younger brother, Thiam-hok, sent from Amoy. Siok-hun, wearing a pair of pants tied tight at the ankles and a scarf wrapped around her head, and holding a bag of rice in her hands, arduously walks onto the stage. Thiam-guan puts the letter down, looking at his wife from the corner of his eye.

SIOK-HUN: *(Seeming to understand his puzzlement, explains.)* It's what your aunt taught me. If you dress like an Emperor's subject when you line up to receive your rice, you get it faster.

THIAM-GUAN: What?

Siok-hun takes the rice to the room inside. Siok-hun comes back holding two cups of tea. She gives one cup to Thiam-guan and drinks the other herself.

SIOK-HUN: Wrapping my pants like this shows that I'm the Emperor's subject. If you get your rice this way, you also get more than others.

THIAM-GUAN: You're not afraid that other people will recognize you?

SIOK-HUN: I studied how Auntie wraps her head in a scarf like this, and bows. Frankly, I was terrified. *(Pause.)* Do you think we'll end up taking Japanese names and become subjects of the Emperor?

THIAM-GUAN: Let's wait and see. *(Pause.)* How can you wear those clothes? Quick, go change.

Siok-hun takes clothing hanging on the wall and prepares to change.

SIOK-HUN: How come you have spare time to hang around the house today?

THIAM-GUAN: We had a big meeting for the neighborhood heads. There's an air raid drill next week. They said it'll be a competition. If our group finishes last, we'll lose face.

Siok-hun realizes that her clothing has a loose thread, and sits down to mend it.

SIOK-HUN: Will there be a real "ooo ..."? *(Imitates the sound of the air raid siren.)*

Tsong-bing, carrying his school bag, comes home.

THIAM-GUAN: This time they're also going to set fires, fake fires. I'm looking for a few neighbors for the exercise.

TSONG-BING: I'm home.

SIOK-HUN: A-bing, how come you're so early today?

TSONG-BING: The school took us to see a movie. We saw *Sayon's Bell*.

SIOK-HUN: How come you have it so good? They take you to see a Li Xiang-lan movie.

THIAM-GUAN: *(Holding up Thiam-hok's letter.)* A letter from Thiam-hok came. He says the situation over there with the war is so tense and chaotic. He's also participating in an organization.

SIOK-HUN: It's very dangerous to do that.

TSONG-BING: What organization?

THIAM-GUAN: Children should have ears, but no mouths.

SIOK-HUN: *(To Tsong-bing.)* A-bing, where's your lunchbox?

TSONG-BING: Oh, darn. I left it at the movie theater.

SIOK-HUN: A child like you, with nothing in your head, you're always losing things. Remember to bring it back tomorrow.

TSONG-BING: I know.

SIOK-HUN: Ah … in the movie you saw today, when Li Xianglan was dressed up like a Barbarian, did she really look like one?

TSONG-BING: *(Teasing her.)* It was pretty good. The movie was really well written, telling that story of the place Lam-o that way.

SIOK-HUN: *(With curiosity.)* What was it like?

TSONG-BING: *(Toying with her.)* Nothing much, just true, pure love, watching a Barbarian woman, in the wind and rain, sending her teacher off to be a soldier. But then she slips and falls to the bottom of the river.

THIAM-GUAN: It's a true story, everyone's talking about it.

TSONG-BING: *(More teasing.)* I must say, they can really tell the story! The way they wrote it, everyone will dash ahead of the next guy to get to be a soldier. Those who haven't been called up yet will be very angry.

THIAM-GUAN: Wasn't it filmed in Bu-sia?

TSONG-BING: It was. Our *sensei* said, that place where the Bu-sia Incident happened, that's the place they picked to film it.

SIOK-HUN: Did they speak in Barbarian?

TSONG-BING: It was all in the national language—I mean Japanese.[5] Yeah, only in the part when Sayon taught the children Japanese, then there was a little in Barbarian.

---

[5] Today in Taiwan, "national language" refers to Mandarin, not Japanese.

SIOK-HUN: There must have been lots of songs.

TSONG-BING: A lot.

SIOK-HUN: When Li Xianglan sings, her mouth opens up, and she sings in a soft, soft sound. It's really beautiful.

TSONG-BING: *(More teasing.)* Those songs—you could never get enough of that part.

SIOK-HUN: The other day, I asked your Third Aunt to go see it with me. *(Pause.)* Is it playing in the Miyako Theater?

TSONG-BING: Yup. *(Pause.)* We don't have to go to class again tomorrow. We're digging an air raid ditch.

THIAM-GUAN: Where?

TSONG-BING: Sin-tshi.

THIAM-GUAN: Are you walking?

TSONG-BING: I don't know.

SIOK-HUN: Your shirt's going to get all dirty. It'll be really hard to get clean.

TSONG-BING: Our *sensei* was so mad. He said this wastes teaching time.

SIOK-HUN: You get to skip class. You students must be really happy.

Tsong-tik enters, carrying a lot of bags and other things.

SIOK-HUN: *(Pointing to Tsong-tik.)* A-tik, why do you have all of those bundles of things?

TSONG-TIK: *(Glancing at his father, Thiam-guan.)* My enlistment orders came.

SIOK-HUN: What?

Silence.

TSONG-TIK: They sent them to the school. *(Pause.)* I have to go in three days.

TSONG-BING: Where are you going?

TSONG-TIK: Burma. I've brought back all of my things from school.

Silence. Thiam-guan lights a cigarette, gets up, and walks downstage.

THIAM-GUAN: How many did they pick to go?

TSONG-TIK: Four. *(Intentionally making light of it.)* Really, so many have gone, now it's my turn. You can't escape it. All the high school students are getting called now.

TSONG-BING: Nearly everyone in your class has been called.

TSONG-TIK: Almost all of them have gone.

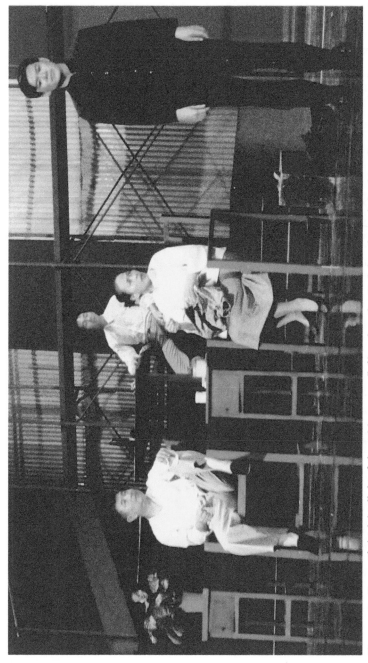

Figure 1.6 Tsong-tik (right) tells his father Thiam-guan (left) and mother Siok-hun (center) that his enlistment orders have come, and he must go to Burma to fight in the war on behalf of the Japanese. Younger brother Tsong-bing looks on.

THIAM-GUAN: *(To Siok-hun.)* Tomorrow morning, take him to the Golden
    Temple to pray to Kuan-te-ia.
SIOK-HUN: I'll also ask Kuan-te-ia for a bit of incense ash for him to take
    with him.

*Siok-hun embraces Tsong-tik. Air raid siren sound plays. The people on stage freeze
in a tableau. The lights change.*

*Various kinds of bombs and gunshots, as well as the sounds of a broadcast of the
Japanese emperor encouraging warfare; the "Song of Exorcism" can also be heard,
and on stage are projected several photographs of Tainan being bombed by the American army and scenes of the remnants of defeat.*

"Song of Exorcism"
    Pure, pure heaven; quick, quick, the earth,
    Lo-tshia's skills were clear at seven,
    Lord's band round his head,
    White clad, strong as ten thousand men,
    On the mountain, beat tigers,
    In the heavens, beat generals,
    Down on earth, save the people.

The lights fade.[6]

---

[6] In performance, this play has always taken an intermission at this point; therefore, there
is no stage direction indicating a change of lights to the next scene.

Scene 10

The sounds of a string of firecrackers. On stage, numerous photographs of the retrocession are projected, with people in every location elated and jubilant.

The retrocession song "Song of Celebratory Clouds" is sung by a chorus in Taiwanese.

"Song of Celebratory Clouds"
　　Taiwan now rejoice in peace,
　　Raise heads to blue sky, white sun,[7]
　　Six million share happiness,
　　Poor in need are welcome too.[8]

The projection of photographs of the Taiwanese retrocession concludes.

The lights change to Scene 11.

---

[7] The expression "blue sky, white sun" refers to the flag of the Republic of China, which includes a white sun against a blue background.

[8] This refers to the poor people fleeing the mainland, particularly the soldiers.

Scene 11

When the lights come up, Hui-ing is teaching her father Thiam-guan Mandarin.

THIAM-GUAN: *(Reading aloud, his pronunciation not very standard.)* Bo, po, mo, fo, de, te, ne, le ...

HUI-ING: Read it again for me.

THIAM-GUAN: *Bo, po, mo, fo, de, te, ne, le* ...

HUI-ING: When you say "*bo*" you have to keep your lips together more, *bo* ...

THIAM-GUAN: *po* ...

HUI-ING: No, that's not right.

THIAM-GUAN: My lips were together.

HUI-ING: *(Pulls out a piece of paper.)* When you say "*bo*," don't let any air come out, you can only do that when you say "*po*." *(Puts the paper in front of her mouth.)* See, *bo* ... the paper doesn't move, now look, *po* ... see, the paper moves.

THIAM-GUAN: It's so much effort. The paper moves, then it doesn't move, *po, po, po*, and we're all still "poor"![9]

HUI-ING: If you don't learn these sounds, how will you ever learn the "national language"!

THIAM-GUAN: If you young people learn it, it'll be fine. Your dad is hopeless.

HUI-ING: Dad, how can you have so little patience? If you stay this way, you'll end up a mute.

THIAM-GUAN: It's no big deal, right now everyone still speaks Japanese.

HUI-ING: *(Pause.)* It's strange, how come Mom's not back yet? In just a bit, I'm going off to see a movie.

THIAM-GUAN: So much free time.

HUI-ING: Today is Sunday. It's been so long since I've seen a movie. Right now so many American movies are really good.

THIAM-GUAN: They talk that blah-blah-blah, how can you understand?

---

[9] In the original script, the pun is with the word for "spit," which is also pronounced *po*. Because the joke would be lost in English, instead of literally rendering it as "the corners of your mouth are full of spit," I have preserved the idea of the pun with this translation.

HUI-ING: They have a translator there who tells the story. Today I'm going to see *Casablanca.* That actress Ingrid Bergman is so beautiful, such great qualities!

Tsong-tik and his coworker Kong Guoxiang come home together.

TSONG-TIK: Dad, this is my colleague at school, *(Pronouncing in Taiwanese.)* Khang Kok-siong.

THIAM-GUAN: Have a seat.

Kong Guoxiang doesn't understand what he means. In the scene below, Tsong-tik and his family speak Taiwanese; with Kong Guoxiang they speak rather nonstandard Mandarin. In this scene, the lines in Mandarin are italicized.[10]

TSONG-TIK: *(To Kong Guoxiang, in Mandarin.) Sit, sit. (To Hui-ing.)* Go bring out some tea. *(To Thiam-guan.)* Dad, he's come from the mainland.

Hui-ing leaves the stage.

THIAM-GUAN: *(As if he suddenly understands.)* Ahh …

TSONG-TIK: *(To Kong Guoxiang.) Come over and have a seat.*

GUOXIANG: *Thank you, thank you.*

TSONG-TIK: *(To Thiam-guan.)* We just left the Miyako Theater. The event welcoming Tan Gi was really unbelievable.

THIAM-GUAN: Did you run into Tsong-bing?

TSONG-TIK: Yup, I saw him on the stage. The students from his engineering school performed, and made it really lively. *(To Guoxiang.) I told dad, we just saw my little brother.*

GUOXIANG: *Zongming*[11] *performed well.*

THIAM-GUAN: What did he say?

TSONG-TIK: He said that Tsong-bing performed well.

THIAM-GUAN: What does that Tan Gi look like?

TSONG-TIK: Pretty fat. Whatever he was speaking, I didn't understand any of it.

---

[10] In the original script, the distinction between Taiwanese and Mandarin would be obvious from certain vocabulary words and grammatical structures. Here, in translation, italics are used to help make the distinction. Italics are not used this way elsewhere in the translation, because the other scenes with Mandarin (Li Xianglan's scenes) do not also incorporate Taiwanese.

[11] Tsong-bing's name pronounced in Mandarin.

THIAM-GUAN: Ah, Mr. Khang, have you eaten yet? ... *(With his hands, he makes eating gestures.)* Eat.

GUOXIANG: *We haven't eaten yet.*

They keep looking at each other, and then at Tsong-tik, and then back at each other.

TSONG-TIK: Dad, do you want him to stay for lunch?

THIAM-GUAN: Definitely.

TSONG-TIK: *My dad wants you to stay for lunch.*

GUOXIANG: *Thank you.*

THIAM-GUAN: I'm sorry, I haven't been able to learn Mandarin, *po, po, mo, mo*, it's too hard to learn.

TSONG-TIK: *(To Guoxiang.) My dad said, he's had trouble learning Mandarin.*

GUOXIANG: *Don't worry, Zongde*[12] *speaks it very well.*

Hui-ing enters to bring the tea, then exits.

TSONG-TIK: *(To Guoxiang.) After retrocession, I came back from Burma, and I began to learn Mandarin so I could teach. Every day, I copied out* Records of the Three Kingdoms *by hand. When I came across a character I couldn't pronounce, I looked it up in the dictionary. (To Thiam-guan.)* I'm telling him, I copied all of *Records of the Three Kingdoms* to practice Mandarin.

THIAM-GUAN: The young have more ways to learn. He got this method from his brother.

TSONG-TIK: *(To Guoxiang.) It was my little brother who thought of this method.*

Siok-hun, holding a blue shopping bag, comes back. When Guoxiang sees Siok-hun, he immediately stands up.

TSONG-TIK: Mom, this is my colleague, one of those mainlanders.

Guoxiang gets up and greets her, with a bow.

SIOK-HUN: Oh, mainlander, hey, hey, sit down, sit down.

THIAM-GUAN: I've invited him to stay for lunch.

SIOK-HUN: I didn't buy anything special, everything has gotten so expensive. *(To Guoxiang, in Taiwanese.)* So sorry.

THIAM-GUAN: Did you buy enough?

---

[12] Tsong-tik's name pronounced in Mandarin.

SIOK-HUN: The prices have gone up so much, it's really scary, one bunch of greens was 5,000 yesterday, today it went up to 8,000. *(Asks Kong Guo-xiang, in Taiwanese.)* Is your food this expensive on the mainland?

THIAM-GUAN: You shouldn't ask people that.

GUOXIANG: *What?*

TSONG-TIK: *She asked you to stay for lunch.*

GUOXIANG: *Thank you, thank you.*

SIOK-HUN: So, so sorry, it's just regular food, *(Uses her hands to explain.)* prices have really become so high.

GUOXIANG: *(Glancing at Tsong-tik.) I'm really putting you to too much trouble.*

TSONG-TIK: *(Explaining to his mother.)* Just cook whatever you've got, we're colleagues, it isn't a big deal.

SIOK-HUN: I'll start right away. *(To Guoxiang, in Taiwanese.)* So sorry, so sorry.

Siok-hun and Guoxiang bow back and forth to each other. Siok-hun exits.

THIAM-GUAN: Where is Mr. Khang from?

TSONG-TIK: My father's asking where are you from.

GUOXIANG: *(In Mandarin pronunciation.) Hebei.*

TSONG-TIK: *(In Taiwanese pronunciation.)* Ho-pak.

THIAM-GUAN: Oh, where's that?

TSONG-TIK: In the northwestern part of the mainland.

THIAM-GUAN: Oh, so far away. He came by himself?

TSONG-TIK: He's married. He has a wife and family.

Tsong-bing enters, holding an ROC flag in his hand. At his side is Hui-ing's classmate Akiko, but she does not walk to the center of the stage with him.

THIAM-GUAN: How many kids?

TSONG-TIK: Two. *(To Guoxiang.) You have two children, right?*

GUOXIANG: *Yes, yes.*

TSONG-BING: *(Shouting offstage.)* Hui-ing, Hui-ing, someone's here to see you.

HUI-ING: *(Offstage.)* I'm coming.

THIAM-GUAN: I have a younger brother in Amoy, he's also been to Shang-hai. These past few years, with the war, we haven't been able to send letters, so we haven't had any news.

TSONG-TIK: *My second uncle is on the mainland. We haven't had any news of him for the past two years. (To Tsong-bing.)* Tsong-bing, this is my colleague, Mr. Khang. *(To Guoxiang.) My younger brother, Zongming.*

GUOXIANG: *My pleasure, my pleasure. I just saw your performance. It was really wonderful.*

TSONG-BING: *We've been practicing a long time, but some people's Mandarin still isn't very good.*

Akiko catches Tsong-tik's eye, and he glances at her out of the corner of his eye.

THIAM-GUAN: *(To Tsong-tik.)* Go ask that young lady to come in.

TSONG-TIK: Oh. *(Walks over toward Akiko.)*

TSONG-BING: *(To Guoxiang.) Please, sit and relax for a while. I'm going inside for just a moment. (Exits.)*

THIAM-GUAN: *(Pointing at the teacup, to Guoxiang.)* Have some tea!

GUOXIANG: *Thank you.*

TSONG-TIK: *(To Akiko.)* Come have a seat!

AKIKO: Thanks, but I'm just about to go.

THIAM-GUAN: *(To Guoxiang.)* When you come here, don't worry about being polite. Just be yourself.

Guoxiang picks up his teacup and drinks some tea. Thiam-guan and Guoxiang have a moment of awkward silence.

TSONG-TIK: I'm Hui-ing's oldest brother. Are you Akiko?

AKIKO: *(Embarrassed, bowing.) Hai,*[13] her classmate.

TSONG-TIK: Come in, don't be polite. *(Bows.)*

AKIKO: I'll just wait here. *(Bows.)*

Tsong-tik bows to Akiko in return, then goes inside.

TSONG-TIK: Hui-ing-a, hurry up.

HUI-ING: OK!

Tsong-bing comes out, holding a cup of tea.

THIAM-GUAN: *(Looking at Guoxiang, speaking to Tsong-tik.)* Your friend seems really nearsighted. His glasses are so thick.

TSONG-TIK: *(To Guoxiang.) My father said, are you very nearsighted?*

GUOXIANG: *My eyes aren't too good.*

---

[13] In the case of the Japanese word *Hai*, meaning yes, the italics indicate Japanese, not Mandarin.

TSONG-BING: *How long has Mr. Kong been in Taiwan?*

GUOXIANG: *Almost half a year.*

TSONG-TIK: *(To his father.)* He's been here half a year, he came to teach Mandarin.

GUOXIANG: *Taiwan has progressed more than I had imagined. When I first got here, even though Taiwan did not yet have a government, public law and order was, much to my surprise, pretty good.*

TSONG-TIK: *(To Guoxiang.) My father used to be a neighborhood head. After the war, when the government hadn't come over yet, we all depended on the old "neighborhood group" to maintain order. (To his father.)* He's commending you for being such a good neighborhood head.

THIAM-GUAN: *(Somewhat pleased with himself.)* It's nothing, really. In this neighborhood, everyone works together, they really cooperate. Just give a holler, and everyone comes. During the Japanese era, we drilled this really well.

Hui-ing hurriedly rushes out.

HUI-ING: Dad, I'm going to the movies.

TSONG-TIK: *(To Guoxiang.) This is my little sister.*

HUI-ING: *(To Akiko.)* I'm so sorry. The hook on my skirt suddenly broke off. It took forever to sew it back on.

AKIKO: It's OK.

Hui-ing and Akiko exit.

TSONG-BING: *(To Guoxiang.) To tell you the truth, when we first went to the train station to greet the Chinese government troops, I was really disappointed when I first laid eyes on them. How could they have no discipline? Some of them weren't fully dressed, or their clothes weren't on right. They had pots in their hands, bowls, ...*

TSONG-TIK: *Some were holding wash basins.*

TSONG-BING: *But, in thinking about Taiwan's retrocession, it was these soldiers who defeated the Japanese. Many people were moved to tears when they saw them.*

TSONG-TIK: *(To his father.)* We're talking about going to meet our nation's soldiers.

THIAM-GUAN: *(To Guoxiang.)* Back then, we all grabbed flags and went to the train station to welcome them. We set off firecrackers, making lots of noise.

GUOXIANG: *At that time, I hadn't come over yet. I haven't had the opportunity to experience that kind of lively scene.*

TSONG-BING: *Some soldiers were just grabbing things here and there. It really made some people furious.*

GUOXIANG: *That ... I'm not too clear about.*

TSONG-BING: *(To his father.)* I said that some of the soldiers were grabbing stuff. I really didn't like seeing that.

Siok-hun enters holding a plate of cakes.

THIAM-GUAN: In that time of transition, it was all such chaos.

SIOK-HUN: Have some cakes. I made them myself.

THIAM-GUAN: *(To Guoxiang, gesturing.)* Help yourself. Eat, eat, don't be polite.

TSONG-TIK: *My mother made these herself.*

TSONG-BING: *(To Tsong-tik.)* Teacher Tan, who used to take us for our Chinese studies, came back here to teach. Today I ran into him at the Miyako Theater.

TSONG-TIK: If Taiwan hadn't been returned, he might have been executed by the Japanese.

THIAM-GUAN: Who?

TSONG-BING: My middle school teacher. During the war, he was arrested by the Japanese. They called him a traitor.

TSONG-TIK: *(To Guoxiang.)* *Today, Zongming ran into his middle school teacher, Teacher Chen, who was arrested and locked up by the Japanese.*

THIAM-GUAN: *(Asks Guoxiang.)* How many years is Mr. Khang going to stay in Taiwan?

TSONG-TIK: *(Asks Guoxiang.)* *My dad asked you, how long do you plan to be here?*

GUOXIANG: *Four or five years. My family is still in Hebei.*

SIOK-HUN: *(Pointing to the cakes, asks Guoxiang.)* Does the mainland have these kind of cakes?

GUOXIANG: *They're tasty, very tasty.*

TSONG-TIK: *(Pointing to the cakes, asks Guoxiang.) My mom asked if you've eaten this kind of ... this kind of* "kue"?

GUOXIANG: *I haven't had ones with this kind of flavor before.*

SIOK-HUN: These steamed cakes are a lot of work. You have to check, check, check to get the time just right. You can't relax for even a moment.

THIAM-GUAN: Mr. Khang isn't going to be steaming any cakes. What's the point of telling him that?

SIOK-HUN: I'm just making conversation.

TSONG-TIK: *(Pointing to his parents, to Guoxiang.) The two of them are (Using his hands to gesture.) arguing.*

Thiam-hok and his wife Bi-ling enter the stage, carrying suitcases.

TSONG-BING: *(Calling to the outside.)* Uncle, Uncle, how it is that you're back?

SIOK-HUN: *(Toward the outside, in a big voice.)* Hey, if it isn't Thiam-hok, *(Shouts loudly.)* Thiam-hok!

Everyone looks in Thiam-hok's direction.

THIAM-HOK, BI-LING: Older Brother, Sister-in-Law, we're back.

Everyone on stage except Guoxiang walks toward Thiam-hok and his wife.

THIAM-GUAN: A-hok, how did you get back?

THIAM-HOK: There just happened to be a boat going, so we could return.

TSONG-TIK: We were just talking about you, and then you came back.

SIOK-HUN: *(Loudly shouting upstairs.)* A-gi, A-buan, your brother is back from Amoy. Hurry down. *(To everyone.)* I'll light some incense, and everyone can make prayers.

THIAM-GUAN: I had thought none of our messages went through.

THIAM-HOK: Yes, but fortunately the war is already over.

Thiam-gi and A-buan come downstairs. Everyone, escorting Thiam-hok and his wife, exits.

The lights change to Scene 12.

Scene 12

On the stage, the final scene of the film Casablanca *is being shown, and being explained by the Translator.*

TRANSLATOR: *(In a radio announcer's voice.)* There are only ten minutes before the airplane has to fly away. There's a thick fog. At the moment, the visibility is only one and a half nautical miles.

(In the translator's own voice.) Just at the moment when the agent announces that the airplane is about to take off, a car drives by in front of him, driving right up to the entrance. At this moment, four people get out of the car. It's none other than Tom-mu, with Jyo-jee and his wife, May-lee, as well as the bodyguard Bu-rang.

(In a handsome man's voice.) Ask someone to escort Jyo-jee to the plane.

(In a nasal man's voice.) No problem.

(In the translator's own voice.) Bu-rang asks someone to first take Jyo-jee to check his luggage. After Jyo-jee leaves, Tom-mu says ...

(In a handsome man's voice.) Sign Jyo-jee and his wife's names on the flight manifest.

(In the translator's own voice.) When she hears Tom-mu say this, May-lee starts with fright.

(In a sweet lady's voice.) What, how can it have my name?

(In a handsome man's voice.) You definitely must go with him.

(In a sweet lady's voice.) Oh, and you?

(In a handsome man's voice.) I can't go. You have a husband. I've already thought it through very clearly.

(In a sweet lady's voice.) No, no, I want to be with you.

(In a handsome man's voice.) May-lee, you must forget what has happened to the two of us. Yesterday, I thought about this all night. I am a MAN. I should be bold like a MAN. I cannot snatch another man's wife. Absolutely not.

(In a sweet lady's voice.) I don't want to hear it!

(In a handsome man's voice.) Calm down, listen to me. If the two of us were together, all of our honor would be lost.

(In a nasal man's voice.) What Tom-mu says, truly shows his conscience.

(In the translator's own voice.) When May-lee hears that Tom-mu is going to break away from her, she feels great pain in her heart. She's loved Tom-mu for many years already. Now the two of them are going to separate. How could she not have a broken heart? She wants to take Tom-mu's heart back again.

(In a sweet lady's voice.) How can you not love me, even a little bit?

(In a handsome man's voice.) May-lee, I could never do that to Jyo-jee.

(In a sweet lady's voice.) I don't want to leave you, Tom-mu!

(In a handsome man's voice.) May-lee, this can't be helped. There's an old saying, "A virtuous woman cannot marry two husbands." For your own honor, for your own happiness, I have to do this. Jyo-jee may not be as handsome as I am, but only he can give you the perfect home. I'm just a wanderer, I can't give you any happiness.

Music from the film.

(In the translator's own voice.) When May-lee hears these words from her lover Tom-mu, tears well up in her eyes.

(In a handsome man's voice.) Don't cry, you must be strong.

(In the translator's own voice.) Just when the lovers are about to embrace, *pah, pah, pah,* a police car rushes in!

(In a handsome man's voice.) Jyo-jee, I have something to say to you.

(In a high, haughty man's voice.) Don't say it. I don't want to hear it.

(In a handsome man's voice.) Your wife loves you, you must believe this. You can leave today. She's thought of everything, and arranged it all herself. Don't be mistaken. She and I don't feel any of the affections a man and a woman might feel for one another. The two of us are pure, unsullied. She wanted to get a passport out of me, so she pretended to love me. In fact, it's not true at all. The person she truly loves is you.

(In the translator's own voice.) When Tom-mu is finished speaking, he takes the passport and gives it to Jyo-jee.

(In a high, haughty man's voice.) Tom-mu, thank you for your help. I'll dote on May-lee, don't you worry.

(In the translator's own voice.) Just at this moment, the three people hear the *kun, kun* sound of the airplane's propellers starting up. They all understand—the time to leave has now come.

(In a high, haughty man's voice.) Let's go, May-lee.

(In the translator's own voice.) May-lee looks at Tom-mu for a moment. Her heart really cannot bear it. She says …

(In a sweet lady's voice.) All right. Tom-mu, good-bye, I'm leaving.

(In a handsome man's voice.) Hurry, the plane is about to take off.

(In the translator's own voice.) May-lee and Tom-mu are finally about to part. May-lee, her heart broken, leaves together with her husband. As her image gradually disappears from Tom-mu's eyes, his heart grows sadder and sadder. He just blames his fate, wondering why fate has left him all alone.

(In a nasal man's voice.) Tom-mu, don't think about it too much. People say, "Even the ends of the earth are filled with fragrant blossoms, you don't have to love just one flower," right? Come on, let's go have a drink and forget the whole thing.

(In the translator's own voice.) Just as the two of them are about to drink a toast, the airplane flies into the air, higher and higher, farther and farther, and finally disappears into the clouds and fog.

That's all for today's movie. In the story, although Tom-mu and May-lee love each other, in the end May-lee is a married woman, and Tom-mu can make prompt and timely decisions. He promptly ends the improper male-female relations between himself and May-lee. This bravery is truly worthy of our study. After watching this movie, I believe that all of us can obtain an enlightening message. What message is that? Precisely this: our womanfolk should adhere to the path of womankind, and absolutely must not seek out men on the side; our menfolk also must not play around, and they must remember to look after their households. We're grateful to everyone for watching today. Thank you, and we'll see you again!

On the movie screen, "The End" appears in English.

The Translator bows to the audience, and exits.

The lights change to Scene 13.

Scene 13

On the stage, people run around in chaos. The words below are spoken by different people.

PEOPLE: *(Shouting.)* Taipei is in chaos, hurry back.

It's rebellion, rebellion.

They're beating mainlanders in An-ping.

Hurry! Hurry!

A bunch of thugs are shooting people.

Tons of people have gathered at the statue, it's really scary.[14]

Child, hurry back!

Quick, get your family back home!

Soldiers are coming, everyone get down, fast.

Tsong-tik, pulling Kong Guoxiang, runs in a flurry.

TSONG-TIK: *(To Kong Guoxiang.)* It's OK, hurry to my house to hide.

Tsong-tik pulls Kong Guoxiang upstage and exits.

The people on stage gradually disperse.

An empty stage, a moment of quiet.

The lights change to Scene 14.

---

[14] The statue in the main circle of Tainan, a site used for executions.

Scene 14

The sound of frogs chirping.

Li Xianglan and Sachiko are wearing prisoners' clothes.

LI XIANGLAN: The frogs outside are crying so loudly.

SACHIKO: Maybe it's going to rain tomorrow.

LI XIANGLAN: This all seems like a dream. Tumbling down from my highest point to my lowest.

SACHIKO: Tomorrow, Kawakita and I are both getting sent back to Japan. *(Pause.)* You'll be the only one left.

LI XIANGLAN: It doesn't matter. I think I'll be OK.

SACHIKO: If you hadn't started out using "Li Xianglan" as your stage name, then maybe you'd be OK.

LI XIANGLAN: Maybe this is fate!

SACHIKO: How could the judge definitively pronounce you a Chinese person, a convicted traitor? You could be put to death.

Silence.

SACHIKO: I'm sorry, what I meant was, they should really investigate things better ...

LI XIANGLAN: No one could have predicted things would go this way. *(Pause.)* Li Xianglan is the name my godfather chose for me. I grew up in China. Since I was making movies in China, using a Chinese name was a totally natural thing, who could have known ... Now, the greatest evidence of my crimes is that I made *Chee-na Nights*. They're convinced I used the film to inspire Chinese traitors in the "Greater East Asia Holy War." Remember when Hasegawa Kazuo slapped me? The Chinese used that slap to establish my guilt. They're convinced I willingly bowed down to the Japanese.

SACHIKO: Even if it were like that, you are Japanese. The authorities should have fully investigated. If you're Japanese, there's nothing wrong with making that film.

LI XIANGLAN: Really? I just don't know. This is all so confusing. *(Pause.)* My parents are still in Beijing. Now, I just hope they're safe and sound.

SACHIKO: They're not leaving?

LI XIANGLAN: They're still waiting for a boat. *(Pause.)* Too many people have to go back to Japan. *(Pause.)* Do you remember, when we filmed *Yellow River*, we lived together with the Japanese soldiers for quite some time. That stretch of the Yellow River made us feel so desolate, so uncertain of the future, just like right now ...

SACHIKO: Making that film was truly a hardship. We were constantly hiding from the bombs.

LI XIANGLAN: That part of the river was pretty much as I had imagined it. Sometimes I felt afraid. At any moment, it seemed like it might breach its dikes and overflow.

SACHIKO: You probably mean that time it rained nonstop for several days!

LI XIANGLAN: That was the first time I came into contact with Japanese soldiers. Some of them looked so young. I wasn't sure if they were clear on why they wanted to come to China.

SACHIKO: They didn't have a choice. It was simply the Emperor's command.

LI XIANGLAN: There was that evening when the moonlight was extraordinarily bright. And we sang for those Japanese soldiers.

SACHIKO: You sang "Moonlight on the Castle Ruins."

Sounds of "Moonlight on the Castle Ruins" waft in on the harmonica.

LI XIANGLAN: One of the privates grabbed his harmonica to accompany me. He played that harmonica so well...

The lights change to Scene 15.

Li Xianglan and Sachiko exit.

Scene 15

Thiam-gi, Thiam-hok, and their wives are in the house, sometimes standing, sometimes sitting.

THIAM-GI: Brother, should we go to the prison to see what's going on? How could those two kids have been gone so long?

THIAM-HOK: My friend from Amoy said it wouldn't be a problem. He's really tight with the police. Everything's been properly arranged. The two kids asked me not to go, otherwise I'd go myself ...

A-BUAN: Letting two children go pick up their father, it just isn't right at all. A-gi, I think your brain is made of concrete.

THIAM-GI: Tsong-tik is a teacher. He's more capable than we are. If he says he wants to go himself, then let him. Quit your whining.

BI-LING: Shh ... a little quieter, Sister-in-Law isn't feeling well.

A-BUAN: This morning I went to the pharmacy to pick up some wood ear powder for her.[15] I don't know if she's feeling any better.

THIAM-GI: Do nothing wrong, and this kind of thing happens.

BI-LING: Sister-in-Law still doesn't know that the two boys went to pick up Brother-in-Law today, right?

A-BUAN: Tell her later, just in case those people go back on their word ...

THIAM-HOK: We already put together all that money. There shouldn't be any problem.

A-BUAN: Right, right. I've already prepared all the stuff for offering thanks to Thinn-kong.

BI-LING: The pig ...

A-BUAN: Already sent to Butcher Tian. We're all very close.

THIAM-HOK: I never thought the retrocession would turn out to be this crazy. In the Japanese era, I didn't want to be Japanese, so I went to the mainland. I came back after retrocession, but I'm less and less sure of what I am!

THIAM-GI: Take people like Older Brother. Kindly getting people together to talk about public safety, and that's also a crime!

---

[15] Wood ear powder (*chuan'erfen* in Mandarin, *tshuan-ni-hun* in Taiwanese), is a traditional Chinese medicine.

THIAM-HOK: If they really want to arrest people, they don't need any reason. Yesterday, some people wanted to protect the mainlanders who'd just arrived at the harbor. They went over to An-ping to help out, and brought them all to the Golden Pine Building in Sin-ting. In the end, they were reported for imprisoning mainlanders, and they were all arrested. Really, no good deed goes unpunished.

Hui-ing, supporting her mother Siok-hun, slowly enters. The others on stage suddenly stop talking about that subject.

A-BUAN: Sister-in-Law, are you feeling any better?

SIOK-HUN: Much, much better.

A-BUAN: A-ing, help your mother come sit over here. I've cooked a pot of red bean soup. I made it for all of you.

Bi-ling and A-buan exit together.

THIAM-HOK: Sister-in-Law, you also have to take care of your own health.

SIOK-HUN: A-hok, did you bring over all the money?

THIAM-HOK: Yes, my friends from Amoy said there shouldn't be any problem!

SIOK-HUN: Yesterday, I was truly scared to death.

THIAM-HOK: Such a coincidence, that man they executed also wearing a gray shirt, just like Brother's shirt.

THIAM-GI: Right now, it's all so chaotic, anyone can be arrested. They can just grab you and shoot you at will. You don't even know why you've been killed. If that person hadn't gone over to the statue area to check things out, and he hadn't been kind enough to come tell us about it, then we never would have gone over to see the executions there. When I looked across from far, far away, and I saw a man in a gray shirt come out to be executed, I couldn't stop shaking.

Bi-ling brings Siok-hun a cup of water.

BI-LING: Fortunately, the person they shot and killed wasn't Brother-in-Law.

SIOK-HUN: Might they go back on their word?

THIAM-HOK: Sister-in-Law, don't worry!

A moment of silence.

Akiko nervously enters, stopping in front of Hui-ing's home.

A-buan sees her, and goes forward to greet her.

AKIKO: Excuse me, is Hui-ing there?

A-BUAN: Yes, please come in and have a seat, I'll go tell her. *(To Hui-ing.)* Akiko's here to see you.

Hui-ing goes to the front and sees Akiko.

HUI-ING: Akiko.

AKIKO: How come you haven't come to school for the past two days?

HUI-ING: We've had a situation at home.

AKIKO: What is it?

HUI-ING: It's nothing. I'll be at school tomorrow.

THIAM-GI: Older Brother, the situation is really bad now, I think that you two should be more careful.

THIAM-HOK: Right, I know. Now the conditions are the worst in Taipei. I've heard that three or four friends have all had situations.

BI-LING: *(To Thiam-hok.)* That's enough, don't talk so much.

AKIKO: Don't worry, I won't tell other people.

HUI-ING: I was so scared, when they came that day to grab him, they pressed the guns against our chests. We didn't dare move.

Akiko gently touches Hui-ing's shoulder.

A-BUAN: What do you all think, would it help to ask that colleague of Tsong-tik's, Teacher Khang, to go testify as a witness?

SIOK-HUN: Right, ask Teacher Khang, he's a mainlander.

THIAM-HOK: That's not the issue they're arresting people for right now. They said Older Brother used to be the neighborhood head, and after retrocession he still often got people together for meetings, so there were suspicions.

Akiko and Hui-ing say their good-byes and part company. Hui-ing comes back into the living room.

SIOK-HUN: He didn't do anything. *(To Thiam-hok.)* When you brought the money, did you speak with him?

THIAM-HOK: I did.

HUI-ING: Mom, don't worry. Dad hasn't done anything. I know that a lot of people were only taken in for questioning, and after just a few days they were let out.

A-buan brings out the red bean soup.

THIAM-GI: That's true. We also went over to Kuan-te-ia to throw the divining blocks, and they all showed good luck. Nothing's going to go wrong.

A-BUAN: Come on, red bean soup, it's hot ...

THIAM-GI: Well, we should be more careful about what we were just saying. It's best not to talk about these things outside.

A-BUAN: Have some read bean soup. Eat it while it's hot.

A-buan and Bi-ling give each person red bean soup.

Tsong-tik and Tsong-bing come home, bringing their father, Thiam-guan.

HUI-ING: *(Loudly.)* Mom, Dad is back.

Everyone quickly stands up.

SIOK-HUN: You're back, you're back. *(Walks toward Thiam-guan.)*

A-BUAN: I'll prepare some offerings for Thinn-kong right away. *(Exits.)*

BI-LING: I'll go prepare pig's feet and rice noodles. *(Exits.)*

THIAM-GI: Older Brother, first sit for a while.

Everyone helps Thiam-guan sit down.

SIOK-HUN: A-ing, go bring Dad a cup of tea. *(To Thiam-guan.)* Do you want to wash your face first?

Thiam-guan does not respond.

Siok-hun looks at her sons, signaling for them to go get him a towel.

Tsong-tik exits to get the towel.

THIAM-GI: Nothing really happened to Older Brother, that's truly good fortune!

THIAM-HOK: Right, as long as you're back, it's all fine.

SIOK-HUN: *(Asking Thiam-guan.)* A-guan, what would you like to eat? I'll go prepare it.

Thiam-guan, as before, does not respond.

Hui-ing gives her father tea.

SIOK-HUN: *(To Thiam-guan.)* First have some tea!

Thiam-guan shakes his head, the look in his eyes showing his complete exhaustion.

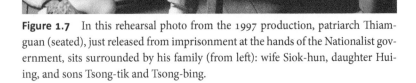

Figure 1.7 In this rehearsal photo from the 1997 production, patriarch Thiam-guan (seated), just released from imprisonment at the hands of the Nationalist government, sits surrounded by his family (from left): wife Siok-hun, daughter Hui-ing, and sons Tsong-tik and Tsong-bing.

Tsong-tik comes in with a towel for his father to wipe his face. Siok-hun immediately takes it, and wipes Thiam-guan's face.

HUI-ING: Dad, have some tea!

SIOK-HUN: *(Wiping Thiam-guan's face for him, and also wiping his hands.)* After we clean your face, first go take a rest. As long as you're home, everything's fine, everything's fine.

The lights change.

Everyone helps Thiam-guan exit.

Hui-ing leaves the group, and stands alone downstage.

The lights change to Scene 16.

Scene 16

On stage, backlit, the women in Siok-hun's family are preparing the things needed for an engagement.

Hui-ing, at the front of the stage, gives a monologue.

HUI-ING: After Dad was released, and came home, he changed. He didn't like to say much anymore. The aunts in our house all told my oldest brother to get married right away. They said, this way, we could "wash in happiness." It was perfect timing that a matchmaker came and proposed someone, and since the intended match was my classmate Akiko, we were all well acquainted. This marriage was quickly settled.

The lighting on stage gradually brightens; can clearly see Siok-hun making paper cuttings, A-buan doing the flowers for the bride's head, and Bi-ling embroidering a veil.

Hui-ing walks to her mother's side, and sits down to make paper cuttings.

A-BUAN: Doing these flowers yourself is so much more beautiful, so much prettier.

HUI-ING: Auntie, how are we supposed to wear so many flowers in our hair?

A-BUAN: Even this, you don't know! Later on, if you are ever a mother-in-law, people will laugh at all of the things you don't know.

BI-LING: That's a long time away. One pair of flowers is for the bride to wear herself, and one pair for her to put in her mother's hair. After that, when she comes over to our home, she'll put a pair in your mom's hair. If there are still more left, she'll give them to us aunties.

HUI-ING: Oh, I get it. *(Asks Siok-hun.)* Is the bakery going to send the cakes here first?

SIOK-HUN: Your uncle said it would only look right if we sent them from our house to theirs.

A-BUAN: It's good to arrange a big spectacle—one hundred twenty cakes— quite a lot.

SIOK-HUN: If someone marries their daughter into our family, how can we not give them the cakes to eat?

BI-LING: Each set of cakes weighs six catties, plus that big round cake for the middle.[16] It all looks so good.

SIOK-HUN: I don't know ... do you think it's fair to Akiko to marry her into our family?

A-BUAN: Come on, why would you say such a thing? Don't you know, because of the "Land Policy" this time around, her Tiunn family was left with nothing but the house. For her to marry into our house is her good fortune.

SIOK-HUN: I'm just saying ...

BI-LING: Our Tsong-tik is a great catch. Plus, he's a teacher. That's the most stable work.

A-BUAN: Right, in these times, having a steady job is the best. What more could you ask for?

HUI-ING: Mom, you shouldn't worry about that. Akiko is my best friend. Her marrying into our family will put her family at ease, too.

SIOK-HUN: I'm just saying, she was originally a million dollar girl ...

HUI-ING: Oh, am I a "million dollar girl"?

A-BUAN: *(Points at Hui-ing.)* Oh, you're not just a million, you're a billion dollar girl. Sister-in-Law, quickly marry off this billion dollar girl of ours, so we can eat cakes, too.

HUI-ING: Auntie ...

Tsong-tik and Thiam-guan enter a different area of the stage.

SIOK-HUN: *(To Bi-ling.)* Bi-ling, how's the embroidery on the veil coming?

Bi-ling holds the red veil up on her hand for Siok-hun to see.

SIOK-HUN: Oh my, it's so beautiful. My Tsong-tik likes the new, Western-style wedding clothes. But having the bride wear a phoenix-crown with a red veil looks so beautiful, so festive.

Siok-hun puts the veil on Hui-ing's head to see how it looks.

A-BUAN: Our billion dollar girl is even more beautiful wearing this red veil.

HUI-ING: Brides these days won't wear this sort of thing. Why are we even embroidering this veil at all?

---

[16] One catty in the Republic of China is equal to 500 grams.

SIOK-HUN: We're assembling presents, assembling presents. They say for an engagement you need to assemble twelve presents.

TSONG-TIK: Dad, you really don't want to invite those friends?

THIAM-GUAN: Don't bother. *(Pause.)* They wouldn't necessarily come.

TSONG-TIK: Those over at the temple ...

THIAM-GUAN: Your uncle will take care of that.

Silence.

Thiam-guan smokes continuously.

THIAM-GUAN: *(In Japanese.)* I'm really sorry, that I made all of this happen.

TSONG-TIK: *(Flustered.)* Dad, you shouldn't say such things, it's not your fault that this happened ...

THIAM-GUAN: In these times, you have to depend on yourself. *(Pause.)* You're about to get married ... Dad can't give you anything ... go take the principal's exam, maybe you can live in the teachers' dormitory ...

TSONG-TIK: I was already planning to take it.

Tsong-bing picks up a coat and walks over to his father.

TSONG-BING: *(Placing the coat over his father's shoulders.)* Dad, put this over your shoulders.

THIAM-GUAN: I'm not cold.

TSONG-BING: *(Giving Tsong-tik a look.)* Dad, I've been thinking ... after Brother gets married ... I want to go abroad.

THIAM-GUAN: Go abroad?

TSONG-BING: I want to go to America.

TSONG-TIK: And for money?

TSONG-BING: I can apply for a scholarship. *(Pause.)* I really want to go and see what it's like.

Silence.

THIAM-GUAN: *(Pause.)* If you go ... don't get involved in any politics ...

TSONG-BING: I know.

The light in the area with the three of them, Thiam-guan, Tsong-tik, Tsong-bing, gradually fades.

HUI-ING: *(Opens up the "double happiness" character she has finished cutting.)* Look at what I made! Isn't it beautiful?

A-BUAN: The billion dollar girl can really cut paper. You take after your mother. She's really good at it.

SIOK-HUN: *(To Hui-ing.)* A-ing, count them up, have we cut enough of them?

HUI-ING: *(Picks up each paper cutting one at a time to count.)* One, two, three, four, five ...

The music for "Fragrant Night" begins.

The lights change to Scene 17.

The characters in Scene 16 exit.

Scene 17

Li Xianglan and Sachiko, each holding a big suitcase, enter. They are preparing to board a ship leaving Shanghai.

On stage, the music of "Fragrant Night," as sung by Li Xianglan, can be clearly heard.

"Fragrant Night"
> I love the vastness of the night,
> When nightingales are singing bright,
> The flowers under the moon, they bloom, they enter into my dreams,
> Leaving the fragrance of the night.[17]
> The wafting sweetness of the dew ...

The music gradually softens, but continues.

SACHIKO: Isn't that you singing?

LI XIANGLAN: It's "Fragrant Night."

SACHIKO: It's a good thing your birth certificate arrived in time, otherwise you wouldn't be able to go back to Japan with us.

The music continues.

"Fragrant Night"
> Fragrant night, I sing songs for you,
> Fragrant night, my heart longs for you.
> Ah ...
> I sing songs for you,
> My heart longs for you,
> Fragrant night, fragrant night,
> Fragrant night ...

The sound of rousing audience applause.

LI XIANGLAN: *(In Japanese.)*
> Sayonara, my Shanghai.
> Sayonara, my China.
> Sayonara, my Li Xianglan.

---

[17] "Fragrance of the night," or *yelaixiang*, is the Chinese name for the tuberose; this song is both about the flower itself and its fragrance, utilizing the double meaning of the name.

In Mandarin.

Good-bye, good-bye.

The ship horn sounds again.

The "Fragrant Night" music gradually quiets, gradually turning into the sound of waves.

The lights change to Scene 18.

Li Xianglan and Sachiko exit.

The sound of the waves gradually turns into the sound of cicadas.

Scene 18

TIME: 1962, the summer of the fifty-first year of the Republic

On stage, slides of images of old Tainan appear. The whole atmosphere is the same as Scene 1.

Thiam-guan, riding a bicycle, carries his Grandson around, meandering from place to place.

GRANDSON: Grandpa, can we buy a television?

THIAM-GUAN: OK, OK.

GRANDSON: I don't want to have to go upstairs to Uncle's place to watch it every time. A-bun is so annoying, he loves to cry.

THIAM-GUAN: Ah.

Thiam-guan stops the bicycle, and lets his Grandson off. Grandfather and Grandson walk together side by side.

GRANDSON: Grandpa, when can we take a boat, and go to An-ping?

THIAM-GUAN: Did you finish all your homework?

The sounds of cicadas are heard.

GRANDSON: As soon as summer vacation started, I finished it all up. ... the cicadas are calling. *(From the ground, he picks up a stone and throws it up toward the tree.)*

THIAM-GUAN: Such a naughty boy. Look, there are fallen leaves and flowers all over the ground.

Grandson picks up a phoenix tree flower from the ground.

GRANDSON: I want to gather them up and make a specimen book. Me and my classmates are competing with each other. *(Continues to search the ground.)*

THIAM-GUAN: If you want to gather these, you should go over to the Ko-xinga Shrine to look. There are a lot more phoenix trees over there.

GRANDSON: I want to find the most beautiful one. *(From the ground, picks up a cicada that is just shedding its cocoon.)* Grandpa, look.

THIAM-GUAN: This cicada is shedding its cocoon.

GRANDSON: So, then, is it going to die?

THIAM-GUAN: After it sheds its cocoon, it will fly away.

GRANDSON: And the cocoon?

THIAM-GUAN: It's left behind.

GRANDSON: In that case, I'll pick it up and show it to my classmates.

THIAM-GUAN: Are you hungry? Let's go to the Circle to eat a bowl of *kue*.

GRANDSON: I want to eat fish soup.

THIAM-GUAN: Let's go!

Thiam-guan, carrying his Grandson, exits.

The lights change for the Epilogue.

The sounds of cicadas gradually conclude.

Epilogue

TIME: 1997, the eighty-sixth year of the Republic

The three siblings Tsong-tik, Tsong-bing, and Hui-ing are still resting at the Weather Observatory.

The sounds of hymns in Taiwanese emanate from the church.

HUI-ING: Walking around this area, it's really pretty nice. *(Takes a bottle of water out of her pocket.)* Do you want to have a drink?

TSONG-BING: I'm not thirsty, you have some.

Hui-ing drinks some water.

TSONG-TIK: Tsong-bing, are you really thinking about coming back?

TSONG-BING: Yes. I'll see how it goes the first year or two. At my age, I want to come back and see.

TSONG-TIK: If you're thinking of coming back, you can move in with me. My house doesn't have lots of big rooms, but it's comfortable. *(Pause.)* These past few years, Taiwan has really changed a lot, the way people act, the whole atmosphere, is much worse. I'm afraid you won't get used to living here. Sometimes, I'm actually nostalgic for the good old days of strict law and order. I felt more free.

TSONG-BING: Wherever you go, it's the same. I don't know how we can really call it progress.

HUI-ING: *(Standing in a relatively high place.)* This land here, with the Emperor's Temple, truly is rather high. I've heard people say that this Emperor's Temple is the highest point in the city of Tainan. No wonder when I used to ride a bicycle up to this area, I would get all out of breath. It was all uphill.

TSONG-BING: They're singing at the Tai-Peng-King Church.

HUI-ING: When I was little, I often went to the Khoan-Sai-Ke Presbyterian Church to hear them sing.

TSONG-TIK: One time, you got lost. Grandpa went everywhere beating a gong to look for the child. Do you know that someone picked you up and kept you at their house for two or three days?

HUI-ING: I didn't know about it until Mom told me.

TSONG-BING: Mom made pig's feet with thin noodles to give to that person.

HUI-ING: How do you know that?

TSONG-BING: You have such a bad memory.

TSONG-TIK: That time, Grandpa went around beating the gong, shouting "have you seen a little girl in a red dress and a red hat?"

HUI-ING: It's so embarrassing. Back then, how could Mom dress me up in red from head to toe?

TSONG-BING: You had pursed lips, pursed lips. So ugly!

HUI-ING: Brother, come on.

TSONG-TIK: It's true! It's getting dark, should we go back?

TSONG-BING: OK, let's go.

They walk toward another part of the stage, as if they are going to the lane with the Heavenly Temple.

HUI-ING: Look, that phoenix tree by the statue is blooming so beautifully.

TSONG-TIK: Now, there's only that one left!

TSONG-BING: *(In Japanese.)* Brother, *(In Taiwanese.)* do you remember, we came here to watch the execution?

TSONG-TIK: At that moment, we thought they were executing our Dad!

TSONG-BING: It all happened so long ago, and now we finally have an official day of remembrance.

TSONG-TIK: These past ten years, after martial law was lifted, Taiwan has been changing every day. I never thought that we'd even be able to choose the president.

TSONG-BING: The times are different. Old folks like us don't have a lot of time left to live. In a few years we'll all be gone. We'll never know what Taiwan will be like.

HUI-ING: If it's peaceful, that's enough.

TSONG-BING: The next generation can figure out their own future. If they're unconventional, I don't mind. You can't think about everything. Someday, if we have a "handover" like Hong Kong, then it'll all be lost, lost, lost.

HUI-ING: *(To Tsong-bing.)* OK, don't talk about what will be, what won't be. Come on, while it's still light, you and Tsong-tik pose for a picture here.

TSONG-BING: Where should we stand?

Figure 1.8 In this production photo of the Epilogue, the now elderly siblings (from left) Tsong-tik, Tsong-bing, and Hui-ing finish their stroll together through the streets of their hometown, the city of Tainan. This scene is set in 1997, the same year this production was performed.

HUI-ING: Use that phoenix tree by the statue as the background.

Tsong-bing and Tsong-tik stand together and let Hui-ing take a picture.

TSONG-BING: The pictures we've taken today, are probably the most we've ever taken together in our whole lives.

Three young people, wearing modern fashionable clothing, holding a camera, enter, taking pictures.

YOUTH A: (*In Mandarin.*) Come on, come on, take a picture here. One, two, three ...

YOUTH B & YOUTH C: (*Making the gesture of posing for a picture.*) Yeah!

YOUTH A: Let's keep going. ... (*After taking a few steps, turns around and says to Hui-ing, in Taiwanese.*) Obasan, your clothes are so pretty!

The three young people exit.

HUI-ING: (*Laughing.*) Young people have such sweet mouths.

TSONG-TIK: Who knew you could still be praised as pretty!

TSONG-BING: You had to get old for people to say you were pretty!

TSONG-TIK: Come on, come on. It's getting dark, let's go back.

HUI-ING: Let's go, let's go!

The choir's song gradually increases in volume.

Tsong-tik, Tsong-bing, and Hui-ing happily walk offstage.

On stage, slides of Tainan's streets and some old family photos are shown, continuing until the choir's song comes to an end.

—*End of play*—

Conversion Charts: Names and Terms

Table 1.1 Title and author

How it appears in this volume's translation	Chinese characters	Mandarin romanization in *pinyin*	Taiwanese romanization in *Tai-lo*
The Phoenix Trees Are in Blossom	鳳凰花開了	Fènghuánghuā kāile	Hōng-hông-hue-khui-liáu
Hsu Rey-Fang	許瑞芳	Xǔ Ruìfāng	Khóo Suī-hong

Table 1.2 Names of characters that appear in the play

How it appears in this volume's translation	Chinese characters and Japanese *kanji*	Mandarin romanization in *pinyin*	Taiwanese romanization in *Tai-lo*	Japanese romanization in *romaji*
A-buan	阿滿	Āmǎn	A-búan	
Akiko	秋子	Qiūzǐ	Tshiu-tsú	Akiko
Bi-ling	美玲	Měilíng	Bí-lîng	
Chen Yunshang	陳雲裳	Chén Yúnshang		
Hasegawa Kazuo	長谷川一夫	Chánggǔchuān Yīfū		Hasegawa Kazuo
Hui-ing	惠英	Huìyīng	Hūi-ing	
Kawakita	川喜多	Chuānxǐduō		Kawakita
Kong Guoxiang	孔國祥	Kǒng Guóxiáng	Khang Kok-siông	
Li Xianglan	李香蘭	Lǐ Xiānglán	Lí Hiong-lân	Ri Kōran, Ri Kouran
Sachiko	幸子	Xìngzǐ		Sachiko
Siok-hun	淑雲	Shūyún	Siok-hûn	
Thiam-gi	添義	Tiānyì	Thiam-gī	
Thiam-guan	添源	Tiānyuán	Thiam-gûan	
Thiam-hok	添福	Tiānfú	Thiam-hok	
Translator (*bianshi*)	辯士	biànshì	piān-sū	benshi
Tsong-bing (A-bing)	宗明 (阿明)	Zōngmíng (Āmíng)	Tsong-bîng (A-bîng)	
Tsong-tik	宗德	Zōngdé	Tsong-tik	

Table 1.3   Names of historical and mythological figures mentioned in the play

How it appears in this volume's translation	Chinese characters and Japanese *kanji*	Mandarin romanization in *pinyin*	Taiwanese romanization in *Tai-lo*	Japanese romanization in *romaji*
Tan Gi	陳儀	Chén Yí	Tân Gî	
Kuan-im	觀音	Guānyīn	Kuan-im	
Kuan-te-ia	關帝爺	Guāndìyé	Kuan-tè-iâ	
(Kuan-kong)	(關公)	(Guān Gōng)	(Kuan-kong)	
Lin Zexu	林則徐	Lín Zéxú		
Lo-tshia	哪吒	Nézhā	Lô-tshia	
Ong-ia	王爺	Wáng Yé	Ông-iâ	
Otaka Yoshiko*	大鷹淑子	Dàyīng Shūzǐ		Ōtaka Yoshiko
Pan Shuhua*	潘淑華	Pān Shūhuá		
Tanaka Kinuyo	田中絹代	Tiánzhōng Juàndài		Tanaka Kinuyo
Thinn-kong	天公	Tiāngōng	Thinn-kong	
Uehara Ken	上原謙	Shàngyuán Qiān		Uehara Ken
Yamaguchi Yoshiko*	山口淑子	Shānkǒu Shūzǐ		Yamaguchi Yoshiko
Yuan Shikai	袁世凱	Yuán Shìkǎi		
Zhou Xuan	周璇	Zhōu Xuán		

*Other names for Li Xianglan; appear in Dramaturgical Notes only.

Table 1.4   Names of fictional characters, including film roles, mentioned
in the play

How it appears in this volume's translation	Chinese characters and Japanese kanji	Mandarin romanization in pinyin	Taiwanese romanization in Tai-lo	Japanese romanization in romaji
A-bun	阿文	Āwén	A-bûn	
A-tsai	阿財	Ācái	A-tsâi	
Bu-rang	布浪	Bùlàng	Pòo-lōng	
Guilan	桂蘭	Guìlán		
Hase Tetsuo	長谷哲夫	Chánggǔ Zhéfū		Hase Tetsuo
Jyo-jee	喬治	Qiáozhì	Kiâu-tī	
May-lee	瑪麗	Mǎlì	Málē	
Sato	佐藤	Zuǒténg	Tsò-tîn	Satō, Satou
Tan	陳	Chén	Tân	
Tiunn	張	Zhāng	Tiunn	
Tom-mu	湯姆	Tāngmǔ	Thng-ḿ	
Tian	田	Tián	Tiân	

Table 1.5   Names of places mentioned in the play

How it appears in this volume's translation	Chinese characters	Mandarin romanization in *pinyin*	Taiwanese romanization in *Tai-lo*	Frequent English renderings
Amitabha Temple	彌陀寺	Mítuó sì	Mî-tô-sī	Mituo Buddhism Temple
Amoy	廈門	Xiàmén	Ē-mn̂g	Xiamen, Amoy
An-ping	安平	Ānpíng	An-pîng	Anping
Bu-sia	霧社	Wùshè	Bū-siā	
Buddhist Ancestor Temple	佛祖廟	Fó zǔ miào	Pút-tsóo-biō	
Chiang Kai-Shek Road	中正路	Zhōngzhèng lù	Tiong-tsìng-lōo	
Chihkan Tower	赤崁樓	Chìkǎn lóu	Tshiah-khàm-lâu	Chihkan Tower
Chinatown	中國城	Zhōngguóchéng	Tiong-kok-siânn	
Circle	圓環仔	Yuánhuánzǐ	Înn-khuân-á	
Clear Water Temple	清水寺	Qīng shuǐ sì	Tshing-tsuí-sī	Cingshuei Temple
Cultural Bureau	文教局	Wénjiào jú	Bûn-kàu-kio̍k	
East Gate	東門	Dōng mén	Tang-mn̂g	
Emperor's Temple	上帝廟 (北極殿)	Shàngdì miào (Běijí diàn)	Siōng-tè-biō (Pak-kik-tiān)	Beiji Temple
Golden Pine Building	松金樓	Sōng jīn lóu	Siông-kim-lâu	
Golden Temple	金華府	Jīnhuá fǔ	Kim-hua-hú	Jinhua Temple
Great Person Temple	大人廟	Dàrén miào	Tuā-lâng-biō	Daren Temple
Hai-an Road	海安路	Hǎi'ǎn lù	Hái-an-lōo	Hai An Road
Heavenly Temple	天公廟 (天壇)	Tiāngōng miào (Tiāntán)	Thinn-kong-biō	Tiantan
Hebei	河北	Héběi	Hô-pak	Hebei
Hong Kong	香港	Xiānggǎng	Hiong-káng	Hong Kong
Hu-tsian Road	府前路	Fǔqián lù	Hú-tsiân-lōo	
Iu-hang-bue Street	油行尾街	Yóuhángwěi jiē	Iû-hâng-bué-ke	
Jade Emperor Palace	玉皇宮	Yùhuáng gōng	Gio̍k-hông-king	
Jin-tik	仁德	Réndé	Jîn-tik	
Khoan-Sai-Ke Presbyterian Church	看西街教會	Kànxījiē jiàohuì	Khuànn-sai-ke-kàu-huē	Khoànⁿ-Sai-Ke Presbyterian Church, Kan Si Street Church
Koxinga Shrine	國姓廟	Guó xìng miào	Kok-sìng-biō	Koxinga Shrine

Table 1.5 Continued

How it appears in this volume's translation	Chinese characters	Mandarin romanization in *pinyin*	Taiwanese romanization in *Tai-lo*	Frequent English renderings
Lam-o	南澳	Nán'ào	Lâm-ò	
Lam-si Canal	南勢港	Nán shì gǎng	Lâm-sì-káng	
Ma-tsoo Temple	媽祖宮	Māzǔ gōng	Má-tsóo-king	
Miyako Theater	宮古座	Gōng gǔ zuò	King-kóo-tsō	
New Sakariba	新的沙卡里巴	Xīnde Shākǎlǐbā	Sin-ê Sa-khah-lí-pa	
Pak-si Street	北勢街	Běishì jiē	Pak-sì-ke	Beishi Street
Phoo-tse Hall	普濟殿	Pǔjì diàn	Phóo-tsè-tiān	
Provincial Girls' Middle School	省女	Shěng nǚ	Síng-lú	Provincial Tainan Girls' Middle School
Sakariba	沙卡里巴	Shākǎlǐbā	Sa-khah-lí-pa	Sakariba
Shanghai	上海	Shànghǎi	Siōng-hái	Shanghai
Sin-long Street	神農街	Shénnóng jiē	Sîn-lông-ke	Shennong Street
Sin-ting	新町	Xīndīng	Sin-ting	
Sin-tshi	新市	Xīnshì	Sin-tshī	
Social Education Hall	社教館	Shèjiàoguǎn	Siā-kàu-kuán	
Tainan	台南	Táinán	Tâi-lâm	Tainan
Tainan Assembly Hall	公會堂	Gōnghùi táng	Kong-huē-tn̂g	Tainan Assembly Hall
Tainan Hospital	台南醫院	Táinán yīyuàn	Tâi-lâm pēnn-īnn	
Taipei	台北	Táiběi	Tâi-pak	Taipei
Temple of the Five Concubines	五妃廟	Wǔ fēi miào	Ngóo-hui-biō	Temple of the Five Concubines, Wufei Temple
Thai-ping-king Church	太平境	Tàipíngjìng	Thài-pîng-kíng	Maxwell Memorial Church
Three Benefits Hall	三益堂	Sān yì táng	Sam-ik-tn̂g	
Three Companies	三郊	Sānjiāo	Sam-kau	
Tua-tiann Street	大埕街	Dàchéng jiē	Tuā-tiânn-ke	
Water Spirits Temple	水仙宮	Shuǐxiān gōng	Tsuí-sian-kiong	Shueisian Temple
Weather Observatory	測候所	Cèhòusuǒ	Tshik-hāu-sóo	Southern Region Weather Center
World Hall	世界館	Shìjièguǎn	Sè-kài-kuán	
Yellow River	黃河	Huáng hé	N̂g-hô	Yellow River

Table 1.6   Names of films, songs, novels, and film companies mentioned in the play

How it appears in this volume's translation	Chinese characters (Japanese in parentheses)	Mandarin romanization in *pinyin*	Frequent English renderings
A Good Name for Generations	萬世流芳	Wànshì líufāng	*Eternity*
"Candy-Peddling Song"	賣糖歌	Mài táng gē	
Cassia Tree of Love	愛染桂 (愛染かつら)	Ài rǎn guì	
Chee-na Nights	支那之夜 (支那の夜)	Zhīnà zhī yè	*China Nights, China Night*
"Fragrant Night"	夜來香	Yè lái xiāng	"Tuberoses"
Manchukuo Film Association	滿洲映畫協會 (滿映)	Mǎnzhōu yìnghuà xíehùi (Mǎnyìng)	Manchukuo Film Association, Manchuria Film Production
"Moonlight on the Castle Ruins"	荒城之月	Huāng chéng zhī yuè	
Records of the Three Kingdoms	三國誌	Sāngúo zhì	*Records of the Three Kingdoms*
Sayon's Bell	沙鴦之鐘 (サヨンの鐘)	Shāyāng zhī zhōng	*Sayon's Bell*
"Song of Celebratory Clouds"	慶雲歌	Qìng yún gē	
"Song of Exorcism"	收驚歌	Shōu jīng gē	
"Suzhou Nocturne"	蘇州夜曲	Sūzhōu yèqǔ	"Suzhou Serenade," "Soochow Evening"
The Yellow River	黃河	Huáng hé	*The Yellow River*
"When Will My Lord Come Again?"	何日君再來	Hérì jūn zài lái	"When Will You Return?", "When Will the Gentleman Come Back Again?"

Table 1.7 Names of foods and other items mentioned in the play

How it appears in this volume's translation	Chinese characters or Japanese kanji	Mandarin romanization in *pinyin*	Taiwanese romanization in *Tai-lo*	Japanese romanization in *romaji*
eel noodle soup	鱔魚意麵	shànyúyìmiàn	siān-hî-ì-mī	
feng shui	風水	fēngshuǐ	hong-suí	
hinomaru bento	日の丸便當	rì (*no*) wán biàndāng		hinomaru bentō
huqin	胡琴	húqín	ôo-khîm	
Kominka	皇民化	Huángmínhuà		Kōminka
kue; cakes; steamed cakes	粿		guǒ	kué
nanguan	南管	nánguǎn	lâm-kuán	
pig's feet with thin noodles	豬腳麵線	zhūjiǎo miànxiàn	ti-kha-mī-suànn	
qipao	旗袍	qípáo	kî-phâu	
rice blood cakes	米血	mǐxuě	bí-huih	
wood ear powder	川耳粉	chuāněrfěn	tshuan-ní-hún	

We Are Here

PENG YA-LING
(1999)

translation by
Wang Wan-Jung and John B. Weinstein

The Uhan Shii Theatre Group premiered *We Are Here* in September 1999 in the Rex Theatre in Wuppertal, Germany, and then in October 1999 in the National Theatre in Taipei, Taiwan, followed by a tour of Hakka regions of Taiwan in 2000.

Director	Peng Ya-Ling
Music Design	Yen Zhi-wen
Narrator/Troupe Producer	Ye Ye

Actors

CHEN XIU-CHUN	WANG CHUN-QIU
DU YI-JIN (Da-tou)	WANG XI-YAN
HUANG SHU-PING	XU YUE-MEI
LIN JU-YING	YE ZHANG-ZENG
LIU JIAO-MEI	ZHANG BI-ZHU
LIU WEN-RUI	ZHANG LI (Dong-dong)
LUO SHU-YU	ZHANG XIN (Pi-pi)
QIU HUI-MEI	ZHENG JING-ZHI
WEN YU-QING	

Figure 2.1 Advertisement for the 2000 production of *We Are Here*, performed by the Uhan Shii Theatre Group.

Dramaturgical Notes for
We Are Here

John B. Weinstein

Playwright/director Peng Ya-Ling developed *We Are Here* through a collaborative process based on oral history interviews. The names that appear in this play are all names of actual people; in the original production, the actors played themselves in their own stories, and also played the supporting roles in the stories of fellow cast members. In addition to the Narrator, the original cast consisted of eleven adult women (Bi-zhu, Chun-qiu, Hui-mei, Jiao-mei, Ju-ying, Shu-ping, Shu-yu, Xiu-chun, Xi-yan, Yue-mei, and Yu-qing), two adult men (Wen-rui and Zhang-zeng), and four children, two girls (Jing-zhi and Pi-pi) and two boys (Da-tou and Dong-dong). All songs in the play, with the exception of the pop song at the end, are traditional Hakka folk songs. As is frequently the case in Chinese poetic and musical traditions, there are specific well-known "tunes" to which multiple songs are written, and the names of these tunes appear in the script together with the lyrics.

The term "mainlander" is used in this play (particularly in Jiao-mei's story) as it is used throughout Taiwan. It refers to someone who immigrated to Taiwan from mainland China around the time of the Nationalist party's retreat to Taiwan in the late 1940s, or a descendant of such immigrants. When speaking about mainlanders, the Hakka in this play sometimes call the mainland by the somewhat archaic name "Tangshan"; marrying a mainlander in Taiwan was certainly not going to lead to the bride's relocation to the actual mainland. Besides the Hakka and the mainlanders, there is a third major ethnic Chinese group in Taiwan, the speakers of the

Minnan dialect (referenced in Zhang-zeng's story) who began immigrating to Taiwan from Fujian Province in the seventeenth century. This group, referred to at various times as Hok-lo, Ho-lo, native Taiwanese, or, simply, Taiwanese, is interestingly absent from reference in *We Are Here*, despite forming the majority of Taiwan's population.

Some of the customs and expressions in this play are equally prevalent among the various ethnic groups in Taiwan, while others are unique to the Hakka communities. As an example, like other people in Taiwan, the Hakka mix in cheaper sweet potato with their rice to make the more desirable rice go further. The rice-based snack *mitaimu*, often eaten cold in the summertime, is also not uniquely Hakka. Nor is the association of prostitution with teahouses (referenced with regard to Hui-mei's husband's questionable behavior). The Taiwanese convention of using the long "A" syllable followed by one of the two characters in a person's given name— such as "A-zeng" for "Zhang-zeng"—also appears in *We Are Here* with some of the Hakka names. A more uniquely Hakka speaking custom is the use of "A-ge," which uses the "ge" that means elder brother, as a generalized term for a Hakka man.

Also more uniquely Hakka are the terms "uphouse" and "downhouse," which refer to those living, respectively, higher up the mountain and further down the mountain. Both terms taken together reflect the mountainous terrain of many Hakka villages, which certainly has not made their agrarian lives any easier. The play references (in Chun-qiu's story) the Hakka tradition of exchanging labor between families, used in particular to help one another when the farm work gets too busy at harvest time for a single family to manage. And the play makes repeated references, in multiple stories, to the Hakka custom of "adopted daughters." Young girls were given away to other families as future brides for the family's sons; in the meantime, they provided a cheap source of labor for the adoptive family. Various terms, such as "huadun girl" and "yahua girl" (the latter, literally "suppressed flower") are used in the play to refer to these girls sent away to other families.

In Zhang-zeng's opening speech, he references his grandfather not being able to speak Mandarin or Minnan. Indeed, his grandfather, like many Hakka elders, speaks only the Hakka language. Though often called "dialects" in English-language discussions of the Chinese language, Hakka, Mandarin, and Minnan (also called Hok-lo, Ho-lo, or Taiwanese), are mutually unintelligible, and they are more like separate languages than the English word "dialect" may suggest. In the original production, the Narrator spoke in Mandarin, while all other characters spoke Hakka throughout the play, aside from a few lines in Ju-ying's story, when she has to speak Mandarin with a shop owner in Taipei. Later in that scene, Ju-ying's use of the Hakka language helps unite her with other Hakka, even in the capital city, far away from her Hakka village.

We Are Here makes ample use of two recurring props, one specifically referencing Hakka customs, and the other a dramatic device without a unique cultural connection. The blue cloths, explained frequently within the text of the play, have been used by the Hakka for centuries as a means of carrying their possessions during their repeated migrations, from the north of China to the south, and then to villages in Taiwan, and most recently to urban locations. The wooden boxes called "reminiscence boxes" are a stage convention, not a cultural one, but one used frequently and to great effect by Peng Ya-Ling in her series of plays *Echoes of Taiwan*, of which *We Are Here* is the sixth installment. *Echoes of Taiwan* includes plays on various ethnic groups within Taiwan, and the reminiscence boxes are used throughout the series to symbolize the characters' memories of the past.

Characters

In order of appearance. The characters' names are the real names of the actors, who acted in their own stories in the original production, and also played supporting roles in others' stories.

Narrator
(Ye) Zhang-zeng (55 years old)
The Children: Da-tou (12), Jing-zhi (11), Pi-pi (5), and Dong-dong (7)
(Liu) Jiao-mei (73)
Yu-qing (66)
(Wang) Chun-qiu (41)
Ju-ying (46)
Xiu-chun (72)
Xi-yan (47)
Bi-zhu (67)
Shu-yu (66)
Shu-ping (43)
Yue-mei (51)
Wen-rui (73)
Hui-mei (44)
Farm Woman (played by Xi-Yan)
Mother in Act II, Scene 1 (played by Ju-ying)
Little Xi-yan in Act II, Scene 1 (played by Pi-pi)
Little Xi-yan's Sister in Act II, Scene 1 (played by Jing-zhi)
Little Xi-yan's Sister's Classmate in Act II, Scene 1 (played by Da-tou)
Grandpa in Act II, Scene 1 (played by Zhang-zeng)
Woman 1 in Act II, Scene 1 (played by Bi-zhu)
Woman 2 in Act II, Scene 1 (played by Xiu-chun)
Adoptive Mother 1 in Act II, Scene 2 (played by Hui-mei)
Adoptive Mother 2 in Act II, Scene 2 (played by Xiu-chun)
Adoptive Mother 3 in Act II, Scene 2 (played by Ju-ying)
Adoptive Mother 4 in Act II, Scene 2 (played by Chun-qiu)
Little Girl in Act II, Scene 2 (played by Pi-pi)
Man in Act III, Scene 1 (played Wen-rui)

Young Chun-qiu in Act III, Scene 2 and Act IV, Scene 3 (played by Jing-zhi)

Mother in Act III, Scene 2 (played by Chun-qiu)

Father in Act III, Scene 2 (played by Zhang-zeng)

Creditor in Act III, Scene 2 (played by Xi-yan)

Father in Act IV, Scene 1 (played by Zhang-zeng)

Younger Brother in Act IV, Scene 1 (played by Dong-dong)

Older Sister in Act IV, Scene 1 (played by Jing-zhi)

Man in the Soldier's Uniform in Act IV, Scene 2 (played by Wen-rui)

Oldest Sister in Act IV, Scene 3 (played by Hui-mei)

Second Sister in Act IV, Scene 3 (played by Xi-yan)

Little Boy in Act IV, Scene 4 (played by Dong-dong)

Little Girl in Act IV, Scene 4 (played by Pi-pi)

The Boss in Act IV, Scene 4 (played by Shu-ping)

Hakka Boss in Act IV, Scene 4 (played by Hui-mei)

Prologue: I Have Come to Taipei

There is a three-tiered platform on the stage.

Four wooden boxes are placed downstage center.

The Narrator stands downstage. Music fades in and the lights come up.

The Narrator walks toward one of the wooden boxes, opens it, and takes out an antique book of records.

NARRATOR: Two thousand years ago, fleeing from wars, disasters, and dynastic changes, the Hakka people gradually migrated from northern to southern China and became known as Hakka, or "guests." In the nineteenth century, they migrated again, from the southeastern most Chinese province, Guangdong, and dispersed all over the world. Living in their own communities, they sustain their own language, religion, and customs. Hakka people often wrap up their possessions with blue cloth. When moving from their homes, the Hakka would likewise use blue cloth to wrap up their bundles and just go on their way. The modern Hakka, migrating once more, do just as their ancestors did. In the Hakka villages in Taiwan today, the migration continues. It has always been this way.

On the platform, the entire family of Ye Zhang-zeng stands frozen: the grandfather, grandmother, father, mother, and their four children, of which Ye Zhang-zeng is one. All of them have bundles of blue cloth either on their backs or hold them in their hands.

ZHANG-ZENG: When I was a child, I lived in the Hakka village in Hsinchu County. My grandfather made a living as a blacksmith. He was the head of the whole family. Later, my father found a job in Taipei, and the whole family migrated there. My grandfather could speak neither Mandarin nor Minnan. When he arrived in Taipei, because he was unfamiliar with the people or the places, my grandfather locked himself up at home and was scared to even take a step out of the house. But the children were overwhelmed with joy when they got to Taipei.

ALL THE CHILDREN: *(Speaking loudly.)* I have come to Taipei.

The four children go toward the four wooden boxes and crouch down in front of them. They open up the boxes and look into them. The lights on stage go down completely, leaving only the flickering lights glowing from inside the boxes, like fire.

Liu Jiao-mei, a seventy-three year old woman, sits on a bamboo stool beside the Narrator. She opens up nine layers of blue cloth, one layer after another.

The music fades in as if it were sounds coming from far-off mountains.

When the Narrator introduces them, all the actors walk slowly to their individually designated spots on stage in the following procession.

NARRATOR: This is Jiao-mei. Jiao-mei left home because she chose to marry a mainlander instead of a Hakka.

All the actors bring their blue cloths up to their eyes and carefully look into the mottled, colored cloths.

They slowly bring the blue cloths to their noses to smell them.

Then they slowly touch their faces with the blue cloths.

NARRATOR: This is Yu-qing. Unlike the traditional Hakka housewives, she went out to make a living to feed the whole family.

Chun-qiu left home, following in the footsteps of her sisters, seeking better opportunities.

Ju-ying came to Taipei from the south. She worked as a dressmaker so that she could be a good housewife and a good mother. She was happy that she no longer had to work in her family's fields as a farmer.

Xiu-chun and Xi-yan were almost sent off as adopted daughters. At that time, it was very common to give away your own daughters as the adopted daughters of others and to take in others' daughters as your future daughters-in-law.

Bi-zhu was given away eleven days after she was born. Her mother had also been an adopted daughter herself.

Shu-yu, as all Hakka mothers expect of their daughters, married a Hakka man.

Shu-ping, as her mother had wished for her, married a Hakka man, though she and her husband seldom spoke Hakka to each other, only when they talked behind other people's backs.

Figure 2.2 In the Prologue of *We Are Here*, 73-year-old Jiao-mei (seated at right) opens nine layers of the blue cloth that Hakka people traditionally used to wrap up their belongings. Behind her, children gaze into "reminiscence boxes" filled with Hakka memories. The ensemble, all portraying their own stories, stands at the rear, in this 2000 performance by the original cast.

There were only a few Hakka people where Yue-mei studied and worked, so she gradually forgot how to speak Hakka.

Wen-rui's family has already been away from Hakka villages for five generations. He, too, seldom speaks Hakka at home.

Hui-mei's father insisted that she pursue higher education. This Hakka father felt there was no future working in the fields all their lives.

The grandfather of Ye Zhang-zeng used to work as a blacksmith in a Hakka village. He had always been the heart of his family's economic and social lives. However, when the whole family migrated to Taipei when Zhang-zeng was ten, the grandfather could speak neither Mandarin nor Minnan. He locked himself in the house all day long and did not want to take even a step out the door. But the Ye family children were all thrilled when they got to Taipei.

The actors turn around and wrap up their blue cloths into bundles, to put on their backs or carry in their hands.

Then they turn toward different directions and slowly look ahead toward the light as if they are looking far into the distance.

Downstage left, the light on the Narrator fades out.

Actors step up onto the platform together, as if they are standing on high mountains.

They gaze far off into the distance.

Lights change.

[Mountain Song] *(Sung by the group together.)*

The lights emanating from the wooden boxes in front of the four children glow brighter. The four children pick up ears of rice and bring them up to their noses to smell them.

SHU-YU *(Solo.)*:
  Eh, my sister,
  My mountain song, I share with you.
  My mountain song, I share with you.

ALL PERFORMERS *(Singing together.)*:
  Eh, my sister,
  My mountain song, I share with you.
  My mountain song, I share with you.

I hear your song, know your heart, I hear your song, know your heart.

Green green the rice, spring begins.

Red red the hills, azalea blooms.

Let us go home, let us return, let us go home, let us return.

The lights change, and the group disappears.

Act I: The Ones Who Ploughed the Fields

The music of farmers' work songs fades in.

Farm women Chun-qiu, Hui-mei, and Ju-ying do a seed-planting movement: planting five seeds each time, they move from stage right to left.

The Narrator walks to downstage left.

Lights come up.

NARRATOR: Farming is the way most Hakka made their living. But many of the young aspired to leave home to earn a living in the big cities. They feared a life in the fields and, even more, they hated that they would have to work so hard in the fields and yet so often not have enough to eat.

Farm scenery: shady trees, rice fields, gentle breezes, and sunlight. Lights come up.

The three farm women chatter about their chores while continuing their seed planting.

CHUN-QIU: A-hui, it seems like just the other day, you were taking the boar to stud, and now I hear you already have new piglets.

HUI-MEI: I sure do! It was great. This time she had ten. Eight sows and two boars.

JU-YING: That's really great!

HUI-MEI: Well, look who raised them! Who else could have so many?

CHUN-QIU: Who would want so many?

HUI-MEI: The sows will fetch a better price. I'll just give the two boars to Ju-ying.

JU-YING: I don't want them. My own sows are about to have their litters. I don't have the money to raise yours.

Ju-ying takes this opportunity to stand up and stretch her arms.

CHUN-QIU: A-hui, the day before yesterday, I saw your husband sneaking around the train station.

HUI-MEI: Oh, great. You saw it two days ago and wait until now to tell me. Don't you know there are some "teahouses" behind the station?

From stage left enters a Farm Woman bringing snacks. She carries two baskets hanging from a pole across her shoulders. One basket has mitaimu, *a snack made of rice, and the other has salted rice porridge. A boy and a girl are catching frogs behind her.*

FARM WOMAN *(played by Xi-yan)*: Hey, folks, come along and have some snacks!

JU-YING: Don't worry about it, sometimes you have to let your husband play around.

HUI-MEI: No way. We'll have a good fight tonight. *(She pulls her feet out of the muddy rice field.)* I'm done here. Time for some snacks. *(She washes her hands and feet with water from the brook beside the field.)* Wow, it's *mitaimu,* my favorite rice snack!

JU-YING: You're always first when there's something to eat. Oh, please! Wash your hands and feet first! What do we have here? *(Ju-ying excitedly goes over to the snack baskets.)*

The children help serve the snacks.

HUI-MEI: *Mitaimu!*

CHUN-QIU: I want salted rice porridge.

JU-YING: I want a bowl too.

The Farm Woman who brought the snacks calls across the mountain to the people up the hills.

FARM WOMAN: Hey, you up there, snack time!

The Farm Woman exits. The little boy, Da-tou, goes along the edge of the rice paddy to catch tadpoles and splash around in the water.

JU-YING: Hey, kiddo, we just finished planting those seedlings. And now you're playing right on top of them.

The little girl, Jing-zhi, collects all the snack bowls.

HUI-MEI: Hey, can't you hear? Hurry home or I'll beat you!

The little boy Dong-dong joins Da-tou to catch tadpoles down by the paddy. The little girls Jing-zhi and Pi-pi jump down the paddy and try to catch up with Da-tou and Dong-dong. All the farm women shout, "We're gonna beat you kids!" The water in the fields splashes in all directions.

CHUN-QIU: Kids today have it better than we did. We had to plow the fields and pull out the weeds. I feared weeding the most. When you knelt down, you got bitten by leeches. So scary! Such misfortune!

The three farm women take off their bamboo hats and flowered scarves.

While they are fanning themselves, they chitchat with each other.

JU-YING: Really, so sad.

CHUN-QIU: Working from morning 'til night, you can't even tell which is which anymore!

JU-YING: The scariest thing is the leeches. It's worth the effort if you get a good harvest. But often just when the rice sprouts have bent their heads and are ready to be picked, the gust of a typhoon or the drizzle of the plum rain will come.[1] The rice sprouts will fall to the ground. They'll either be empty inside or they'll have already sprouted, and then you'll have no white rice to eat. You'll have to keep on eating sweet potato rice.

CHUN-QIU: I've really had enough of sweet potato rice. Such misfortune!

HUI-MEI: My parents would always warn us brothers and sisters while we were weeding the fields. Work harder, study harder. Earning your living with a pen and brush is better than tanning your feet while plowing the fields and pulling up weeds.

CHUN-QIU: Your father had more education than most people.

JU-YING: Your fate is better if you get to study. You don't have to plow the fields to be able to eat. If we get a harvest, we'd be thrilled. We'd have many bowls of white rice to eat. When you eat white rice, you don't need to eat anything with it. When you eat it, you don't even realize you're full.

CHUN-QIU: I tell you, I can eat three bowls of white rice. I don't need anything with it. One time, I ate too much. My mother and brother saw me sitting in the doorway, holding my stomach, crying. They asked me, "A-qiu, what happened to you? Holding your stomach, crying and crying?" I answered, "Oh, can't you see I am too full?"

JU-YING: Such misfortune! Maybe we didn't cultivate good karma in our past lives!

The lights on stage fade out and the light on Chun-qiu goes up. Chun-qiu starts to sing her inner monologue.

---

[1] In Taiwan, the rainy season often comes in May while the plum trees are blossoming, thus it is called the plum rain.

[Pingban Tone] *(Sung by Chun-qiu.)*

CHUN-QIU *(Singing.)*:

> Way way back,
>
> Rushing, cutting crops,
>
> Grown-ups and little ones,
>
> All at once,
>
> Farming fields,
>
> Can't wait for harvest,
>
> All this for three square meals,
>
> Work won't stop.

The lights on Chun-qiu fade out. Ju-ying walks down stage right, and the lights come up on her.

[Pingban Tone] *(Sung by Ju-ying and others.)*

JU-YING *(Singing alone.)*:

> Since young, 'fraid to plow the fields.

Four children slowly walk on stage and stand beside the three farm women. All of them walk up the stairs. They either wear a bamboo hat wrapped with a scarf or they carry shoulder poles and plows.

(Singing together.):

> Since young, 'fraid to plow the fields.
>
> Since young, 'fraid to plow the fields.
>
> Since young, 'fraid to plow the fields.
>
> Since young, 'fraid to plow the fields.

Lights fade out.

Act II: The Ones Who Were Given Away

Scene 1: The Story of Xi-yan

NARRATOR: Because there were plenty of children in Xi-yan's family, the eldest sister in the family had to take her little brothers and sisters to school with her so that they wouldn't disturb their mother's work. Several times, Grandpa brought Xi-yan up the mountain and tried to give her away. But since Xi-yan was too thin and small at the time, in the end, he couldn't give her away.

Xi-yan sits on the stairs watching her childhood memories played on stage. In her memory, Xi-yan's mother is doing some work with her hands, while Little Xi-yan is playing hide-and-seek with a group of children. In the middle of their chase, Little Xi-yan runs to her mother and holds her tight from behind. But her mother forcefully pushes Little Xi-yan away and coughs heavily.

MOTHER *(played by Ju-ying)*: Don't get too close. Take care of the little ones. Go play somewhere else, A-yan.

Little Xi-yan (played by Pi-pi) hugs her mother tight for the second time, and her mother pushes her away again.

MOTHER: I'm contagious! Go play by yourself!

Little Xi-yan's face shows confusion. And Big Xi-yan, sitting on the stairs, can't bear to see it. For the third time, Little Xi-yan tries to hug her mother. Big Xi-yan jumps out from behind and tightly holds Little Xi-yan and her mother.

BIG XI-YAN: Mommy, I want to give you a hug so badly. Why don't you want me?

Mother pushes Big Xi-yan and Little Xi-yan away together. Little Xi-yan is so afraid that she crouches at the side. Big Xi-yan holds the little one tight from behind.

MOTHER: It's not that Mommy doesn't want you. I want to hug you tight in my arms, too.

BIG XI-YAN: *(Sitting on the floor, her face full of shock and confusion.)* Why won't you give me a hug?

MOTHER: Mommy is so afraid that she'll give you her disease. I can't help it.

Little Xi-yan crouches on the floor and slowly moves backwards. Big Xi-yan sits back down on the stairs and watches herself in her childhood memories again.

[The Children's Song: Moon Bright Bright]

CHILDREN *(Singing together.)*:

> Moon bright bright, time's just right,
> Ginger's done, bamboo begun,
> Bamboo blooms, melon looms,
> Melons swell, time to sell,
> Sell for three cents each.

All the children play finger guessing games and chase each other around.

DA-TOU: Jing-zhi, time for school. *(Jing-zhi plays Little Xi-yan's sister.)*

MOTHER: Not yet, you have to carry your younger brother to school with you.

Jing-zhi goes to her mother. Mother uses the blue cloth to wrap the younger brother onto Jing-zhi's back.

JING-ZHI: Mommy, the teacher said we need to pay the school fees.

MOTHER: It doesn't matter. We'll pay in a few days.

JING-ZHI: The teacher said I can't take younger brother to school with me.

MOTHER: Can't take your younger brother to school? How will Mommy work? Unless you just don't go to school.

JING-ZHI: My classmates will laugh at me. *(Jing-zhi begs her Mother.)*

MOTHER: They won't. They won't.

Jing-zhi and Da-tou are about to leave. Little Xi-yan grabs her elder sister Jing-zhi's hand and also wants to go with her.

MOTHER: A-yan, stop that, you can't go. Stay at home and play. A-yan, come on, don't go, play at home.

Xi-yan's Grandpa takes a small bundle of blue cloth and an empty powdered milk can. He puts two little stones in it and shakes it to make sounds. Little Xi-yan loves to drink milk, and on the road she jumps up and down and tries to get the milk can from Grandpa's hand. While he walks up the mountain, he uses the milk can to trick Little Xi-yan.

GRANDPA *(played by Zhang-zeng)*: A-yan, come here, Grandpa has candy for you. I'll take you up the mountain to play. At the top, the auntie up there has *ameidama*[2] candy, your favorite kind. Yummy!

---

[2] *Ameidama* is derived from a Japanese word for candy.

Grandpa and Little Xi-yan come across a farm woman working on the mountain.

GRANDPA: Sister, good morning.

WOMAN 1 *(played by Bi-zhu)*: Good morning. Can I help you?

GRANDPA: This is my little granddaughter.

WOMAN 1: You want to give this child away?

GRANDPA: I don't know. Does anyone want her?

WOMAN 1: This little girl looks so pretty. But why is she so thin, and so small? Why do you want to give her away?

GRANDPA: We have too many kids at home, we can't afford to raise them. So we are giving a little girl to someone else.

WOMAN 1: Actually, I have many kids in my house, too. I have a newborn baby, a little one that needs to be held, another one always on my back, and one this big, this big, and this big. I really couldn't afford another one. Sorry about that.

GRANDPA: Do you know anyone who might want a little kid?

WOMAN 1: Yes. Auntie A-chun in the neighboring village has plenty of rice fields. She might need some extra hands. Maybe she wants a little kid. You can go ask her.

GRANDPA: Thank you. A-yan, let's go. I'll buy some candy for you. Let's go up that mountain to play, to play. Good girl, keep going, hurry up.

Big Xi-yan, who has been sitting on the stairs, walks toward Little Xi-yan and crouches by her. They combine their shadows and the two of them raise their heads to look at Grandpa.

BIG XI-YAN: Grandpa, my feet are sore, I can't walk anymore.

GRANDPA: We're almost there, hang in there, we'll get there soon.

Big Xi-yan goes back to the stairs.

GRANDPA: Good morning, Sister.

WOMAN 2 *(played by Xiu-chun)*: Good morning.

GRANDPA: I want to give away this little girl. I don't know, does anybody want her?

WOMAN 2: She is so thin and so dark, no way. My hands are full with my own kids. I have a two-year-old, a three-year-old, and a five-year-old. I have one this big and one this big. Do you have many kids? *(She takes a close look at the teeth of the little girl.)* This little girl of yours looks very

Figure 2.3 Big Xi-yan (far right) cannot bear to watch her own painful story. She embraces her younger self during her memory of the time her grandfather (center) brought her up the mountain to try to give her away to various Hakka farm women.

tiny and skinny. *(She shakes her head. Little Xi-yan closes her lips very tightly and refuses the woman's "check-up.")*

GRANDPA: I know.

WOMAN 2: There's nothing I can do. It looks like she couldn't help with the housework.

GRANDPA: Do you know anybody who might want kids?

WOMAN 2: You can go to Auntie A-qing in the neighboring village. She has no kids in the family. See if she wants her.

GRANDPA: Thank you so much.

He pulls Little Xi-yan toward him, but Little Xi-yan crouches on the floor and refuses to go.

GRANDPA: Grandpa will buy some candy for you. Come on, let's go, be a good girl. Good girl. A-yan, let's keep going. Good girl. *(Shaking the milk can, he slowly walks onward.)*

Big Xi-yan, who has been sitting on the stairs, walks toward Little Xi-yan's side, and she holds Little Xi-yan.

BIG XI-YAN: Grandpa, don't give me away to other people. I don't want to be given away.

Big Xi-yan and Little Xi-yan look at Grandpa with pleading eyes.

Lights fade out.

Scene 2: *The Story of Jiao-mei*

At stage left, the lights come up on the Narrator.

NARRATOR: There were ten brothers and sisters in Jiao-mei's family. Five older brothers, four older sisters, and she was the youngest. At that time, Hakka people had a custom of giving away their own daughters to others, and then adopting other people's daughters. From a young age, these little girls were made to do lots of housework, farm work, and other hard labor. When they grew up, they would marry their older brothers from their adoptive families. Jiao-mei's four sisters had been given away to others. At the same time, her family adopted four daughters to work for them. Originally, Jiao-mei was going to be given away, too. Fortunately, her father came back just in time to stop that. These adopted little girls lived their undignified lives full of scolding, abuse, and complaints.

Jiao-mei sits on a bamboo stool stage left. Jiao-mei's mother sits center stage with her head down.

Low-pitched, somber music fades in.

JIAO-MEI: There are ten brothers and sisters in my family. I have five older brothers and four older sisters. *(When Jiao-mei finishes talking, a little girl gives the baby girls, wrapped in flower-patterned cloth, to Jiao-mei's mother, one after another, during the following scene.)* My older sister was given away to others to be their daughter-in-law. If she were still alive, she would already be eighty-six years old. *(Adoptive Mother 1, played by Hui-mei, carrying a bamboo basket for selling vegetables, comes out. She takes away a little girl from Jiao-mei's mother's arms.)* My second oldest sister was given to others to be their daughter-in-law when she was young. If she were alive, she would be seventy-eight. *(Adoptive Mother 2, played by Xiu-chun, walks out from stage right and takes away a little girl from Jiao-mei's mother's arms.)* My third oldest sister was given away as a *huadun* girl—an adoptive daughter and future daughter-in-law—when she was one year old. If she were alive now, she would be seventy-six. *(Adoptive Mother 3, played by Ju-ying, walks out from stage right and takes away a baby girl from Jiao-mei's mother's arms.)* The fourth oldest sister of mine was taken away by others when she was young. She lives in Hsinchu now and she has a wonderful life. She is seventy-four. *(Adoptive Mother 4, played by Chun-qiu, walks out from stage left and takes away a baby girl from Jiao-mei's mother's arms.)* When I was young, I was supposed to be given away, too. But it happened that father came back from outside, just at that moment, and he said this girl should stay. That's why I was never sent away to be someone's future daughter-in-law. I grew up at home.

ADOPTIVE MOTHER 1: Ah, you unfortunate one, you just cry all day and won't take any milk. So thin and dark. Do you know we have a big family and tons of work waiting for you? You don't deserve to live!

ADOPTIVE MOTHER 2: Eat more so you'll grow up faster and you can be a wife for your older brother.

ADOPTIVE MOTHER 3: Even your own mother doesn't want you. You'd better behave now. When you're with me, you'd better accept your fate.

ADOPTIVE MOTHER 4: Eat or not, I don't care. If you piss me off, you'll have nothing to eat. Eat faster.

The focus of the light shifts to Jiao-mei.

JIAO-MEI: After all this happened, when our sisters returned home for reunions, we would talk about how they had been abused and tortured. It really breaks your heart.

Four adoptive mothers each hold their little baby girls in their arms. Lights change.

Zhang-zeng, Xi-yan, Shu-yu, Shu-ping, and Bi-zhu walk on stage. Each one holds a little baby girl wrapped up in flower-patterned cloth in his or her arms and narrates his or her own adoptive experience.

ZHANG-ZENG: A-hui, let me tell you. My mother was an adopted daughter. She married my father when she was sixteen.

XI-YAN: Let me tell you. My mother was an adopted daughter, too. When she was little, she was sent away as a *yahua* girl, a daughter adopted to be the future bride of the adoptive family's younger son. I was taken out twice when I was little. Once my grandpa tricked me to go up the mountain and almost got me sent away up there.

XIU-CHUN: Let me share this with you. Twice I was almost given away to others as an adopted daughter.

BI-ZHU: I was given away to my adoptive mother when I was only eleven days old. And my adoptive mother was an adopted daughter herself.

SHU-YU: My mother was sent away to be a future daughter-in-law when she was young. I was almost sold off by my grandma. Fortunately, my father loved me so much that he hid me in the closet.

Figure 2.4 Jiao-mei wraps a white cloth around the head of a little girl symbolizing all of the adopted daughters. By Hakka custom, these girls were sent away from their homes at young ages to live as other families' future daughters-in-law.

JU-YING: My auntie was an adopted daughter. Meanwhile, she herself adopted a daughter.

Lights change. Each person holds a baby girl in her right arm and raises her left hand as if she is going to hit the baby girl. Then they slowly press down their palms against the face of the baby girls. Slowly, each turns away her face to the left to avoid seeing the face of the baby girl.

The somber music grows louder.

Each woman on stage turns her back to the audience and holds her baby girl tight in her arms, as if she feels sympathy for the sad destiny of these adopted daughters.

Lights fade out and music fades out to a complete stop.

[The Song of the Adopted Daughters]

Lights come up.

Stage left, a little girl (played by Pi-pi) sits in front of Jiao-mei. Bi-zhu, Xiu-chun, Yu-qing, Hui-mei, Ju-ying, and Shu-ping, one by one, pull out a large white cloth. They approach the little girl slowly and hand the white cloth to Jiao-mei. She then binds it around the little girl's head. All the female performers pass the white cloth to one another as if in a ritual. They are sending out a kind of message—each of them is comforting the untreasured lives of all the adopted daughters.

[The Song of the Adopted Daughters #1, Old Mountain Tone] *(Sung by Shu-yu.)*

SHU-YU *(Singing.)*:

Adopted daughter sings to you,
Warning all the parents here,
Your own children, treasure them,
Don't give them to other folks,
Adopted daughters break your heart,
Not dressed warmly, not well fed,
Doomed to fate, unfortunate,
Holding grudges, no way out.

[The Song of the Adopted Daughters #2, Old Mountain Tone] *(Sung by Chun-qiu.)*

CHUN-QIU *(Singing.)*:

Adopted daughter sings to you,
Warning all the parents here,

Your own children, treasure them,
Don't give them to other folks,
Adopted daughters break your heart
Not dressed warmly, not well fed,
Doomed to fate, unfortunate,
Holding grudges, no way out.

At the end of the song, all the female performers walk slowly toward Jiao-mei and the little girl. Together they form a tight circle. They watch over both of them with profound sympathy.

Lights fade out slowly and music fades to a complete stop.

Act III: The Ones Who Got Married

Scene 1: *Marrying a Hakka Man*

Lights come up on the Narrator downstage left.

NARRATOR: Are you a Hakka? Does your family plow the fields? Do you have lots of brothers and sisters? Do you live together with your big family? If your answer is "yes," I won't marry you, yet my mother's greatest wish is for me to marry a Hakka man.[3]

A man, played by Wen-rui, stands center stage, wearing a black velvet hat and holding a bunch of fresh flowers in his hands. He is surrounded by five brides-to-be.

One of the women, Jiao-mei, goes toward this man center stage.

JIAO-MEI: Mister, are you a Hakka?

The man nods.

Consecutively, those women go toward the man one by one and question him.

JU-YING: Mother said if I marry a Hakka man, it will be easier to communicate.

YU-QING: You have so many brothers. I can't take it.

CHUN-QIU: Mother said it doesn't matter who I marry, as long as I like him.

SHU-YU: My mother told me not to marry any mainlander or Ho-lo man. I should only marry a Hakka man.

JU-YING: I heard you grow a lot of tobacco in your family. Growing tobacco, it's just horrifying.

YU-QING: I don't want to plow so many fields. I can't take this kind of life.

All these women walk toward the man one by one and turn their heads away, in the opposite direction away from him. They walk away.

JIAO-MEI: I will not consider any Hakka man.

CHUN-QIU: I don't like Hakka men myself.

JU-YING: I won't consider any men who grow tobacco.

CHUN-QIU: I don't have any interest in Hakka men.

JIAO-MEI: I won't consider any Hakka man.

---

[3] The Narrator, if male (as was the case in the original production), should deliver this line as if speaking from a female viewpoint.

Figure 2.5 As Shu-yu weds a Hakka man, her community joyfully sings the "Song of Falling in Love."

YU-QING: So much work. I can't take it. *(All these women turn their heads away with determination.)*

SHU-YU: Mister, you are really handsome. Will you cherish your wife?

MAN: Yes. *(He gives the bunch of fresh flowers to Shu-yu, and Shu-yu accepts it, full of joy).*

SHU-YU *(Singing in Pingban Tone.)*: A-ge gives her all his heart, Love each other years and years.

ALL PERFORMERS: Come see the bride! Come see the bride! *(Lights come on in full brightness.)*

[Song of Falling in Love] *(Sung by the group together.)*

All of the performers surround the bride and the groom in a circle, dance with colorful streamers, and sing happily together:

When third month comes, fall in love,

Dress third sister up, dress third sister up,

Dress third sis up, sister is the bride.

A-ge loves her, she loves him.

They are hand in hand, they are heart to heart.

Sis wants to wed, wed a Hakka man.

When they finish singing, the bride and the groom sit at the left side of the stairs. The lights come from the side, forming a silhouette.

Scene 2: Chun-qiu's Story

Lights come up on the Narrator.

Three silhouettes are seen on stage. One is on the stairs upstage left, the silhouette of a Hakka couple. One is on the stairs center stage, a mother working with her head looking down, while a father sits on the bench with one of his knees up. The other one is a silhouette of a little girl, sitting in front of the wooden box on the stairs downstage right (Jing-zhi plays the role of young Chun-qiu).

NARRATOR: In the night, Chun-qiu usually overheard her parents whispering. It was always the same story: no money. The story always ended the same way. Father wanted to save face and managed to stay calm. No matter how much she didn't want to do it, Mother would have to go out to borrow some money.

Lights change. Father and Mother converse, in a voice-over.

MOTHER *(Played by Chun-qiu.)*: A-zeng, we're running out of rice again.

FATHER *(Played by Zhang-zeng.)*: Again? How's it running out so fast?

MOTHER: Our family has so many people, if the rice weren't cooked with sweet potatoes mixed in, it would be long gone. How could we wait this long to harvest?

FATHER: We still need to wait another month to harvest this season's rice. We'd better go borrow some first.

MOTHER: Do you want to borrow from the farmers' association or from the people downhouse?[4]

FATHER: We still haven't paid back what we borrowed from the farmers' association, right? I think it's better to borrow some from the people downhouse this time.

MOTHER: Sure. When are you going to do that?

Chun-qiu, playing her mother, carries a shoulder pole with two baskets filled with heads of unmilled rice. She goes to borrow some milled rice. The creditor (played by Xi-yan) takes out many loan receipts to show her that there are still many unpaid bills. Chun-qiu, playing her mother, with her head bowed down, repeatedly begs the creditor and keeps on pushing her baskets toward him. The creditor rejects the baskets and kicks them away.

FATHER: Me, borrow the rice? For the next two days I'm going to barter labor with others, so I won't have time. As a woman, you are freer. I think it's best for you to go do the borrowing.

MOTHER: What do you mean as a woman I'm freer? I raise a whole herd of pigs, and also the hens, cocks, and ducks at home. Besides, there's a ton of housework that I'll never finish in my life. Every time, when it's time to borrow money or rice, you ask me to do it. Why don't you go give it a try?

FATHER: Speaking of borrowing money, it's time to pay the kids' school fees. I don't know if you've gotten that ready?

MOTHER: I'm not afraid of that this time. We have nice pigs. If we don't have enough money, we can just sell two of them.

FATHER: So, when will you go do the borrowing?

---

[4] "Downhouse" refers to those living further down the mountain.

MOTHER: I'll go when I'm free.

FATHER: When you're finished borrowing the rice, you need to come back quicker. There's still a lot to do at home.

MOTHER: You, what a useless man!

Chun-qiu takes off the bamboo hat and puts down the shoulder pole with baskets. Lights change.

[Mountain Song Tone] *(Sung by Chun-qiu.)*

CHUN-QIU *(Singing.)*:

Dull knife, cracked stick, life too hard.

Borrow, borrow, no way out.

House front, house back, spinning 'round.

No end to it, all year long.

Lights fade, leaving only the three silhouettes from the beginning of the scene, that of a newlywed couple, that of a quarreling couple, and that of the little girl Chun-qiu in front of a reminiscence box.

Scene 3: Yu-qing's Story

The three silhouettes from the last scene remain on stage. Lights come up on the Narrator.

NARRATOR: Yu-qing and Ju-ying have many complaints about their husbands. They both think their husbands lack the shoulders to carry their families. Neither Yu-qing nor Ju-ying wants to be a tragic woman. They want to seek out their own independence.

There are a lot of books, clothes, and chairs scattered around the stage. On the stairs upstage, a father sits with his back to the audience. Four children are playing hide-and-seek. Yu-qing comes back from outside.

YU-QING: You little bastards throw everything around and make a mess everywhere. All you know how to do is kid around. You don't want to study, you just want to play. I have to do everything inside the house and outside the house. The old man isn't responsible at all. He doesn't take care of anything. All he knows how to do is help other people write official documents.

Yu-qing curses and cleans up at the same time. Ju-ying sits on a small bamboo stool and helps clean up.

JU-YING: My husband is no better than yours. Whenever he opens his big mouth, he's always saying how great he is. He's always the first in line for drinking or gambling.

YU-QING: I ride my own bicycle to Kaohsiung and also to Pingtung. I go everywhere to sell things for my little business.

JU-YING: If there wasn't enough money to pay the children's school fees, he would just ask them to quit school. I'm paying all the bills at home, but he still has the nerve to say I don't help out.

YU-QING: I have to be the father and the mother at the same time. If I don't take responsibility for this family, how will the kids have food to eat? They'll starve to death!

Yu-qing angrily shoves a whole pile of books to the floor. The books fall to the floor with a great crash, arousing similar anger in Ju-ying's heart.

JU-YING: My whole life, I've never seen a man like this.

YU-QING: If it wasn't for me, how could this family survive?

Lights get darker.

[Pingban Tone] *(Sung by Ju-ying.)*

JU-YING *(Singing.)*:

Pondering fate, bitter sighs,
Parents chose the groom for me.
Painful feelings, cannot speak,
When night falls, shed endless tears.

Lights go to complete darkness.

There are four boxes on the stage. Four children each slowly open a wooden box—a reminiscence box.

The reminiscence boxes glow with flickering light from within.

The voices of their fathers and mothers, in their memories, come out of the boxes.

JU-YING: Mother said if I marry a Hakka man, it will be easier to communicate.

SHU-YU: My mother said never marry any mainlander or Ho-lo man.

CHUN-QIU: A-zeng, there's no rice again.

YU-QING: The old man is never responsible for anything.

The four children quickly close the boxes with a big bang.

Lights change. All the children cover their ears tightly, and the sounds all disappear.

The children open the reminiscence boxes again, and the fire glowing from within and the quarrelling sounds again come out.

CHUN-QIU: *(Singing.)* Dull knife, cracked stick, can't get out.

Borrow, borrow, no way out.

SHU-YU: My mother wants me to marry a Hakka man.

JIAO-MEI: So many brothers and sisters, I can't take this.

YU-QING: I have to do everything inside the house and outside the house. I have to be the father and the mother at the same time.

SHU-YU: Whenever he opens his big mouth, he's always saying how great he is. When it comes to drinking or gambling, he's always the first in line.

All the children quickly close the boxes with a big bang.

Lights change. The children cover their ears tightly, and the sounds disappear.

The children open the reminiscence boxes again.

The lights glowing from within grow even stronger, and the voices coming out grow even louder.

CHUN-QIU: *(Singing.)* House front, house back, spinning 'round,

All year round, no end to it.

YU-QING: If this family didn't have me to support it, how would the kids have food to eat? They'd all starve to death!

JU-YING: I'm paying all the bills at home, and he still has the nerve to say I don't help out. My whole life, I've never seen a man like this.

The children close the boxes again with a bang. All the voices disappear.

Lights change. The children cover their ears.

All the lights go down.

Act IV: The Ones Who Left

Scene 1: Yu-qing Leaves

Lights come up on the Narrator.

NARRATOR: In order to pay off huge debts, Yu-qing left her home. She was willing to take any job, as long as it made money. She did not want to live the kind of life where she couldn't even get fifty yuan when she needed it.[5]

The father (played by Zhang-zeng) sits on the long bench on the stairs with his back turned to the audience.

The younger brother (played by Dong-dong) has a fever and is wrapped up in a blanket. His older sister (played by Jing-zhi) wraps her younger brother's head with a wet towel. Da-tou and Pi-pi are playing near the bed. Books, towels, and blankets are scattered on the floor.

YU-QING: You kids are playing with things that aren't even any fun. You're even playing with the blanket.

OLDER SISTER: Little brother has a fever.

YU-QING: Let me take a look. So hot. Mama's going to take you to see the doctor. *(Reaches into her pocket.)* Ah, I don't have any money, what am I gonna do? What am I gonna do when the little one has a fever? Where can I borrow some money? Where is your father?

PI-PI: Papa just went out.

YU-QING: Watch your brother. I'll go look for Papa.

(Facing the man sitting on the long bench.) All you can do is help others write those official documents. Do you know your own little boy is sick? Give me fifty yuan. I need to take him to a doctor. I sold the rationed rice and flour to get the money to see the doctor last time. I have nothing left to sell now. If I sell anymore, we'll all starve. What's your problem? Didn't you hear me? How can you not answer? What kind of man are you that you don't answer me? *(The man still remains silent. Yu-qing*

---

[5] These yuan, or "dollars," are New Taiwan (NT) dollars. One U.S. dollar is generally the equivalent of approximately twenty-eight NT dollars; therefore, the amount of money that Yu-qing needs is less than two U.S. dollars.

just can't wait any longer.) I'm not going to rely on you anymore. I'll figure out a way myself. *(Yu-qing goes back to her children.)* You, older sister,
take care of your younger brother. Mama will go out to borrow some
money.

Yu-qing goes out to borrow money. Yu-qing brings back some medicine.

YU-QING: Older sister, go get some water for your brother to take his med-
icine. Older sister, there's some food in the kitchen, go heat it up.
When your brother takes a bath, don't let him play with the water.
Mama will go out to make some money.

If I don't go out to make some money for this family, we'll have nothing to eat. We'll starve to death.

Older sister, younger brother, watch the house. Take good care of it. If
this family didn't have me to go make some money, we would have
nothing to eat.

*Yu-qing pulls out the blue cloth from the untidy home. She wraps it up into a bundle
and puts in on her shoulder. She walks out toward the light with determination and
ease.*

Lights fade out.

Scene 2: Jiao-mei Leaves

Lights come up on the Narrator.

NARRATOR: Jiao-mei left because she chose to marry a mainlander instead
of a Hakka man.

On the stairs stands a man (played by Wen-rui) wearing a soldier's uniform and hat.

Whispering voices of village women come out from backstage.

WOMEN'S VOICES: Don't go! You can't do that! You'll be a laughingstock!

Female vocal music fades in.

*Jiao-mei leaves, carrying her blue cloth bundle on her back and holding a big suitcase.
The blaming sounds follow behind her. Jiao-mei walks to center stage. Suddenly, ten
women with flower-patterned cloth wrapped on their heads rush to surround her
completely. They fight to grab her while they give her advice.*

HUI-MEI: A-jiao, don't marry a mainlander, think clearly. You don't want to marry a mainlander. *(She pulls Jiao-mei to her side.)*

YUE-MEI: Sister A-jiao, if you marry a mainlander, I won't go have fun with you anymore. *(She pulls Jiao-mei to the other side.)*

SHU-YU: Don't marry a mainlander. You can't speak their language and you'll be a laughingstock.

JU-YING: Sister A-jiao, Tangshan is too far, you don't want to go there. Sister A-jiao, you are such a beautiful woman, why should you be afraid that nobody will want you? Why do you have to marry a mainlander?

XI-YAN: Auntie, nobody wants to marry a mainlander. Don't marry a mainlander.

BI-ZHU: Sister A-Jiao, go home, let's go home. *(She grabs Jiao-mei and takes her to go inside.)*

CHUN-QIU: If you marry a mainlander, Tangshan is so far away, how could you come home from there? *(She blocks Jiao-mei's way and pushes her to the back.)*

XIU-CHUN: Tangshan is way too far. Besides, you can't speak their language, people will laugh themselves silly. *(She grabs Jiao-mei's hand.)*

SHU-PING: You are being too selfish. Don't marry as far away as Tangshan, how are you going to come back from so far away? *(She grabs Jiao-mei's other hand.)*

Yu-qing grabs Jiao-mei's hand and forcefully drags her forward. She scolds her loudly in front of everyone.

YU-QING: Jiao-mei, listen to me carefully. I have told you many times that you can't marry a mainlander, but you insist on marrying one. If you don't listen to me this time, I will chop you up and feed you to the pigs. From then on, you'll never be allowed to return to your mother's house. Do you hear me?

Jiao-mei turns around slowly. She turns left and right to look at those women around her.

Xiu-chun and Shu-yu shake their heads slightly, point their fingers at her, and tell her to be careful.

Among the other women, some are angry, and some are sad to say goodbye.

After taking a close look at each of them one by one, suddenly Jiao-mei takes off the flower-patterned cloth wrapped on her head and throws it down heavily on the floor.

ALL: *(Shouting.)* Oh, no!

Some shake their heads, some curse.

Some stamp on the floor, some throw down their hands.

Jiao-mei picks up her suitcase.

All of the women come up to her and try to take away her suitcase with all of their strength.

JIAO-MEI: *(Shouting loudly.)* That's enough! I'll decide this for myself.

All the women let her go but continue to complain and curse as they are exiting the stage.

Jiao-mei holds her suitcase and walks forward. Suddenly two people rush out to stop her.

XI-YAN: Don't do that. Don't marry a mainlander. No one marries mainlanders these days.

HUI-MEI: The more I tell you not to, the more you want to go. Think more clearly about it.

She blocks Jiao-mei's way and grabs her shoulder. Jiao-mei turns around and takes another path. Suddenly another two people rush out to stop her.

JU-YING: You are so beautiful. Do you really have to marry him? Don't do it! Don't marry someone so far away.

CHUN-QIU: Don't go! Don't marry a mainlander. People will laugh themselves silly.

Two people hide beside the road to talk behind Jiao-mei's back. When Jiao-mei comes near, they duck out of the way.

Jiao-mei walks toward the man in the soldier's uniform. The man takes her suitcase and turns around. They walk to center stage. Lights change.

JIAO-MEI: Just like that, I took my bundle and left my home. My husband and I worked hard together to build our own family. When I got married, none of my family or friends came to my wedding.

Lights fade out.

Scene 3: Chun-qiu Leaves

Lights come up on the Narrator.

NARRATOR: Since her childhood, Chun-qiu had always known, sooner or later, she would follow in the footsteps of her brothers and sisters and leave her home. Because at home, she'd never get enough to eat by farming, she'd never get anywhere working in a factory, and she'd never get the opportunity to go to school.

Chun-qiu, sitting on the center of the stairs, is picking vegetables. At stage right, there is a swing. Young Chun-qiu (played by the little girl Jing-zhi) is swinging on the swing. Chun-qiu's oldest sister and second sister stand at stage right and stage left. They have their blue bundles wrapped on their backs.

Lights on the oldest sister (played by Hui-mei) come up. Music fades in.

OLDEST SISTER: A-qiu, think about it. If you live in the mountains, you will be like Mom and Dad, who work so hard their whole lives and have no money. Such a hard life they have. Study harder, and when you graduate from middle school, come to Taipei and take the joint entrance exam to get into high school here, either day school or night school.

You can work part-time to pay for school part-time. Look at your older sister, I'm making my own money now. It's much freer here.

When you come to Taipei, your own family can take good care of you. Come, just come. Listen to your oldest sister, come to Taipei! Come to Taipei!

Lights fade on the oldest sister.

Lights on the second sister (played by Xi-yan) come up.

SECOND SISTER: A-qiu, come up to Taipei. Don't work as a factory girl. People laugh like crazy at factory girls. People will say, look at the girl who lives uphouse, it's so disgraceful that she's a factory girl.[6] All she knows how to do is watch TV so much that she's become so stupid. She loves to fool around. After you graduate from middle school, you have to study hard. Come up to Taipei!

---

[6] "Uphouse" refers to those living further up the mountain.

Lights fade on the second sister.

Lights come up on Chun-qiu.

CHUN-QIU: Ever since I was a little girl, I have always known that I will leave home when I grow up. If I don't go away, I'll have no school to go to, and no work to do at home.

My mother says we have a hard life and they can't support my going to school. So, when I grow up, I have to leave home.

I can still remember my mom told me that our neighbor's geese were missing and they thought we had stolen from them.

Although we Wangs were very poor and led a hard life, we would never steal other people's geese.

I've always known since I was young that when I grow up, I will leave to work hard and make a lot of money for my family.

I've always known I have to go away, I have to go away!

Chun-qiu picks up her blue cloth, makes it into a bundle, and puts it on her back.

OLDEST SISTER: A-qiu, come up to Taipei!

SECOND SISTER: A-qiu, come up to Taipei!

The little girl comes down from the swing and walks toward the lights downstage. The oldest sister, the second sister, and Chun-qiu raise their arms straight up as if they are going to fly high into the sky. Lights come up on the faces of Chun-qiu and the little girl. Lights fade out and music gradually stops.

Scene 4: Ju-ying Leaves

Lights come up on the Narrator.

NARRATOR: Ju-ying came to Taipei from the south. She needed a job she could do while also being a housewife and a mother. She chose to be a dressmaker.

Lights change.

Ju-ying comes in upstage with a little boy (played by Dong-dong) and a little girl (played by Pi-pi).

The three of them, the mother and the two children, carry their blue bundles on their backs and walk slowly from center stage toward downstage.

JU-YING: I couldn't get used to Taipei when I first came. Taipei was often very rainy. The kids were still little, and it was hard for their diapers to dry. I thought everything was so inconvenient. I had nothing in life. With all my heart and soul, I only wished I could find a job as soon as possible. So I went to the nearby dressmaking shops and asked them one by one. Some said: How are you going to do this when your kids are so small? It was very difficult for me to find a Hakka woman who let me bring some clothes back home to give it a try. I could take care of my kids and do my work at the same time. I felt very happy.

Ju-ying brings her children with her and goes toward a dressmaking shop.

JU-YING: *(Speaking in Mandarin.)* May I ask if you have any work for me to do?

THE BOSS *(played by Shu-ping)*: Of course. There's a lot of work inside, needed in a hurry. But can you do the work with two children with you?

JU-YING: I will try to work it out.

THE BOSS: You can't work it out because they are just too small. I've been working hard to catch up with my work here. I'm very busy. You can go ask around at other places.

Ju-ying walks out to the street with disappointment.

She goes to another dressmaking shop.

JU-YING: *(In Mandarin.)* May I ask, do you ... *(In Hakka.)* Hey, kids, don't touch other people's stuff.

HAKKA BOSS *(played by Hui-mei)*: Hey, you speak Hakka, where are you from?

JU-YING: I come from Meinong.

HAKKA BOSS: I come from Gongguan, Miaoli. We are all Hakka people.

JU-YING: Do you have any work that you can let me take home to do?

HAKKA BOSS: Sure, sure. I have several pieces here, I just cut out the patterns. You can take them home and sew them up. Bring them back in a week and let me see what your work is like.

JU-YING: Thank you!

HAKKA BOSS: Your kids are very cute. I have some candy here. Come, take some.

JU-YING: Don't trouble yourself.

The children take the candy, and their faces are full of joy.

HAKKA BOSS: Stay close to your mother, don't just eat.

Ju-ying walks up to the stairs, and the children sit down on the stairs and eat candy.

JU-YING: I felt so excited when I found the job. Whenever I saw scissors before, I used to think I was quite unfortunate. But now with this set of scissors, I could make a living in Taipei and settle down here. I felt so proud of myself.

Music begins to play.

Many women come on stage, dressed up in glamorous fashions.

They are all Ju-ying's models, symbols of beauty.

Ju-ying adjusts their outfits one by one, and everyone dances happily.

Lights fade out and music concludes.

Epilogue: Open Up the Bundle of Memories

Lights come up and music begins.

The music is Yan Zhi-wen's song "Taking Off."

NARRATOR: Hakka people often wrap up their possessions with blue cloth. When moving from their homes, the Hakka would likewise use blue cloth to wrap up their bundles and just go on their way. Inside the blue bundle, they might have their clothes, photos, books, babies, or any other stuff … The modern Hakka migrate once again, just as their ancestors did. When these people leave their homes in the Hakka villages to go to the big city, what do they have in their blue bundles?

On the stage, group one appears. Ju-ying and her two children carry blue bundles on their backs.

Group two appears. Chun-qiu and her two sisters carry blue bundles on their backs.

Group three appears. Yu-qing and her two children carry blue bundles on their backs.

Group four appears. Jiao-mei and all the other performers carry blue bundles on their backs.

Downstage center, there are two open reminiscence boxes.

Downstage left, Jiao-mei sits on a bamboo stool.

All the performers go up to the rear of the stage, open up the blue bundles they had been carrying on their backs, and hold them in their hands.

One by one, they go to the reminiscence boxes to speak.

Jiao-mei opens up the nine layers of her blue bundle, layer by layer.

BI-ZHU: When I open up my bundle, it is full of the love that my adoptive mother has for me.

XIU-CHUN: This picture is the one that I took with my seven brothers and sisters when I was little.

None of my sisters have been given away to others.

Everyone grew up together.

To me, this is so meaningful, so precious.

WEN-RUI: I throw away all my past worries.

SHU-YU: When I open up my bundle, I see a photograph

    that I took with my parents, brothers and sisters.

    My father loved me dearly. When my grandmother tried to sell me to others,

    he hid me away.

ZHANG-ZENG: This bundle contains my old clothes.

    They give me warm feelings and nostalgic memories.

XI-YAN: This bundle contains the memory, from when I was eight,

    of my father once carrying me on his back to cross the swinging bridge.

    On his shoulders, I felt overwhelmed with warmth.

HUI-MEI: When I left home,

    in my bundle, there were the school fees and living costs

    that my father sold all his rice for.

    I have never been given so much money before that.

    Now I have made more money than what I was given back then.

    I don't have to kneel down in the fields, cut the weeds,

    or get sunburned on the soles of my feet from doing farm work anymore.

CHUN-QIU: My family was so poor that I didn't have much to bring along.

    Only this old bundle has followed me through all these years.

    Now I have my own house,

    my own family, and children, too.

JU-YING: Opening up the bundle, I see my diary from my youth.

    In it, there are many of my hopes and dreams.

    With every step I take, I carry them with me.

YU-QING: When I open up my bundle, it contains the debts from my youth.

    But I have paid all of them off.

    My children have all grown up.

    I have no more worries, no more cares.

YUE-MEI: In the blue bundle,

    I have all my diaries from childhood to adulthood.

These diaries have given me

tremendous courage and strength.

SHU-PING: There is one small photo I have in my blue bundle.

My mother holds me in her arms standing in the center,

my father stands way in the back.

My brothers and sisters stand at the two sides.

Whenever I see this picture,

I feel my mother loves me the most.

I am the happiest person in the whole world.

After each performer finishes their own monologue in front of the reminiscence boxes, they hold their blue bundle with both hands and circle around the stage with big, slow, steady strides. Then they step down from stage left, walk through the audience, and go straight out of the auditorium.

JIAO-MEI: I take this bundle

and work hard with my husband all my life.

The decision I made back then, to this very day, I have no regrets.

Da-tou and Jing-zhi carry their blue bundles on their backs, walk up the stairs, and stand still on the top level.

Pi-pi and Dong-dong walk toward the reminiscence boxes. The flickering lights glow from inside. They take out two candles and go toward Jiao-mei. She lights the candles.

Pi-pi and Dong-dong carry their blue bundles on their backs, and stand in front of the reminiscence boxes, holding their candles.

The music of the song "Taking Off" grows louder and louder.

Lights fade out. Only the two candles remain, flickering for a long, long time.

—*End of play*—

Conversion Charts: Names and Terms

Table 2.1 Title and author

How it appears in this volume's translation	Chinese characters	Mandarin romanization in *pinyin*	Hakka romanization in *Hakka pinyin*
We Are Here	我們在這裡	Wŏmen zài zhèli	Ngo[1] mun[2] cai[4] zê[3] li[1]
Peng Ya-Ling	彭雅玲	Péng Yǎlíng	Pang[2] Nga[3] Lin[2]

Table 2.2 Names of characters that appear in the play

How it appears in this volume's translation	Chinese characters	Mandarin romanization in *pinyin*	Hakka romanization in *Hakka pinyin*
(Zhang) Bi-zhu	(張) 碧珠	(Zhāng) Bìzhū	(Zong[1]) Bid[5] Zu[1]
(Wang) Chun-qiu (A-qiu)	(王) 春秋 (阿秋)	(Wáng) Chūnqiū (Āqiū)	(Vong[2]) Cun[1] Qiu[1] (A[1] Qiu[1])
Da-tou	大頭	Dà Tóu	Tai[4] Têu[2]
Dong-dong	冬冬	Dōngdōng	Dung[1] Dung[1]
(Qiu) Hui-mei (A-hui)	(邱) 惠美 (阿惠)	(Qiū) Huìměi (Āhuì)	(Hiu[5]) Fi[4] Mi[1] (A[1] Fi[4])
(Liu) Jiao-mei (A-jiao)	(劉) 蕉妹 (阿蕉)	(Liú) Jiāomèi (Ājiāo)	(Liu[2]) Jiau[1] Moi[4] (A[1] Jiau[1])
(Zheng) Jing-zhi	(鄭) 淨之	(Zhèng) Jìngzhī	(Cang[4]) Qiang[4] Zi[1]
(Lin) Ju-ying	(林) 菊英	(Lín) Júyīng	(Lim[2]) Kiug[5] Yin[1]
Pi-pi	皮皮	Pípí	Pi[2] Pi[2]
(Huang) Shu-ping	(黃) 淑蘋	(Huáng) Shūpíng	(Vong[2]) Sug[5] Pin[2]
(Luo) Shu-yu	(羅) 淑郁	(Luó) Shūyù	(Lo[2]) Sug[5] Yug[5]
(Liu) Wen-rui	(劉) 文瑞	(Liú) Wénruì	(Liu[2]) Vun[2] Sui[4]
(Wang) Xi-yan (A-yan)	(王) 璽嬿 (阿嬿)	(Wáng) Xǐyàn (Āyàn)	(Vong[2]) Xi[1] Yan[4] (A[1] Yan[4])
(Chen) Xiu-chun	(陳) 秀春	(Chén) Xiùchūn	(Cen[2]) Xiu[4] Cun[1]
(Wen) Yu-qing	(溫) 玉清	(Wēn) Yùqīng	(Vun[1]) Ngiug[6] Qin[1]
(Xu) Yue-mei	(許) 月梅	(Xǔ) Yuèméi	(Hi[3]) Ngiad[6] Moi[2]
(Ye) Zhang-zeng (A-zeng)	(葉) 張增 (阿增)	(Yè) Zhāngzēng (Āzēng)	(Yab[6]) Zong[1] Zên[4] (A[1] Zên[4])

Table 2.3   Names, places, foods, and other items mentioned in the play

How it appears in this volume's translation	Chinese characters	Mandarin romanization in *pinyin*	Hakka romanization in *Hakka pinyin*	Frequent English renderings
A-chun	阿春	Āchūn	A¹ Cun¹	
A-ge	阿哥	Āgē	A¹ Go¹	
A-qing	阿清	Āqīng	A¹ Qin¹	
ameidama	呵妹搭嘛	āmèidāma	a¹ moi⁴ dab⁵ *ma²*	
downhouse	下屋	xiàwū	ha⁴ vug⁵	
Gongguan	公館	Gōngguǎn	Gung¹ Guon³	
Guangdong	廣東	Guǎngdōng	Guong³ Dung¹	Guangdong, Canton
Hakka	客家	Kèjiā	Hag⁵ Ga¹	Hakka
Ho-lo	河洛	Héluò	Ho² Log⁶	Ho-lo, Hok-lo
Hsinchu	新竹	Xīnzhū	Xin¹ Zug⁵	Hsinchu
huadun	花墩	huādūn	fa¹ dun¹	
Kaohsiung	高雄	Gāoxióng	Gau¹ Hiung²	Kaohsiung
Meinong	美濃	Měinóng	Mi¹ *Nung²*	
Miaoli	苗栗	Miáolì	Miao² Lid⁶	
Minnan	閩南	Mǐnnán	Mên² Nam²	Min Nan
mitaimu	米苔目	mǐtāimù	mi³ toi² mug⁵	
Pingtung	屏東	Píngdōng	*Piang²* Dung¹	Pingtung
Taipei	台北	Táiběi	Toi² Bêd⁵	Taipei
Tangshan	唐山	Tángshān	Tong² San¹	
uphouse	上屋	shàngwū	song¹ vug⁵	
yahua	壓花	yāhuā	ab⁵ fa¹	

Hakka pinyin romanizations in italics were extrapolated from romanizations of similar characters.

One Year, Three Seasons

WANG CHI-MEI
(2000)

translation by
Yawtsong Lee, John B. Weinstein, and Wang Chi-Mei

The Tainaner Ensemble premiered *One Year, Three Seasons* on April 15, 2000, in the National Tainan Living Art Center in Tainan, Taiwan, followed by a tour of cultural centers and universities in Chiayi, Kaohsiung, and Taichung.

Director	Wang Chi-Mei
Producer	Hsu Rey-Fang
Stage & Lighting Design	Lin Keh-Hua
Costume Design	Lin Ming-Hsia
Make-up	Chen Zhao-Yin
Production Manager	Lee Wei-Mu
Executive Producers	Tsai Mei-Chuan, Kao Si-Chao
Playwright Assistant	Lu Yi-Hsin
Properties Manager & Rehearsal Assistant	Chang Huei-Wen
Assistant Stage Designer	Tang Yi-Lei
Assistant Lighting Designers	Ren Huei-Ling, Lin Li-Chuen
Stage Managers	Hung Chia-Dai, Su Chin-Wen
Lighting & Sound Engineer	Pai Ke Audio & Lighting Contractor
Photography	Huang Hua-An, Keh Hsiao-Dong
Poster	Huang Yu-Wen

Actors

QIU-YUN	Wu Li-Chuen
MAO-XIONG	Wang Yi-Ren
HARUKO	Deng Li-Chi
LITTLE QI	Huang Wan-Chi
XIANG-LIAN	Kao Si-Chao
YU-ZHEN	Chen Huei-Huang
WEN-TAI	Huang Wen-Tai

Customers played by students from the Department of Television & Film, Nan Ying Vocational High School of Business & Technology

Figure 3.1 Program cover from the original production of *One Year, Three Seasons,* performed by the Tainaner Ensemble in the year 2000.

Dramaturgical Notes for
One Year, Three Seasons

BY JOHN B. WEINSTEIN

From the 1950s to the 1970s, enterprising young women in Taiwan could find professional success and personal fulfillment by opening their own dressmaking shops. After undergoing a formal apprenticeship that lasted three years and four months, a female tailor would seek out employment, either working in another tailor's shop, or opening one of her own. Her customers would often bring their own fabrics, and while flipping through pattern books and fashion magazines, the tailor would guide women of all ages to choose the perfect style of dress. At the time, the ready-to-wear dress industry—an industry in which Taiwan would later become a major player worldwide—had not yet developed in Taiwan. The traditional Chinese *qipao*, with its body-hugging silhouette and high mandarin collar, was still the domain of male tailors, but Western-style dresses were often made by women. These female tailors, working in tiny spaces, and playing with color, design, and shape, helped their fellow women realize the dresses of their dreams. Act I of *One Year, Three Seasons* centers on two dressmaking shops and on the female tailors who run each shop, Xiang-lian and Qiu-yun. Playwright Wang Chi-Mei is passionate about portraying these exemplary women, who use their artistic, interpersonal, and entrepreneurial skills to support themselves and their families through dressmaking.

Beyond dressmaking, the play presents other ways Taiwanese women have shown their entrepreneurial spirit. In Act I, set in the 1970s, Haruko and her granddaughter Little Qi make "mini-bulbs" (in American parlance more often called "Christmas lights") and plastic flowers, the kinds of inexpensive products associated with "Made in Taiwan" in the early days of Taiwan's economic development. Groups of family members or neighbors would join together to compete for subcontracts, and each of the women in the group would have a quota to fill, which they would do as piecework in their own homes. At that time, Haruko also does *wanmian*, a traditional method of removing facial hair by using strings. In Act III, set in the 1990s, granddaughter Little Qi earns her living from the contemporary successor to *wanmian*: she runs a beauty salon offering facials and sauna treatments. Her grandmother has also kept up with the times, opening an English-language center, where children come after school to learn the language, which Haruko herself does not speak. To compete with her many competitors, Haruko has designed her space to look like a fantastical castle.

All of this action occurs against a backdrop of time and place. The place is the city of Tainan, considered the most traditionally Taiwanese of the island's major cities, and a major center of the Taiwanese language in which this play was originally written and performed. Xiang-lian and Wen-tai contribute to the local flavor by reciting, in Taiwanese, poetic couplets by Tang Dynasty poet Li Shangyin (813–858), and by singing lyrics from the Taiwanese opera version of that most classic of Chinese romantic plays, *Romance of the Western Chamber*. The passage of time is reflected, among other ways, through the famous pop songs Little Qi sings, some in Taiwanese and some in the official language of Mandarin. "Wild Goose on the Wing" and "I Am Just a Cloud," two of the songs Little Qi sings in Act I, were made famous in the 1970s by singer Fong Fei Fei, with lyrics in Mandarin by novelist Chiung Yao. In Act II, Little Qi enters humming a favorite from the 1980s, "Farewell at the Shore," the most famous song by Jody Chiang. Known as the "Queen of Taiwanese music," Chiang sang songs in Taiwanese expressing the emotions of everyday working class Taiwanese people. Even in culturally traditional Tainan, the residents show interest in Western culture, as seen in Act I when Xiang-lian and her friend Yu-zhen sing a favorite American pop song, or when they swoon over French film actor Alain Delon.

Local flavor literally appears in the play through references to local food and drink. At the start of the play, a peddler is selling *miancha*, a drink made by adding water to fried flour. Little Qi wants a bowl, but instead Haruko feeds her rice congee with brown sugar. Haruko also refers to dried-up pieces of yam, which could sustain poor families when there was not enough rice. As with everything else, cuisine becomes more internationalized over time. Little Qi goes from loving *miancha* in Act I to drinking coffee in Act III. When Xiang-lian opens her dressmaking shop at the end of Act I, Wen-tai offers to take her and Yu-zhen out for a Western-style steak dinner to celebrate. However, traditional foods in Taiwan do not truly go out of style. In Act II, Wen-tai offers to run out to the famous Sakariba night market to buy local delicacies such as eel noodle soup and steamed buns stuffed with five-spiced meat, garlic, ground peanuts, and Chinese parsley. Sakariba, with origins going back to the 1930s, was torn down by the city government in 1993, in part because its narrow lanes were so crowded with shops, mostly old-style wooden buildings that were often lost to fires, but also because the government wanted to build the underground shopping mall that remains unfinished at the end of the play.

Taiwan was under Japanese occupation from 1895 to 1945, and vestiges of that political and cultural occupation occasionally appear in this play. One vestige is the grandmother's distinctly Japanese name, Haruko. Though the play was originally performed nearly entirely in the Taiwanese language (also called Min-nan, Hok-lo, or Ho-lo), Haruko does use a few Japanese words here and there. Because those words—*radio* and *boyfrrendo*—happen to be loan words adopted into Japanese from English, the viewer might not readily realize that the flavor they offer is as much Japanese as it is Euro-American. Another element reflecting Taiwan's period of Japanese occupation is the use of the *ping* to measure the size of a room, instead of square meters or square feet. The *ping* is equal to the size of two *tatami* mats, the standard-size mats used to line floors of traditional Japanese rooms; one *ping* is roughly thirty-six square feet. In more recent years, the use of English words has become trendy—already seen in Act I in the choice of the English word "Spring" as the name for Xiang-lian's shop. When Little Qi says "Come on, you can make it!," she is drawing on a famous Taiwanese beauty salon's popular English slogan, "Trust me, you can make it!" The presence of Japanese and English words by no means detracts from the Taiwanese feel of the play, but instead enhances it, for Taiwan is a land of cultural syncretism.

Located in the southern part of Taiwan, the city of Tainan enjoys a warm climate. In the eyes of playwright Wang Chi-Mei, the city also enjoys a warmth of spirit in its people. Taiwan as a whole is known for balmy weather, and the expression "four seasons like spring" is often used to describe the island, even though the south in particular can be sweltering in the summer, while there is a chilly, damp winter up north in Wang's hometown of Taipei. When Wang came south to teach in Tainan, the lack of winter was striking to her, and her title *One Year, Three Seasons* reflects her own belief that Tainan only has spring, summer, and autumn. Those three seasons resonate in the names of the three leading female characters in the play. The character pronounced "haru" in Haruko's name means spring, in both Japanese and Chinese. Xiang-lian's name means "fragrant lotus," a flower associated with summer, the season when the sweet-smelling lotus flowers bloom in abundance. The "qiu" in Qiu-yun's name means "autumn," completing the trio of Tainan's seasons. For Wang, climate is both literal and metaphorical. When mainland settlers first came to Taiwan four hundred years ago and established Tainan as their first city, she believes the sunny weather gave them a sunny disposition. Climates can change, however. If the environment around the warm, friendly people of Tainan were to change, might that diminish their happiness?

Against this cultural backdrop, *One Year, Three Seasons* celebrates the achievements of women, working together to develop themselves and their homeland. The feeling of closeness between the characters is paramount, and certain naming conventions underscore that. One is the use of the term "sister" to indicate a close relationship outside the actual family. The younger women often add a word that means "older sister" ("younger sister" is a different word) to the names of their older female friends. Although there are no actual sisters portrayed, the play offers a strong feeling of sisterhood. Another naming convention especially frequent in Taiwan, and used for both men and women, is the use of the syllable "A" (pronounced as "ah") at the beginning, followed by one of the two syllables in the person's given name. Xiang-lian becomes A-lian; Wen-tai becomes A-wen. This kind of nicknaming gives the feeling of a close relationship, and is often used within a family or, in this case, among close friends. Given the prevalence of this particular convention within Taiwan, it further contributes to the Taiwanese flavor of *One Year, Three Seasons*, a play eulogizing the moments of fulfillment, and the moments of loss, in the lives of a close-knit group of Taiwanese women, the unsung heroines behind so many of the labels marked "Made in Taiwan."

Characters

In order of appearance.

Qiu-yun An experienced tailor. When Act I begins, she is a mother in her thirties. Her name means "autumn clouds." Her husband is Mao-xiong; the name of her shop, "Qiu Mao Garments" combines their two names.

Mao-xiong Qiu-yun's husband. A few years older than she, he has no regular employment. His name means "prosperous hero."

Haruko Born in Taiwan during Japanese occupation, she has retained the Japanese name Haruko, the first part of which means "spring." Her storefront is across from her neighbor Qiu-yun's; she rents it out to Xiang-lian for her to open a dress shop.

Little Qi Haruko's granddaughter. The word "qi" signifies a pretty kind of jade, commonly used as a girl's name.

Xiang-lian The leading character, Xiang-lian was born in the mid-1950s, when Taiwan's economy was transitioning from agricultural to industrial. Xiang-lian was elementary school classmates with Yu-zhen and Wen-tai, and they were the first generation to benefit from the nine years of government-run compulsory education offered after the end of World War II. Unlike her two classmates, Xiang-lian had to forgo the opportunity to continue in school, and she instead went to work to help her parents raise their family. Following the master-apprentice system used in the handicrafts industry, she became an apprentice to a master tailor in Tainan. After that, she set out on her own to open a dressmaking shop on Hai-an Road. She later develops her own business enterprises. Her name means "fragrant lotus," a reference to the sweet-smelling lotus blossoms that bloom in abundance during the summer. The three names of the women Haruko, Xiang-lian, and Qiu-yun represent the seasons spring, summer, and autumn, respectively. On one level, this use of seasonal words reflects a customary practice among traditional families when naming children. On another level, these names bring to mind the life forces of these three seasons within the year.

Yu-zhen Xiang-lian's elementary-school classmate and her best friend. Heeding the wishes of her traditional family, she gets married, but she is still able to follow her own heart. Her name means "precious jade."

Young Lady A A customer who comes to have a dress made.

Girl B and Girl C High school girls who come to Xiang-lian's shop to leave their school bags and change into their dresses.

Wen-tai Xiang-lian's childhood sweetheart, he is the beloved who remains faithful to her while she builds her career in the garment industry. His name means "refined peace."

Customer D, etc. Female customers, including students, who come to have clothing made.

Act I
The Year She Opened Her Own Dress Shop

The scene is set in the early 1970s in an alley off Hai-an Road in the Western District of Tainan. Qiu-yun's house and the old dwelling of Grandma Haruko are separated by an alley. Qiu-yun's home with the sign Qiu Mao Garments sits on the left. Haruko's house is on the right. The doors of both houses are ajar. The scenery consists of Tainan's old-style two-story buildings, as they might appear in one's memory. As the curtain rises, a light in Qiu-yun's house still glows in the morning twilight. One can hear the humming of a sewing machine, a dog barking in the neighborhood, and the distant hissing of the boiling kettle of a peddler of mian-cha, *a porridge-like drink. As the new day dawns, Qiu-yun gets up and peeks out the door, checking the color of the sky to see the time and weather. She feels a piece of lining material hanging outside, but leaves it there because it is not yet dry. Yawning, she walks back to her worktable and tries to catch a quick nap. Mao-xiong comes out from an interior room.*

MAO-XIONG: Don't you need any sleep? *(Qiu-yun, startled, turns off the light.)* At least you know it's time to turn out the lights! With that light burning all night, I couldn't even open my eyes in my dreams. *(Qiu-yun gently pulls the door open.)* So are you coming to bed or are you on your way out?

QIU-YUN: I'm not going out. *(She brings in a piece of lining from outside.)*

MAO-XIONG: Now what are you doing? You think you'll live forever by depriving yourself of sleep? *(Tugs at her, but Qiu-yun deftly maneuvers out of his reach and mumbles an answer, while continuing to tidy up her worktable.)*

QIU-YUN: I'm coming.

MAO-XIONG: What's that sound I hear? You're picking up those scissors again. Why start a whole new dress at this ungodly hour? Woman, you don't know how to prioritize your time. Your work is so slow.

QIU-YUN: The kids will be up soon. Once they're off to school, I'll get some sleep.

MAO-XIONG: That's hours away. The kids won't be out of bed before the sun toasts their butts.

QIU-YUN: I'll come to bed after I make their lunches.

MAO-XIONG: Forget about the damned lunches! Your first duty is to your man's belly. If you don't come this minute, I'll drag you in by your hair. *(Qiu-yun looks down with a smile, unties her ponytail and fluffs up her hair. Mao-xiong changes his tone.)* All right, why don't you go get me a bowl of porridge if the peddler is still around.

QIU-YUN: He's already gone. You can't hear the hissing of his kettle anymore.

MAO-XIONG: Hmmm—Hey! Come back here!

On the other side of the alley, Haruko's house is also stirring. Her granddaughter Little Qi seems to have just jumped out of her wood-plank bed.

LITTLE QI: Grandma, I'm hungry. Can we get a bowl of porridge too? I can take a shortcut to catch up with the peddler. Grandma, give me some change! Grandma—*(Her pleas falling on deaf ears, she mimics in a flat tone.)* if you don't come this minute, I'll drag you in by your hair—

HARUKO: *(Gives her a little slap.)* Hush! Stop that nonsense!

LITTLE QI: *(Mimics Mao-xiong's imperious tone.)* If you don't come this minute, I'll drag you in by your hair—*(Picks up a towel to imitate the gesture.)*

HARUKO: *(Pretends not to understand.)* What, are you going off to join the opera troupe?

LITTLE QI: I wanna be a pop star. *(Imitates pop singers on TV, singing "Wild Goose on the Wing.")*

HARUKO: You have a toothache or something? That racket at this hour would be enough to give the big-bellied Buddha a stomachache. Now, get dressed. We have a lot of plastic flowers to put together or we won't get paid this afternoon. Fat Auntie Hui-qin will be happier if we can deliver them ourselves. *(Notices that her granddaughter is heading back to bed.)* What's the matter with you? The moment I ask you to do something, you suddenly need to go back to sleep. I thought you were hungry?

LITTLE QI: *(Looks very upset.)* Fat Auntie Hui-qin is so mean, especially to me. She's easy on other people, but she always rejects my work. She says I didn't do a proper job. She's always complaining, "Defects, defects!"

HARUKO: You should be grateful that you are told of the defects.

LITTLE QI: She just picks on me because I'm young and you're—

HARUKO: What? Old? Most people who work for Fat Auntie Hui-qin are older than me. If not for her, our neighborhood wouldn't have gotten the subcontract. *(Hands Little Qi her dress.)* Maybe you should just go across the street and learn dressmaking instead. This kind of work is unpredictable. You can never tell when it'll end. There's no security in it. We should prepare for lean times. Put away some grain for future famines.

LITTLE QI: Don't worry, Grandma. I'll become a pop star! *(Sings and gesticulates.)* "Mama, mama, yah, listen to my guitar!"

HARUKO: Stop that racket! You're breaking my ears. Listen here, I want you to learn a solid skill so that you won't be pushed around or have to depend on others. I only nag you because I don't want to see you sold off, to see you suffer. You don't want to spend the rest of your life eating nothing but dried-up yam bits.

LITTLE QI: *(Becoming serious.)* These days, people don't go for traditional facials anymore.

HARUKO: I'm not talking about doing traditional facials.

LITTLE QI: People don't send out their stockings to be mended anymore, either.

HARUKO: That's not true. I did some last month, yes, five pairs!

LITTLE QI: You didn't do that many.

HARUKO: I did too. Well, OK. It was five stockings, not five pairs. You sneer at everything. You don't even want to learn dressmaking.

LITTLE QI: I don't wanna be an apprentice. I'm a big girl now. Besides, I don't think she'll be open much longer.

HARUKO: You're wrong there. She has so much work she's even hired another dressmaker for extra help.

LITTLE QI: Really? The one who comes around lunchtime? I like her. But I still don't want to be a dressmaker's apprentice. I'd rather learn hair styling at a beauty salon. I'd get paid from the start. I'd have a salary!

HARUKO: A salary? So when do you start?

LITTLE QI: I'm stuck here making plastic flowers and assembling mini-bulbs with you, and learning how to remove facial hair with pieces of string.

HARUKO: I give up. Go wash your face. *(At this, Little Qi moves toward backstage.)* Warm up some congee for breakfast.

LITTLE QI: *(Yells back.)* I'll have two bowls, and with brown sugar too! *(Comes back out and asks.)* Do we have any of those baby fish?

HARUKO: *(Scolds her.)* Enough!

They both freeze. The lights dim.

On the other side of the alley, Qiu-yun takes out some cash from her waist pocket and counts it before handing it to Mao-xiong. He grabs it from her, and turns his head to speak.

MAO-XIONG: What about this week's money? Why so little?

QIU-YUN: We don't get paid until the dresses are delivered to the customers.

MAO-XIONG: You're so slow! The customers need their dresses. They come here every day, asking you to hurry up. Their patience is wearing thin. This is no way to be a dressmaker. No wonder we're not saving much money.

QIU-YUN: My customers aren't complaining. I know how many orders I can handle.

MAO-XIONG: Fine, fine. What about that girl you hired to help you? Why hasn't she come lately?

QIU-YUN: She only comes when she has free time.

MAO-XIONG: Does she do a good job for us?

Xiang-lian enters from the right, carrying the dresses farmed out to her. She walks in slow motion along the front edge of the stage toward Qiu-yun's house. Thoughtful and purposeful, she carries just the hint of a smile.

QIU-YUN: She does great work. She's so good the master tailor at her current job kept her on even after her apprenticeship ended.

MAO-XIONG: So young, and already making a dressmaker's salary. Younger than you when you started out! Where is she from? She's not from around here, is she? *(Qiu-yun walks toward backstage without answering.)* Is she even twenty yet? *(She reemerges with some fashion magazines, whose worn pages she tries to repair.)* Woman! I'm talking to you. Are you deaf? *(Grabs a thick magazine and threatens her with it. When he sees pages falling out from the magazine, he throws it back.)* These magazines are falling apart and you didn't even bother to glue the pages back. *(Qiu-yun shows him the pot of paste in her hand.)* You think you're so smart, huh? *(Suddenly enraged, he grabs the pot of paste and hurls it at her.)* You think you know how to do everything? You think you can play dumb when I speak to you? *(As Qiu-yun backs away, Mao-xiong strides toward her.)*

Xiang-lian arrives at center stage. Hearing the banging inside, she stops short. Snapping back into reality, she makes a quick retreat, disappearing into the wings. Music fades in, accompanying the actions below. Mao-xiong comes back out and rummages around for money hidden by Qiu-yun. After finding one hundred yuan in a box of tailor's chalk, he makes a big show of picking up the box and dumping out its contents. He curses. Walking out, he looks down at his feet, and goes back inside to change into his street shoes. He walks outside again and passes Haruko's door.

Haruko and Little Qi stare at him. He pauses nonchalantly, taking out a comb and preening. The grandma and granddaughter turn away from him. He exits to the right, grunting. Haruko mumbles a few words, and then segues into a parody of Mao-xiong's rage, imitating his facial expressions and gestures. Little Qi effortlessly mimics her grandma's histrionics as she edges toward Qiu-yun's house. She pauses in front of the house but refrains from going inside, despite her deep sympathy for Qiu-yun. Grandma wears a grim expression and remains silent. As they slowly turn toward the left, they see Xiang-lian reenter with more dresses and pass by Haruko's door.

XIANG-LIAN: Good morning, Granny! You haven't gone out today?

HARUKO: Not yet. I'm leaving in a while to do A-cai's face. You know, the matchmaker. Her business hasn't been doing well lately. She wants to see if a clearer, smoother complexion will bring her better luck. Are you wearing any makeup?

XIANG-LIAN: No ...

HARUKO: If you let me do your face, I'll give you a discount.

XIANG-LIAN: Qiu-yun's waiting for me ...

HARUKO: I know. How many dresses have you done for her today? You are really good with these dresses. Such fine work! You're such a hard worker! You think you can teach my Little Qi a thing or two? She's not really lazy. She's just too young to know what's good for her. By the way, how much does Qiu-yun pay you for a dress? ... I can't get my granddaughter to do anything. It would be wonderful if you would take her on as your apprentice. How much do you charge? The going rate or ...

XIANG-LIAN: For some of the dresses, she cuts out the patterns and I just assemble them ... we don't necessarily follow the going rates ...

HARUKO: I think you should let me do your face sometime. Look at the powder I use. It's so white, so fine. I guarantee you would be even fairer, even prettier ...

XIANG-LIAN: Granny, if there's anything you need, I'll help you, too.

Looking around, Xiang-lian sees Little Qi, who suddenly becomes bashful. Squatting down, Little Qi sings a few lines from the popular melody "I Am Just a Cloud." Then she dashes off and disappears into a small alley. As Xiang-lian enters the shop, Qiu-yun appears, looking flustered. Trying to compose herself, she puts on a smile.

QIU-YUN: Have you finished them all?

XIANG-LIAN: They're all here. The suit, two dresses, and three skirts.

QIU-YUN: I didn't think you'd have time to come by today. I was planning to go to your shop tonight.

XIANG-LIAN: Have your customers been pressuring you?

QIU-YUN: No ... It's my husband ... he wants the money badly. ... He ...

XIANG-LIAN: I was here before. I didn't come in because he seemed upset ... I decided I'd come back later and bring them all at once. Is there anything else I can do for you? I still have some free time.

QIU-YUN: Have you had lunch yet?

XIANG-LIAN: I'm fine. I had some bread. I didn't wait for lunchtime in the shop. It's better to come outside at this hour anyway. The boss's wife goes out to eat, and the boss pays no attention. No one really notices me coming over here.

QIU-YUN: *(Looks at the dresses brought by Xiang-lian.)* Your work is so fine. You even stitched the edges of the lining.

XIANG-LIAN: Oh, I forgot. We always do that in our shop. Is it a problem?

QIU-YUN: No, not at all. My customers will be delighted. You've also sewn in a hidden pocket. *(She tries out a sleeve.)* It's cute. And useful, too.

XIANG-LIAN: I hope it's OK. Day after day, my boss stresses that hidden pockets are the most exquisite aspect of ladies' dresses. I just made the cuts without thinking. Next time I'll use a different pattern, without the hidden pockets. I can save some trouble ...

QIU-YUN: With your skillful hands, I wonder when you are going to open your own shop. When you do, I won't be able to ask you to help me anymore.

XIANG-LIAN: Don't say things like that. No need to worry, I'll still be here ... My own shop. Of course I've thought about it. I'm working day and night with hopes of leasing a storefront. When I was an apprentice, I made eighty yuan a month. (*Little Qi begins walking back but pricks up her ears for any tidbits worth recounting to her grandma.*) Now I make eight thousand yuan a month. Besides paying for night school, I still spend only eighty each month. I save the rest. My three sisters are working their way through school. Only my two little brothers still need financial support. My parents have asked me to come back to our village to open a ...

QIU-YUN: You'd go back to the countryside?

XIANG-LIAN: What my folks have in mind is a fabric store, where I'll also make clothes.

QIU-YUN: Out in the countryside you can probably buy a storefront for a hundred thousand yuan or so. But I don't think you should go back to the country.

XIANG-LIAN: Me neither! Here in the city, the clientele has finer taste. I can work with a wider range of fabrics and try novel cuts and styles. The trouble is a suitable storefront is hard to find. Most building owners would rather try some business of their own downstairs, and if it doesn't make money they don't really care. So they're not eager to rent it out. I've been looking around. In the better neighborhoods around here, there are lots of available storefronts, but they're so expensive. And I want to stay away from any place with shops selling rice, coal or tofu. It's too messy.

QIU-YUN: And the ambiance is all wrong.

XIANG-LIAN: If there are fabric stores, jewelry stores and dressmakers nearby, so much the better. While shoppers are out and about, they would naturally walk through my door!

QIU-YUN: *(Smiles as she observes Xiang-lian's face light up with hope.)* There aren't as many dressmakers as before. Men still have their suits made to order but women are starting to buy off the rack.

XIANG-LIAN: Dresses off the rack don't look as nice, so some women will come back to dressmakers. Tainan has no shortage of ladies with lots of money. Qiu-yun, when you have the time, can you find out if anyone's looking for a partner in the dressmaking business?

QIU-YUN: If ... I ... , were it not for *(Gestures with her hand, toward the inside.)* you-know-who, I'd go into business with you right away. But there's no way around it. *(Sighs.)* You know, clearly I run the shop myself, do all the tailoring myself, and even go out myself to get things hemmed, just like an apprentice. When I'm too busy to handle all the orders I get, my "boss" takes me to task. He's stricter than the master tailor I apprenticed under, and that man once threw an iron at me. He wouldn't dare mistreat the girls with a husband or a family here in Tainan, but he had no problem abusing country girls like us, all alone in the city. Look, I still have this scar. Back then, I thought when I get married, I'd have my husband to back me up. I'd open my own shop, and things would be better.

XIANG-LIAN: I don't know much about marriage, but having one's own shop ...

QIU-YUN: OK. Let's not talk about me. Of course, when you have your own shop, you'll have plenty to worry about. But you get to do what you like and when customers make special requests, you get to decide. You can fulfill them all.

XIANG-LIAN: Yes! I'll pour my heart and soul into my work. I won't rest until all my customers are elegantly dressed.

Music fades in. Haruko and Little Qi take a few steps toward Qiu-yun's shop. When Haruko waves her hand, Little Qi carries over a tray of teacups. Qiu-yun comes out to greet them. Xiang-lian also rises slowly.

HARUKO: You are already very elegant. *(Qiu-yun and Xiang-lian exchange glances.)*

XIANG-LIAN: I said *(Raising her voice.)* I wanted to make my customers elegant.

HARUKO: I see. I wanted to invite you two over for tea. Qiu-yun, come here. Can you put in a good word for me with—what's her name—Xiang-lian? Maybe she could be persuaded to open a dress shop at my place. The location is good and my rent will be reasonable. Besides, my granddaughter and I can lend a hand.

Qiu-yun explains Haruko's offer to Xiang-lian using exaggerated intonations and gestures. The two discuss and bargain, keeping parts of their conversation out of the earshot of Haruko and her granddaughter. Haruko likewise vigorously uses somewhat odd-sounding, archaic intonations to make her sales pitch. Occasionally a couple of key phrases can be heard, but most of it is in expressive tones and gestures. Little Qi serves tea and sings "Coral Love" to spice up the atmosphere. Italics that follow are suggested lines only. Actors are to improvise.

HARUKO: *Qiu-yun, tell your friend that my place is convenient to everywhere. The neighborhood is good, and the rent is cheap. I've got good feng shui here, well-suited for a business catering to ladies.*

QIU-YUN: *How much are you charging?*

HARUKO: *I'll let her have it for only three thousand yuan a month. You are both very nice and decent folks, and I know you won't give me any trouble. So I'm giving her a good deal. I'm charging only three thousand.*

QIU-YUN: *Let me explain your offer to her.*

Qiu-yun nods impassively to Haruko. Turning around, she excitedly pulls Xiang-lian aside and gesticulates to her. Haruko stays still.

XIANG-LIAN: It's still a little high. Please explain to her that her place is in an alley and not on a busy street. What about utilities? Is hot water available? Since I am just starting out, can she give me a break?

Xiang-lian wants to go over to take a look.

QIU-YUN: Look the place over first. I'm sure the rent is negotiable.

Little Qi takes Xiang-lian on an inspection tour of the house while Qiu-yun bargains with Haruko.

QIU-YUN: *It's hard to find a decent tenant like her. She's capable and sensible. You'll get along fine. It's a waste not to rent out unused space. You don't want to rent to another kind of business. Dress shops are cleaner and more respectable. If you can charge a bit less ...*

HARUKO: *Hmmm! Less ... Tell her I'll take off five hundred. I'll charge her twenty-five hundred a month. We'll split utilities fifty-fifty. That's as low as I can go. Take her that offer.*

Xiang-lian comes back and stays behind Qiu-yun.

QIU-YUN: *She's lowered the rent by five hundred and is charging you only twenty-five hundred a month. You'll pick up half the utilities bills. I think it's reasonable. What do you think?*

XIANG-LIAN: *Twenty-five hundred? That's not bad and I'll have you as neighbor. All right, it's a deal.*

Little Qi, still singing, helpfully brings out a table. In the meantime, Haruko and Qiu-yun agree on the deal.

Xiang-lian rushes inside excitedly to set up her new tailor shop.

LITTLE QI: Is this table OK? Or do you want to order a new one?

QIU-YUN: No need for a new table. Just add a wooden board as a tabletop.

LITTLE QI: OK. We happen to have one in the back.

XIANG-LIAN: Let's go get it.

QIU-YUN: When you're just starting out, you don't want to spend too much money. You want to save wherever possible.

XIANG-LIAN: *(Sets up the table with Little Qi.)* Let me wipe it clean. The height is just right. Now that I have my worktable, I can get started.

LITTLE QI: What about the sewing machine? Grandma, didn't we used to have one? Where is it now?

HARUKO: Oh, that one. Your aunt took it with her when she got married. It's long gone. Gone since you were five years old. *(Laughs.)* Where have you been?

LITTLE QI: Really ...

XIANG-LIAN: I'll get a second-hand machine. A new one would cost over ten thousand yuan.

LITTLE QI: Oh, I know. There's a woman a few doors down who just quit dressmaking. Her machine is practically new. I'll ask her about it. Five or six thousand yuan should clinch the deal.

QIU-YUN: You mean A-gui? I know her well. Leave it to me. *(Immediately turns around and exits down the alley on the left.)*

LITTLE QI: How does this look?

XIANG-LIAN: Great! Let's tidy this place up a bit.

As Qiu-yun slowly wheels a sewing machine up from the back of the alley toward Xiang-lian's shop, she dispenses advice and good wishes to Xiang-lian from afar.

QIU-YUN: A-lian, this alley is very close to the temple, and to the bustling streets. Once you have your own shop, no matter what time it is, you can do as you please. You can do whatever you think best to give your clients whatever they wish for. *(Filled with dreams, as if brought back to the days when she first opened her own shop.)* You can dress each and every customer so elegantly ... *(Softly sighs, and then smiles. She wheels the sewing machine over to the doorway of Xiang-lian's shop, and hands it over to them. She then returns to her own shop and sits down. She gazes across the alley, toward the new shop opposite her.)* When you've got the time, you can still come over to visit with me.

LITTLE QI: *(Handing the tray to her grandmother, she runs over to Qiu-yun's side to take a look, and then runs back.)* But don't ever, ever get married.

Haruko thrusts the tray back into Little Qi's hands and pinches her arm surreptitiously. She speaks to Xiang-lian.

HARUKO: Make some money first. Don't rush to get married. Do you have a boyfriend?

XIANG-LIAN: Don't worry, Granny, I already have my hands full taking care of myself.

HARUKO: You really don't have a *boy-frrendo*?

XIANG-LIAN: When I was an apprentice, my master was very strict. We learned to act and speak according to the rules. There was no going out at night, and dating boys was forbidden. Granny, I have nothing but admiration for my master. I hope to run a ladies' dress shop even more elegant than his. My work is my passion. The dresses I make here will fit perfectly, and they will never lose their shape. When my customers slip them on, their faces will be filled with smiles. Granny, don't you worry.

As the fabric hanging over the stage is gradually lowered, Xiang-lian rushes into her shop where the worktable is piled high with fabric. She darts back and forth, in one moment picking up a yardstick nervously, and then wielding it back and forth; in the next moment, grabbing a pair of scissors and treasuring them with a foolish grin; then finally tossing a chalk stick and bobbin of thread into the air, as if she were a juggler. Balancing a bulky book of fashion patterns on her head, and with three or four pieces of fabric draped gracefully over herself, she pretends to show splendid dresses one by one to her customers. She sits on her worktable with a silly smile. She rolls around in the pile of fabric. Finally, sitting on a stool in the front, she sighs sweetly ... she takes out a measurement chart and scribbles a bit on it ...

XIANG-LIAN: I've truly opened my own shop. I got thirty-eight orders on the opening day. Customers kept streaming in, one after the other. I must have seemed like an idiot, all tongue-tied, more jittery than on my first day out from my apprenticeship. On top of that, when I was taking my customers' measurements, my hands would unexpectedly start trembling. When making the cuts, I kept pulling out the charts to check and double-check. I was so worried that I'd gotten the measurements wrong ... Now I work and work, often continuously through the night, without any sleep. But I am happy, and I'm not worried at all about being able to finish the dresses. It's fine if I don't get to sleep. I can definitely get it all done, and make sure every dress is beautiful and fits perfectly. I want all of my customers to be satisfied ... I'm fine without any sleep ... *(When she says that, she suddenly slumps back and seems to doze off.)*

Yu-zhen, fashionably dressed, enters. She was Xiang-lian's classmate in elementary school and now studies music in Tainan. She checks the address on the envelope in her hand to make sure she has come to the right place. When she walks in and sees Xiang-lian, she smiles. After a pause, she brings over a chair and sits by Xiang-lian. Xiang-lian stirs, and then slumps onto Yu-zhen's shoulder, continuing to sleep.

YU-ZHEN: You wrote me a letter asking me to come patronize your shop, but do you really need more patrons? Look how exhausted you are!

XIANG-LIAN: *(Even with Yu-zhen rocking about, she still seems completely asleep.)* Yu-zhen, so you've come. Did you bring your fabric?

YU-ZHEN: How could I not?

XIANG-LIAN: How many pieces?

YU-ZHEN: Four or five.

XIANG-LIAN: Where did you buy them?

Figure 3.2 In this production photo from the original production of *One Year, Three Seasons*, an alley off of Hai-an Road is flanked by the dressmaking shops of Qiu-yun on the left and Xiang-lian on the right. In her newly opened shop, Xiang-lian (right) enjoys catching up with childhood friend Yu-zhen, who has come to bring Xiang-lian business by ordering custom-made dresses.

YU-ZHEN: Gifts from relatives.

XIANG-LIAN: Wow, it's such high quality. I don't want to take any chances with your imported fabric.

YU-ZHEN: Don't be ridiculous.

XIANG-LIAN: Yesterday, I nearly ruined a piece of fabric imported from Hong Kong. It became discolored after I ironed it. I cried my eyes out because I didn't know where I could buy a replacement piece.

YU-ZHEN: So what are you going to do?

XIANG-LIAN: Actually, after drying my tears, I discovered that the color had come back!

YU-ZHEN: You told me that just to scare me! You've always liked pulling my leg.

XIANG-LIAN: I swear it's all true. *(She turns to face Yu-zhen. The two friends look at each other fondly.)* You've changed—you're even prettier than when I last saw you. Where did you get your hair done? Did your mother take you?

YU-ZHEN: Oh no, my mom doesn't bother with such things anymore. You've changed too—a lot. It seems like you've gotten taller. How can that be?

XIANG-LIAN: Really? I can't have grown any taller! I don't know. Since our graduation, I've gained twenty kilos and grown fifteen centimeters. When I first came here, I paid half fare. Within half a year, I'd shot up like a balloon and had to pay full fare. Even my mom didn't recognize me. But that was when I first came to Tainan. I haven't grown at all since.

YU-ZHEN: Maybe you've added two more centimeters, now that you're the boss. *(Looks at Xiang-lian again.)* I think you've become thinner. How can you do everything on your own? You should hire someone to help you out. Don't overwork yourself.

XIANG-LIAN: I did put an ad in the paper looking for help. I got four responses but nobody was suitable. These days, there aren't a lot of people both able and willing to work in this trade. Apprentices are even harder to find. They prefer working in beauty salons, where apprentices make seven or eight hundred a month. With the comings and goings, it's more lively, and more fun. Those who know how to say the right things can also get tips.

YU-ZHEN: I thought your landlady's granddaughter would come lend a hand.

XIANG-LIAN: That's what she said in the beginning, that she wanted to come learn the trade from me. But Qiu-yun warned me not to believe it. I still feel like I let down her grandma, but the granddaughter now says she knows how to make magic bras. *(She outlines one using hand gestures.)*

YU-ZHEN: Oh, magic ... bras ... oh, really? *(They dissolve into laughter.)*

XIANG-LIAN: Really. First she saw it in a magazine, then she picked one up in a boutique that sells imported stuff in Taipei. After taking it apart and putting it back together, she now claims she knows how to make them. Soon she's going to put up a sign here and start selling them.

YU-ZHEN: What are you going to do? Your customers will think you're in a partnership with her.

XIANG-LIAN: There's nothing I can do about it. They give me a discount on the rent, and they're really not that calculating. Once my customers have their dresses made by me, they'll know. They won't be confused.

YU-ZHEN: Seriously, if I hadn't asked you about it, I would have come in for a magic bra, because of your sign outside.

XIANG-LIAN: *(Jokingly.)* You don't need one. *(Unfolds the fabric in admiration.)* This is excellent fabric. It's light and drapes well. The color is beautiful. It's pretty even without an embroidered hem.

YU-ZHEN: How about this piece? Do you think a blue hem would look good on it?

XIANG-LIAN: It would look better if the hem is the same color as the fabric. I can edge it with lace. What do you think of this pattern? The hemline can be made a little lower and it would look very elegant. *(Puts Yu-zhen's fabrics aside.)*

YU-ZHEN: You work so fast!

XIANG-LIAN: That's because I know what styles you like—

YU-ZHEN: And you also know what my mom likes—

XIANG-LIAN: It's even more important to please her *(Intentionally using the intonations of Taiwanese opera.)* ladyship! So how is your mother doing these days?

YU-ZHEN: She is as active as always. *(Sighing.)* And more eager than ever.

XIANG-LIAN: Just follow your heart. Pick the one you like the most.

YU-ZHEN: I'm already so confused.

XIANG-LIAN: What? Too many guys to choose from? *(Puts down the fabric in her hands and turns forward to listen.)*

YU-ZHEN: No, it's not like that at all.

The two friends carry on an animated conversation punctuated by spirited gestures. As in the scene where Qiu-yun helped Xiang-lian rent space from Haruko, they use indistinguishable sounds and gestures to express their emotions and illustrate their dialogue. Yu-zhen describes her mother's efforts to find a doctor to marry her. As she describes the medical school students who come to the arranged parties, she alternately displays affection, interest, or resignation. Xiang-lian, laughing profusely, tries out the fabric on Yu-zhen in various ways, instantly turning her into a pretty doll.

Following italics are suggestions only. Actors are to improvise.

YU-ZHEN: *One of them is a tall guy with glasses. He's OK, but he interns in Taipei and doesn't have much time to spend with me. When he smiles, he looks like Alain Delon.* (She giggles.) *One of my mother's favorites is very short, only up to here. On the second visit, he brought a pair of bracelets studded with rubies. My mother was thrilled and immediately suggested a trip to Kenting. It was really hilarious!*

XIANG-LIAN: *Did you have fun on the trip?*

YU-ZHEN: *It rained in Kenting so we could only walk around in the hotel, and we drank so much coffee our eyeballs popped out.*

XIANG-LIAN: *Doesn't your mother tag along?*

YU-ZHEN: *She doesn't anymore. Now she says young people should spend more time by themselves.*

XIANG-LIAN: *How about your Alain Delon?*

YU-ZHEN: *He wrote to me, asking for a date. He wants to take me to a concert next Saturday ...*

XIANG-LIAN: A concert date! Sounds great. I'll finish this dress in time for you to wear it to the performance. You'll look divine in it.

YU-ZHEN: There's no rush. If you have other customers to take care of first—

XIANG-LIAN: I can handle it. If I get any new customers, I can always refer them to the dress shop across the street or just invite Qiu-yun to come over here and help out. Things over there have been rather complicated lately ...

Xiang-lian is reluctant to talk about Qiu-yun's problems at home. At this point Young Lady A enters. Holding a paper wrapped package, she walks briskly to Xiang-lian's shop.

YOUNG LADY A: Is the tailor in? I'd like to have a dress made out of this fabric.

XIANG-LIAN: That's me. Are you in a hurry? When do you need it?

YOUNG LADY A: Next week. I'm wearing it to a dinner.

XIANG-LIAN: What day next week?

YOUNG LADY A: Wednesday.

XIANG-LIAN: I see. In that case, I don't think I can make it. This week is almost over.

YOUNG LADY A: Can you please just help me out?

XIANG-LIAN: I'm so sorry. Since it's your first time here, I should try to squeeze you in, but I am really terribly behind, and all these dresses here have to be done by me, all by myself. Your dress would take two to three weeks to finish ...

YOUNG LADY A: I was thinking a new shop like yours would definitely be willing to do a rush job ...

XIANG-LIAN: I am very sorry. I really should help you. Well ... why don't you try Qiu Mao Garments *(Pointing Young Lady A in the right direction.)* across the street. The tailor there is also experienced, with fine handiwork, and also a woman.

YOUNG LADY A: *(As she walks toward Qiu-yun's shop, she turns around and says.)* You're an interesting one. I've never heard of a tailor sending business to a rival. *(Asks at the door.)* Is this Qiu Mao Garments?

QIU-YUN: Do come in! *(Ushers Young Lady A in. When he hears the sound, Mao-xiong comes out and sits at another side of the table.)*

YOUNG LADY A: Ma'am, do you have time to help me out? I need this in a hurry.

QIU-YUN: When do you need it? Show me your fabric.

YOUNG LADY A: How about next Wednesday?

QIU-YUN: I'll try my best. Wow, this is excellent stuff. *(Opens a fashion book.)* Do you like this style? How much fabric do you have here?

YOUNG LADY A: About seven and a half feet. Is that enough?

QIU-YUN: It's enough for a dress like this, sure! How do you like this style?

YOUNG LADY A: The neckline is too low for me. I wouldn't dare.

QIU-YUN: How about this one? No? Or this? It's got this cute little pocket here. I think it suits you.

YOUNG LADY A: Really? I'll go with this then.

Qiu-yun and Young Lady A look at the fashion book together, amicably deciding on a style, but when Qiu-yun takes her measurements, Young Lady A feels embarrassed by Mao-xiong's proximity.

QIU-YUN: Mao-xiong, don't you need to go over to Poker Zhang's to talk about something? On the way, you can help me deliver these uniforms to Mrs. Chen on Minzu Road?

MAO-XIONG: What are you talking about?

QIU-YUN: *(Calmly packs the uniforms and hands them to him.)* Minzu Road, the third house. You've been there before.

Mao-xiong takes the uniforms. As he passes by Xiang-lian's door, two high school girls, customers B and C, hurry by. His eyes follow them. The two high school girls enter Xiang-lian's shop.

GIRL B: Ma'am, are our dresses ready? We'll change into them here.

GIRL C: Is it okay if we change in the back?

GIRL B: Can we leave our school bags here?

XIANG-LIAN: Sure, that's fine. *(Girls B and C exchange a contented look.)*

GIRL C: Thanks!

GIRL B: We'll let ourselves out the back. *(They chat and go behind the curtain.)*

YU-ZHEN: *(Sotto voce.)* Times sure have changed!

XIANG-LIAN: It blew my mind when they asked me about this.

YU-ZHEN: Their families probably have no idea what's going on.

XIANG-LIAN: Nor their school. Oh my ... I envy them. They get to go to school and still go out and have fun.

YU-ZHEN: Are they going out with boys?

XIANG-LIAN: College boys.

YU-ZHEN: College boys? They come back here to change back into their school uniforms before heading home? At what hour?

XIANG-LIAN: *(Jokingly.)* That's none of your business. You sound like your mother. It depends really. Sometimes they come back a few days later,

Figure 3.3 Qiu-yun (center) discusses a party dress with new customer Young Lady A. As Qiu-yun takes the customer's measurements, her husband Mao-xiong pokes around near the table, getting uncomfortably close.

but since they've left their school bags this time, I imagine they'll be back later this evening.

Yu-zhen: You're doing them a big favor.

Xiang-lian: I don't know. I never really had the chance to be so young and carefree.

Yu-zhen: Never mind that. Whatever happened to your boyfriend A-wen?

Xiang-lian: Wen-tai? I wouldn't call him a boyfriend. He's more like a little brother.

Yu-zhen: Has he completed his military service yet? Watch out! Any day now he'll be knocking on your door asking for your hand in marriage.

Xiang-lian: He wouldn't dare.

Yu-zhen: He's totally infatuated with you, isn't he?

Xiang-lian: Ask him yourself. He'll be here shortly.

Yu-zhen: Oh?

Xiang-lian: Oh—.

Yu-zhen: Oh, oh—. *(Sings: "Oh, oh, yeah, yeah, love you more than I can say—.")*
As Yu-zhen sings, Little Qi emerges, bounding from the alley.

Little Qi: It's here, it's here! *(Seeing Mao-xiong walk on the other side, she lowers her voice, speaking to Xiang-lian.)* Our sign is ready. Grandma had it made.

Young Lady A comes out of Qiu Mao Garments. As she passes by Xiang-lian's shop, she glances in, and is about to say something but then thinks better of it. As Mao-xiong passes by, she gives him a wide berth. He stomps into his shop. Two workers carry the sign in and gesture at the front eaves. The sign says "Spring! Elegant Tailoring, Fashionable Lingerie, Adorable Babywear, Imported Fabrics." The word "Spring" is in English.

Little Qi: A-lian, what do you think?

Xiang-lian: Not bad at all!

Yu-zhen: Why do you have an English word on the sign? Whose idea was that? It looks like exotic calligraphy!

Xiang-lian: "Spring"—it's the English word for Granny Haruko's name.

Little Qi: A-lian wanted Grandma to decide on the name of the shop. Grandma thought about name combinations like "Chun Lian," "Chun Xiang," or "Xiang Qi"—but she couldn't make up her mind.[1] Then she

---

[1] Each of these combinations combines one syllable each from two of the women's names,

came up with the idea of the English word "Spring" and we all agreed. We never imagined it would look so good!

YU-ZHEN: I can understand "elegant tailoring" and "fashionable lingerie," but why "adorable babywear"?

LITTLE QI: I'm not good enough to make adult clothing, but I can handle babywear. And Grandma is good at it, too.

YU-ZHEN: What about "imported fabrics"?

LITTLE QI: Oh, that. That's you! Didn't you bring imported fabrics to order new dresses?

Yu-zhen walks over to Xiang-lian's side and smiles. From Qiu-yun's house, the sounds of yelling and things being smashed are heard. Little Qi and Yu-zhen go over to take a look, but then come back, unable to help. Xiang-lian's boyfriend Wen-tai enters through the alley. Yu-zhen sees him approach as she turns around.

YU-ZHEN: What a coincidence! Bumping into you in a tiny alley like this! What brings you here?

WEN-TAI: Yu-zhen, I see you've come to bring more business to A-lian. I don't know how to cut patterns and make skirts, so I'm here as a handyman. I'm sure there are tasks I can help with ... *(To Little Qi, pointing at the sign.)* Leave this to me. How high do you want it?

Little Qi happily comes over to join Wen-tai in attaching metal wires to the sign.

WEN-TAI: It's not every day that we can have such a school reunion. Tonight I'd like to treat my two dear classmates to a steak dinner.

XIANG-LIAN: I don't have time for that. I need to meet the deadline on two jackets.

YU-ZHEN: And I'm sure you won't take me out without Xiang-lian.

WEN-TAI: Of course I would.

YU-ZHEN: I don't believe you. I remember one time when we were little, you hid pieces of sweet sugar cane in your school bag to give to Xiang-lian, and Xiang-lian only. You wouldn't even let me have one when I begged you for a piece.

WEN-TAI: I wouldn't have remembered that at all if you hadn't brought it up.

---

using the names Haruko, Xiang-lian, and Little Qi. "Chun" is the Mandarin pronunciation of the first character in Haruko's name.

More racket erupts in Qiu-yun's house.

YU-ZHEN: That's so scary. Sure makes you think twice about getting married.

XIANG-LIAN: Don't worry. Just make sure you marry a decent man. Nowadays, there aren't many men as bad as Mao-xiong.

WEN-TAI: Well, I'm a decent man. *(No one pays attention to him. The racket at Qiu-yun's house gets louder. Wen-tai, turning serious, asks.)* What should we do? One of us should go over there and save Qiu-yun from another beating.

LITTLE QI: Oh, I'll go. No one ever invites me out for steak dinners, but when there's this kind of trouble, everyone turns to me. I'll give it a shot ... *(Loudly, in front of Qiu-yun's house.)* Hey, cool it! *(Eliciting no response, she withdraws. Mao-xiong is pushed out the door. He sits down in a chair, still in a rage.)*

MAO-XIONG: You tell me—why can't I stay in my own damn house? I wasn't leering at anyone. You were just taking measurements. Besides, she was so ugly, what was there to see? Did you get rid of me to hide the money you're making? Is that it? *(Storms back in toward Qiu-yun, yelling at her and hitting her.)*

Little Qi comes back to ask the others what they should do, before running back to Qiu-yun's house.

Amid the ruckus, Grandma Haruko enters from the left and stands right by the doorway. When Haruko signals with her hand, Little Qi begins hammering on the window—a ruse to get Qiu-yun out. The others join in.

LITTLE QI: Qiu-yun, Qiu-yun, your kid's been hurt! He fell from a swing at school. *(Qiu-yun rushes out from the rear, all disheveled. Little Qi drags her toward the rear of the alley.)* The teacher says they'll be sending him home early. *(Little Qi and Qiu-yun talk in whispers and move farther away. As Mao-xiong comes out in a huff, Grandma stares him down in the doorway.)*

Customers D, and so forth, enter, and then go into Xiang-lian's shop, looking over her dresses and selecting patterns from her fashion magazines.

MAO-XIONG: *(Pretending nothing happened, he walks over to Wen-tai, who is hanging up the sign.)* Hey, buddy, that's quite the sign you've got there. Business will get better and better ...

Wen-tai does not even acknowledge his presence. Haruko ignores him. Snubbed, Mao-xiong slinks away.

YU-ZHEN: *(To Xiang-lian.)* You've got so much work to do, I'd better get going. Take it easy and don't overdo it. *(Comes out and speaks to Wen-tai teasingly.)* Wen-tai, take your time doing your job, too, otherwise our class leader might decide you didn't make the grade, right?

Customers continue to stream into Xiang-lian's shop.

HARUKO: *(Standing near Xiang-lian's window, as if muttering to herself.)* A-lian, since you are doing such brisk business, why don't you renew the lease for another year? I'll charge only five hundred more a month. All right, fine—only three hundred more a month. You are doing so well and your friends are all here in Tainan. You wouldn't think of moving back to your village now, would you?

More and more girls and young ladies appear at the door of the shop.

HARUKO: Wow! She's got so many customers!

Music fades in. The lights change, gradually dimming until the scene fades to blackout.

Act II
The Eve of Her Departure

There are no lights on in Qiu-yun's house. Xiang-lian's shop is almost empty, with everything wrapped in packing paper, or under blue cloth, or canvas drop cloth. Wen-tai, dressed in a light-colored shirt, appears more mature and formal. He quietly pours two glasses of wine and sets them down on the table. It is now the mid-1980s.

Romantic music can be heard playing softly in the background.

WEN-TAI: A-lian, everything's all set out here. Do you need help with your packing?

XIANG-LIAN: *(Appears in a dress, relaxed and mature.)* I'm almost finished. I'd like to give the hemming machine to Qiu-yun but I don't know if she'll want it.

WEN-TAI: Won't Little Qi want it?

XIANG-LIAN: She runs a beauty salon that offers facials and sauna treatments. She doesn't do hemming anymore.

WEN-TAI: When her Grandma did the traditional facials, she only got a few bucks. Now, Little Qi charges a thousand for a facial with massage. That's easy money!

XIANG-LIAN: *(Nodding.)* Yes, but she's had to work very hard to get to this point. Now she doesn't have to do anything much herself. She has three girls doing backrubs and shiatsu massages and two other trained professionals doing delicate face massages. All she does is sit by the cash register, chatting with clients and promoting beauty products. On the anniversary of the opening of her salon, she even treated me to a free session.

WEN-TAI: Was it like the traditional facial?

XIANG-LIAN: No. Not at all! It was my first facial ever. Little Qi wanted me to go in every week, but I haven't.

WEN-TAI: You don't need it anyway.

XIANG-LIAN: She wanted you to try it out, too.

WEN-TAI: Me? Men don't go to beauty salons!

XIANG-LIAN: Sometimes women bring their husbands with them.

WEN-TAI: I wouldn't be caught dead in such a place. Well, maybe if you took me. *(Xiang-lian smiles.)* No, not even then. I can maintain my good looks on my own. *(Strikes a manly pose.)* Don't I look young and dashing? *(Xiang-lian is amused and hugs him from behind.)*

XIANG-LIAN: You're handsome enough. *(Chatting intimately.)* This hemming machine is practically new and I can't even give it away. It cost me so much at a time when I had so little. My old boss wouldn't buy one, even though he had a big shop. He'd send the most junior apprentice to take the dresses out for hemming; it cost a buck and a half per piece. When I first started out, I had to run those errands two or three times a day. Some days it was so hot out that I'd hold up the bundle to shield my face from the sun. *(Pantomimes shading her face with an imaginary bundle.)* But then I'd worry that the sunlight would ruin the dresses, so I'd run the whole way. The heat was unbearable.

WEN-TAI: Those errands should have been fun. *(Holding her.)* When I was doing my military service, I would have jumped at any chance to go off the base on an errand. Your boss was giving you the chance to get some fresh air and you didn't even appreciate it. You should have taken your time.

XIANG-LIAN: I wouldn't have dared.

WEN-TAI: *(Looking into her eyes and kissing her hand.)* You're so dedicated.

XIANG-LIAN: Back then I decided that when I have my own shop, I'd never make my apprentices run back and forth so many times a day. There would be a fixed schedule, with all errands at the end of the workday, or maybe once first thing in the morning and again at the end. New hemming orders could be dropped off and finished ones picked up all at the same time.

WEN-TAI: You're one of a kind.

XIANG-LIAN: *(Standing up on a chair.)* I wish I could go to a place where everyone follows through on their plans.

WEN-TAI: I know. I know what you mean.

XIANG-LIAN: Do you really?

WEN-TAI: Yes. That's why I've never asked you why you have to leave this place.

XIANG-LIAN: So you really don't know what I'm thinking.

WEN-TAI: Who can penetrate Your Majesty's innermost thoughts? *(Sitting her on the table.)*

XIANG-LIAN: Every time I see you, I remember all the moments, the past, the present, each and every moment we've spent together. When we were together in grade school, the hour-long walks to and from school ...

WEN-TAI: The sight of you always brings back fond memories. *(Kissing her, hating to part with her but feigning nonchalance.)* Maybe you didn't know this, but during those walks to school, I would wonder how you managed to get all your homework done ...

XIANG-LIAN: And I would wonder how you *hadn't* managed to get all your homework done. I'm just kidding. To be honest, I never paid much attention to how anyone else was doing in school. But I do remember how every day a dozen students were caned by the teacher and ordered to stand at the back of the room to be punished.

WEN-TAI: You would turn around to look at me and, if I was caught looking back, I'd pretend to be gazing at Sun Yat-sen.[2]

XIANG-LIAN: So tell me, why did you stop walking to school with me when we were in fifth grade? Were you afraid the other boys would tease you?

WEN-TAI: That's right. There was graffiti in the boys' bathroom about me being a "girl liker." A-feng and his gang were badmouthing us, saying we were "bathing in the river of eternal love."[3]

XIANG-LIAN: Did they really say that? The only graffiti I heard about was: "A-wen has no pride. He sharpens pencils for A-lian."

WEN-TAI: Yeah ... there was also graffiti about us getting married. But I started walking with you again in sixth grade.

XIANG-LIAN: Your skin was thicker by then.

---

[2] At that time, the portrait of Sun Yat-sen was hung in the back of every classroom in elementary schools. Sun Yat-sen is considered the father of the Chinese nation in both Taiwan and mainland China.

[3] "Bathing in the river of eternal love" is often written on wedding cards and/or on strips of paper hung on the wall at wedding ceremonies to wish the bride and groom good fortune and happiness.

WEN-TAI: Well, I didn't mind anymore if they talked about A-wen and A-lian getting married. I started to think that someday we really would get married.

XIANG-LIAN: Please don't say you're going to wait for me.

WEN-TAI: Okay, I won't say that.

XIANG-LIAN: *(Deeply touched.)* Out of all the people in the world who've been kind to me, really, out of everyone—my parents and grandmother included—you have been the kindest. Knowing you exist, no matter where you are, makes me feel safer. Whatever happens, no matter what difficulties I may encounter, as long as I know you are here, so far away, thinking of me ...

WEN-TAI: I'm going to miss you.

XIANG-LIAN: Will you be moving back home to the village?

WEN-TAI: Most of my family is gone. I wouldn't know what to do with myself back home.

XIANG-LIAN: So there's no pressure for you to ... ?

WEN-TAI: There's some pressure, but it's no use at all.

XIANG-LIAN: Seriously, if one day, I mean, if I should ever ... Then you ...

WEN-TAI: I won't ever fall in love with anyone else.

XIANG-LIAN: But I'm about to go away. I'll be gone by tomorrow.

WEN-TAI: You mean today.

XIANG-LIAN: Oh, right, today ...

WEN-TAI: Today, we are here. When did you start sounding like an old granny? You're right here in front of me, and yet you tell me to find someone else. You've gone abroad before and you've always come back. It's not as if you're going to the moon. And even if you were, you'd still have to come back eventually.

XIANG-LIAN: But this time I've closed up my shop for good. There's nothing left for me to do here. I can't imagine ever coming back to work in Tainan.

WEN-TAI: When we were kids, we never imagined we'd grow up so fast, that time would fly by like this. No one thought A-lian, the top student in the class, would give up school for work. I never expected to attend vocational school in the city, and had no idea I'd bump into you here in Tainan. Who could predict that you'd progress so fast from apprentice to master tailor, and then become your own boss? I never guessed that your dedication, experience, and flair for design would win you so much recognition that a company would send you overseas to set up a new factory, and that's how you'd build up your own career. So many great things have happened that we never imagined. We can't predict the future, but there's no reason to think it won't be good ...

XIANG-LIAN: But don't you think I've become a bit reckless? It's frightening.

WEN-TAI: In the past, we didn't always know what we were doing or where we were going. We just relied on our wits and our will to see us through. You've carefully thought about every step along the way. That's not being reckless. One day you'll decide you want to come back, and then you will. But that's for the future. We're never completely in the dark about things to come. At least we know the important things. Like when I first came to Tainan to see you, I knew that you'd be happy to see me.

XIANG-LIAN: *(Reminiscing.)* You stood at the door of the tailor shop, wearing a khaki uniform.

WEN-TAI: By then, you were second in command at the shop. I didn't want to go inside, so the other girls kept calling for you. When you finally came out, you looked like a fresh-faced little girl.

XIANG-LIAN: A big girl.

WEN-TAI: A beautiful big girl. I was just about to begin my military service and I had come to ask that beautiful big girl to be my fiancée. Do you still remember what you said to me then?

XIANG-LIAN: No, I've forgotten. What did I say? Do you dare repeat it?

WEN-TAI: *(Reciting a line of classical Chinese poem by Tang Dynasty poet Li Shang-yin.)* "My body lacks the wings of the bright-colored phoenix / But my heart beats with the spirit of the unicorn."

XIANG-LIAN: Impossible! I never said any such thing.

WEN-TAI: You didn't just say it, you sang it!

XIANG-LIAN: I don't believe you.

WEN-TAI: "Sharing our love by brush and ink / We assuage our mutual longing."

Xiang-lian remembers these lines in the Duma tune from the Taiwanese opera version of the classic love story Romance of the Western Chamber, and she starts singing along with Wen-tai. The two look at each other with tenderness and deep affection.

WEN-TAI AND XIANG-LIAN: "In the moon-lit Western Chamber / We await the perfect moment."

Wen-tai hugs her.

WEN-TAI: Everything's packed. Daybreak is only a few hours away. Why don't we get some sleep?

XIANG-LIAN: All right. But let's have one more sip of wine. *(Wen-tai pours and they drink.)*

WEN-TAI: Your face is getting hot.

XIANG-LIAN: Yours, too. The hotter the better.

WEN-TAI: It's even hotter in here. *(He unbuttons his shirt and places her hand over his heart. With her hand on his chest, Xiang-lian watches him take off his shirt.)*

XIANG-LIAN: *(Intoxicated.)* You have no idea how wonderful you are ...

WEN-TAI: And I'll only get better and better ... *(She takes off her dress, leaving her slip on. Leaving their clothing on the floor, they walk arm in arm toward backstage, exiting together.)*

Music fades in softly and lighting changes. Little Qi enters from the right, humming snatches of the Taiwanese popular song "Farewell at the Shore."

LITTLE QI: I can't believe how narrow this alley is. You can't even drive a car through it. When we were kids, the alley seemed so wide. There was enough room to draw several hopscotch boards ...

Qiu-yun enters from the left. She stops in front of her house and gazes in the direction of A-lian's shop. Little Qi is about to open the door, but when she sees Qiu-yun, she walks over to chat with her instead.

LITTLE QI: Sister Qiu-yun, you're home early.

QIU-YUN: Not really, this is when the night shift lets out now. We don't have long night shifts anymore. If the factory can have the short night shifts, that's pretty good.

You're dressed so fashionably these days. I barely recognized you.

LITTLE QI: *(Laughing.)* Right, so many factories have moved across the Strait. Isn't it tough being the forewoman?

QIU-YUN: It's not so bad.

LITTLE QI: I have a hard enough time supervising three employees. I don't dare criticize them. I just give them compliments and treat them to late-night snacks. Let me tell you, now my Grandma is the really fashionable one. She'll be here shortly because she doesn't trust me to close out the lease on my own. When's the last time you saw her? She doesn't wear magnolia flowers anymore, she prefers Christian Dior's *Poison*. *(Qiu-yun laughs heartily when she hears that.)* I mean, what's there to worry about? A-lian is like a sister to me. She's always been so responsible. *(As they approach the door of A-lian's shop, Little Qi turns around and asks Qiu-yun.)* By the way, do you want her old Mitsubishi sewing machine? How about it? A-lian has taken such good care of it, it looks practically new. That old brand still does the job. *(Comes back toward Qiu-yun's house.)*

QIU-YUN: Did A-lian say she would give it to me?

LITTLE QI: Do you want it or not?

QIU-YUN: Will it be a gift ... ?

LITTLE QI: If you want it, we'll bring it over to your place. Who knows? Maybe one day an old customer will drop by and ask you to make a new dress for a wedding banquet, a dress for a bride's "lady of good fortune," whatever.[4] With that machine, you'll be able to help them out.

QIU-YUN: My old sewing machine still works.

LITTLE QI: That one's too old. The belt should have been replaced ages ago. Are there still people that even fix old machines like that anymore? I don't think so. Take that Mitsubishi over to your place. And do you want that hemming machine?

QIU-YUN: A-lian did ask me about that.

LITTLE QI: Why don't you take both? This building will be vacant now and we're so busy with our business at the other place. Who knows what

---

[4] The "lady of good fortune," usually a female relative from the bride's side, serves various functions during the wedding events.

we'll do with it in the future? It's best not to leave too much stuff lying around here. Sister Qiu-yun, have you ever thought about opening a café?

QIU-YUN: No, I haven't. It would cost too much to start up. Were you thinking of opening a café here?

LITTLE QI: No, not here. We'd need a larger space. I was thinking of a piano bar and café. Brewing coffee is so easy. You see, I'm learning from my Grandma and considering all kinds of business ideas.

QIU-YUN: I guess you don't like drinking porridge nowadays?

LITTLE QI: I still crave porridge whenever I'm really hungry. I remember the aroma, the taste. I still like it, but I don't have time to make it. I don't even have time to buy it. Grabbing a cup of coffee is much easier. *(When they reach Xiang-lian's door, Little Qi stops and asks.)* So, do you think A-lian is brewing up something special with her coffee-mate?

QIU-YUN: *(Slaps Little Qi's back, laughing.)* She might not be back yet. I heard she had a big meeting—

LITTLE QI: No, she's definitely back. The big bosses never have long meetings. They like to leave the real work to the little guys. Let's drop in on her and see how she's doing.

QIU-YUN: I need to go home first to drop off my stuff and wash my face and hands. I'll join you later.

She walks toward home. Little Qi turns and watches her, and then follows along.

LITTLE QI: Well, I'll wait for you then. That way we can continue our chat. *(She sits down at the table. The sewing table of yesteryear has been replaced by a smaller one, which serves as a dining table.)* So, where's your husband?

QIU-YUN: Must have gone to bed. His health's not what it used to be. He has heart trouble, and problems with his liver, and his kidneys. And he's chronically drowsy. He brightens up only when that old dog A-gou and Poker Zhang take him gambling.

(Qiu-yun takes off her coat. Little Qi finds her not much changed from when she was younger.)

LITTLE QI: He's an old man now, yet you're still young at heart. He can't possibly keep such tight reins on you anymore.

QIU-YUN: *(Again lightly slaps Little Qi's hand.)* He has the same bad temper and foul mouth he's always had, but he can't control me like he used to. He doesn't have much strength, and even less of a voice. He grumbles a lot less, since there's not much he can do about anything.

LITTLE QI: If he's in such bad shape, why do you keep him around at all?

QIU-YUN: What do you expect me to do? *(Stabs Little Qi's head with a finger, laughing with a look of self-satisfaction.)* Let's have some wax apple!

Yu-zhen emerges hurriedly from the far end of the alley, carrying two big bags. She pauses at Xiang-lian's door, as if she's hesitating. She arranges her dress, examines herself, then lightly knocks on a window. Little Qi and Qiu-yun carry on their small talk absent-mindedly, all the while watching ... and listening ...

YU-ZHEN: A-lian, are you home? *(Not getting any response, she turns and stands forlornly by the wall. She fiddles with the dresses in the bags and heaves a heavy sigh. After deep reflection, she makes up her mind to try again in a louder voice.)* A-lian, are you home? A-lian, it's me! A-lian—

XIANG-LIAN: *(Comes out barefoot and hastily dressed.)* Yu-zhen, I'm glad you're here. Tomorrow, no, today, I'll be flying out— What's wrong?

YU-ZHEN: I'm sorry. I didn't want to bother you in the middle of the night—

XIANG-LIAN: It's all right. What happened? *(Sees her big paper bags.)* These clothes—

YU-ZHEN: I can't take it anymore. *(With her old friend before her eyes, she becomes very emotional.)*

XIANG-LIAN: What's going on? What did he do to you this time? *(Sits her down.)* Tell me the whole story.

YU-ZHEN: *(Wiping away her tears, she pours her heart out.)* I can't go on living with his family. It breaks my heart, how he doesn't even think about me. I bet he'd say that now that we're married, I'm obliged to serve every member of his entire family. What about his obligations to me? I never get to see him. He's at the clinic all day with his father and uncle. I'm home by myself with the kids and my mother-in-law, who doesn't like this, and doesn't like that. It's like living in a prison, where I'm not even free to step out the door. If it's not an errand for the kids, she doesn't even understand why I'd need to leave the house.

XIANG-LIAN: When the kids grow older—

YU-ZHEN: When the kids grow older, you think it will get better? That's what everyone says. But how long will I have to wait? I shouldn't have given birth to those two kids. Now all I want is to get out of there. No one understands how I feel. No one can help me.

XIANG-LIAN: Can you really leave just like that? Where would you go?

YU-ZHEN: *(Standing up.)* I feel so alone, with no one at my side. When you go abroad, I'll be even more isolated. But I've made up my mind about one thing. Can you please alter these clothes for me?

Xiang-lian opens the bags and looks up at Yu-zhen. Yu-zhen turns her face away and takes a few steps backward, then, turning toward Xiang-lian, she speaks, forcing herself to remain calm.

YU-ZHEN: I'm pregnant again. *(Pulls her dress tight to show her.)* My clothes are getting a little tight. Can you let them out two centimeters on each side? I can't let the family find out, especially not my mother-in-law. I'm going to get rid of it. It's not too late. I may have to go to Taichung, since all the doctors in Tainan will recognize me. I just can't have another child. *(Bursts into tears.)* A-lian, do you know how much pain I am in? It breaks my heart. I love my baby, but I can't allow another baby to become one more reason to keep me in that house.

XIANG-LIAN: *(Immediately gets out her sewing kit, scissors, awl, thread, and needle.)* Don't be too hard on yourself. I'll do your alterations right away. Even if it takes me up to the second I board the flight, I'll finish them all.

Wen-tai appears with a glass of water, at first not sure to whom to give it. He decides to hand it to Yu-zhen, tapping her on the shoulder.

XIANG-LIAN: If you've thought it through, and you're clear about it, then do what you have to do. *(Suddenly hitting on an idea.)* I can postpone my departure for two more days to accompany you to the clinic. *(Yu-zhen looks up at her, shaking her head.)* Or Wen-tai can take you.

YU-ZHEN: *(Returning the glass to Wen-tai and looking at both of them.)* No, that won't be necessary. *(Hugs Xiang-lian and, looking at Wen-tai, speaks soberly.)* It'll be better if I go alone.

Qiu-yun and Little Qi, after hotly debating over whether or not to go in ... finally walk over to the door of Xiang-lian's shop.

LITTLE QI: Sister A-lian. *(Those in the shop look startled. Little Qi tries to look relaxed.)* I can't believe you have so much work left to finish on the eve of your departure. All these need to be altered? Good thing I've brought Qiu-yun along with me. She's an expert at alterations.

Qiu-yun hits her in jest.

QIU-YUN: Are you implying that I don't get new dress orders anymore, so all I'm good for is alterations?

LITTLE QI: Not at all! Alterations are in great demand these days. Fashion-minded women young and old are having the hardest time finding qualified tailors to do their alterations. If they do find one, the tailor might still not have time to help them.

QIU-YUN: That mouth of yours is really something— *(The two enter the shop, one behind the other, and get ready to help.)*

LITTLE QI: I'm being serious! I found veteran tailor Qiu-yun to help. I used to make magic bras, so I can help too. See, Qiu-yun, you should take these machines. Who knows if you'll have old friends coming in the night asking for alterations.

QIU-YUN: A-lian, you might still need these machines in the future, right?

XIANG-LIAN: Hard to say. You take them for now. I'd planned to give them to Little Qi, but she has no use for them now that she's so successful. I'd have felt a little awkward bringing them over to your house.

Each person takes out a dress, and without any need for discussion, they immediately start examining them, cutting threads, and ripping out seams. Yu-zhen also joins in.

LITTLE QI: Wow! This evening gown is made from really fine fabric ... Are you sure you can trust me with it? My sewing skills are a bit rusty. I might ruin the dress ... *(Pleading for help.)*

YU-ZHEN: *(Exchanging dresses with Little Qi.)* Let me do that one then.

LITTLE QI: Good. This one's made of cotton, so it won't slip and slide so much ...

QIU-YUN: *(To Yu-zhen.)* Yu-zhen, you know how to sew, too! That's pretty impressive.

YU-ZHEN: Don't underestimate me. I've studied dressmaking too. The patterns and color schemes I designed won praise from my teachers. I should do more of this. This skill may come in handy someday ...

QIU-YUN: *(Looks fondly at her.)* Don't you worry. Self-reliance will see you through.

YU-ZHEN: Sister Qiu-yun, you're so kind to people, so generous and forgiving. You've stomached so much unhappiness. You never argue with your husband, and you take such good care of your family. I could never measure up to you. I don't have the temperament to be a dutiful wife or daughter-in-law.

QIU-YUN: I'm doing so-so. I don't have to look after my in-laws or the rest of his family. Marriage is payment for debts from a previous life. I'm just a fool! I cling to the hope that one day Mao-xiong will become a little gentler with me. Don't be too hard on yourself. We're in different situations. You're still young. You have even less reason to be scared.

YU-ZHEN: I am scared. But I'm also determined to find a way out.

XIANG-LIAN: Hey, what's going on here? One whole dress per person? That's so inefficient. According to my own guidelines for quality control, each person should do one specific task, and we'll be faster and better. The way you ladies are each doing this step, then that step, and all grabbing for the same tools, you're wasting lots of time. Come on, let me organize an assembly line.

QIU-YUN: We're doing just fine without your "guidelines"!

LITTLE QI: I think our way is faster. But maybe that's because I'm working on an easy one. *(Giggles.)*

YU-ZHEN: My dear lady, save your assembly line for your new brand-name clothing company. It's not like we have an order of thirty thousand items to fill here.

XIANG-LIAN: *(Correcting her in a whisper.)* More like three hundred thousand—

QIU-YUN: Wow. The garment factories in Tainan are closing down one after another. They can't afford the labor here anymore, so they're all moving to places like Indonesia or mainland China.

YU-ZHEN: Master A-lian, you don't have to act like the boss today. Nobody here is listening to you anyway.

XIANG-LIAN: The best time to implement a new system is now, while morale is high. But— *(Conceding defeat with a hearty, self-deprecating laugh.)* alright then, I'll leave you ladies to run the shop today. I won't lift a finger. I'll just monitor your performance from this "headquarters." *(Sighs as she turns around and sees Wen-tai.)* See how I got "demoted"?

Wen-tai pours water for all of them.

WEN-TAI: Does anyone want a bite to eat? I'll pick something up at the Sakariba night market.

QIU-YUN: Don't go to any trouble.

YU-ZHEN: We don't have any free hands—we can't pick up the food!

WEN-TAI: Little Qi, don't you want a bowl of eel noodle soup? Or a steamed bun? I'm sure you can find a spare hand for a late-night snack.

LITTLE QI: *(Appears to be working hard.)* I'm on a diet now.

XIANG-LIAN: *(To Wen-tai.)* Don't bother.

WEN-TAI: Well, then ... I'll just go home for a while so I don't get in anyone's way. *(To Xiang-lian.)* I'll come pick you up later this morning.

XIANG-LIAN: I'll walk you out to the street. I could use the exercise. Besides, they have no use for me here now. *(Looks around with affection as she takes Wen-tai's arm.)* Who knows when I'll see this little alley again? *(As the two start walking together toward the rear, going down the alley, they run into Grandma Haruko.)*

HARUKO: A-lian, are you leaving? I'm glad I caught you before your departure.

XIANG-LIAN: I'm not going quite yet— *(Inside, Little Qi beckons, but Haruko ignores her.)*

HARUKO: This red envelope is for you. *(Handing her a red envelope containing cash.)* It will help keep you safe on your travels everywhere, to America, to mainland China.

XIANG-LIAN: Granny, you shouldn't have—

HARUKO: Don't act all polite with me. I'm giving you this as your elder—

XIANG-LIAN: It will bring me good luck. I know it. I'll keep the red envelope itself—but what's inside— *(Tries to give the money back to Haruko.)*

HARUKO: A-lian, you're just heartless, with no feelings for me at all. You were making plans to go abroad, and I didn't hear even a peep about it from you. This old lady won't hold that against you. I still come by to say hello, and I still come here to see you off. I treat you like family, just like my own Little Qi, but you're still so formal with me. Have a heart! *(Refuses to take money back.)*

XIANG-LIAN: *(All flushed.)* Alright, I'll accept it. Granny, you're so gracious. When I left home at fourteen, my mother and grandfather each gave

Figure 3.4 On the eve of Xiang-lian's (at left) departure for a new professional job abroad, her longtime landlady "Granny" Haruko (center) gives her a red envelope with money, a farewell gift usually from elders in one's own family. Xiang-lian later shares with Wen-tai (right) her sentiments about this place she is about to leave.

me a red envelope with one hundred yuan. I came to Tainan carrying only a single suitcase. Back then, Tainan seemed a world away from home. To this day, I still have those two red envelopes. Granny Haruko, I'll always keep this red envelope, too, as a token of your good wishes. Your house has been my home here in Tainan.

HARUKO: *(Hugging her in Western style.)* I'm going inside. You two carry on with your chat.

XIANG-LIAN: *(Overwhelmed by the affection bestowed on her.)* A-wen, I can't bear to leave now.

WEN-TAI: My queen! Our beloved A-lian! With peace in your heart, fly away on your new adventure. Fly away!

He kisses her as they walk upstage, slowly walking along the alley. Those in the tailor shop are still working around the big table, busily altering the dresses.

Music. Curtain falls.

Act III
Return to Hai-an Road

After the intermission or a short break, curtains rise amid the rumble of cars driving over steel plates. It is now the late 1990s. Steel fences can be seen surrounding the work site. The audience can also see green and gray roadblocks bearing warnings such as "People Working—Sorry for Any Inconvenience" and "Unauthorized Entry Prohibited." The widened street appears deserted and in disrepair. Silhouettes of buildings loom in the background. Grandma Haruko and Little Qi stand by the fences to the right; Qiu-yun and her wheelchair-bound husband are found on the left. Wen-tai is in the center. They all have their backs to the audience.

Lighting changes as Wen-tai turns around.

WEN-TAI: Many years have gone by. Needless to say, I am still waiting for A-lian. A-lian is also waiting—waiting for the day when she can finally come back here, when she can settle down in one place, and when she need not always be on the go. It's true, her return isn't solely for my sake, yet she is coming back for me. In the depth of my heart, I know that I remain the footprint of her childhood, whether in the rice paddy or in the schoolyard. I was right there with her, when she started working in the prime of her youth. When she was just one person doing the work of many, I was the person closest to her heart.

Xiang-lian appears to the right.

XIANG-LIAN: Many years have gone by. We are inseparable, though the days we've spent together have not been many at all.

WEN-TAI: For a time after she went abroad—

XIANG-LIAN: We only saw each other twice a year. My heart ached from missing him.

WEN-TAI: My heart ached from missing her. She's always hated the hot summers, ever since she was a little girl, but for each vacation, she'd come back here to Tainan.

XIANG-LIAN: Sometimes a full month's vacation—

WEN-TAI: All smiles, happily chatting away with me, even as she complained about the heat.

XIANG-LIAN: All smiles, happily chatting away with him, even as I complained about the heat.

WEN-TAI: When my year-end vacation finally came, it was always in the dead of winter. I would brave the bitter cold in China or in Europe to visit her. When I had her in front of me, talking about whatever she wanted, I would feel warm all over.

Yu-zhen appears to the left.

XIANG-LIAN: Friends all blame me. They say he's still single because of me, because I keep putting things off. But he doesn't mind. He says we're both so busy, even if we bought a new home, anticipating a wedding, the place would just sit there breeding mosquitoes.

YU-ZHEN: I didn't say anything. It's just that, these past few years, I've been freer to come and go, and when I'd visit A-lian, staying in her apartment, drinking wine and watching the sunset together, my thoughts would often go to poor A-wen.

WEN-TAI: I've never worried about our putting it off for so long. She and I are meant for one another. And now she's coming home. She's finally made up her mind.

XIANG-LIAN: I'm coming back to settle here in Tainan, not in Taipei, not in Kaohsiung. I think he must have been surprised.

WEN-TAI: I was a bit surprised, because she'd once said she didn't know what on earth she could do in Tainan. But it looks as though she's got it all planned. The thing is she wanted to come back first to this neighborhood to visit the old house of Granny Haruko. Does A-lian not know that this place has transformed beyond recognition?

XIANG-LIAN: I—want—to—come—home—

LITTLE QI: *(Turning around, she walks forward in a mature, leisurely way. She is fashionably dressed.)* I told her, if she wants to buy a place, she should look in my part of town, or in Yongkang or Dawan. ... They've got new houses there, spacious and comfortable. There's good business in those new communities, too. ... If she wants to go back to the Hai-an Road of before, well, that place is long gone. It's so different now.

WEN-TAI: I've come first, to find my bearings. I'm afraid I won't be able to find our old alley when I bring her here. It's going to feel strange. I don't want it to be too much of a shock to her.

Lighting changes. Wen-tai, Yu-zhen, and Xiang-lian turn away, with their backs to the audience.

QIU-YUN: *(Turns and takes a couple of steps toward the center.)* I think I understand how A-lian feels. She's done so well abroad, with all her success, but she can't ever forget, can't ever stop thinking about those young girls who make dresses right here. She has never taken an apprentice. If she comes across a talented young girl, good with her hands and good with her mind, she brings her right in to learn on the job, working by her side. It's like when I first saw her, just as talented, just as likeable. Her shop was just next door. I watched her take such good care of her customers each day. I couldn't stop singing her praises. I wished with all my heart she would forge a path even more successful and more prosperous than my own.

Now she has a dozen people just to handle pattern and sample making, and many assistants who buy fabrics, choose colors, and select materials, all under her command. Whatever she envisions, she can make it happen. Having that kind of freedom, that kind of power, is something I could never even imagine. But when it comes to buying a home, she seems just as uncertain, just as inept as before. Buy here? Wrong investment!

LITTLE QI: *(Looking at her old neighbor from years ago.)* Sister Qiu-yun's life is much sweeter now. She doesn't need to work anymore. As long as she just collects the rent on her properties, she'll always have plenty. She's never dieted, and yet her figure's still as trim as before. She practices the iron fan dance and does *waidan* kung fu. She teaches dressmaking and embroidery at the Community Center, and even counsels women who have no luck with marriages.[5]

QIU-YUN: Not really. I just participate in group activities and discussions.

LITTLE QI: Hey, I am one of those unlucky women, too.

QIU-YUN: Not you. You want no part of marriage.

LITTLE QI: You mean I refuse to get married. Like you, right, Grandma?

HARUKO: What were you saying? *(Approaches Little Qi and Qiu-yun.)*

---

[5] An "iron fan" is a fan made of metal used in a martial dance. The *waidan*, or "external," form of kung fu, was originally connected to Taoism, but is now a popular physical exercise among everyday people in Taiwan. The women have had "no luck" with marriages due to death, divorce, or other life challenges.

LITTLE QI: Sister Qiu-yun, how's your old man been doing lately? *(Qiu-yun pushes Mao-xiong's wheelchair.)* Oh, so he's taking a stroll too? His color's looking a lot better.

MAO-XIONG: Haruko, it's been a long time since you last came this way. *(After his stroke, he speaks slowly in a flat tone.)* A-qi, you've never come back to visit, have you come back for a look even once?

LITTLE QI: What for? What's there to see? This place was torn down the day after they started demolishing the neighborhood.

MAO-XIONG: You have all been very busy, I know.

HARUKO: I'm not busy anymore. In the mornings, I don't need to go get groceries or cook. In the afternoon, when the kids and the teachers come over to our English school, I go out to have a good time. You all live too far from my place. *(Little Qi speaks softly into her Grandma's ear.)* No, I do not play mah jongg.

LITTLE QI: Fine, if you say so. *(To Mao-xiong.)* I'm not like you. I didn't want to sign up for store space in the underground shopping mall. I haven't been as interested as you.

QIU-YUN: We took our names off the list a long time ago. It was his idea to sign up. I wasn't interested at all. I just can't get used to the idea of paying for something I haven't seen with my own eyes. When I buy a house, I always go for preowned ones. Some people tried talking me into buying presale properties. I politely sent them on their way, saying I couldn't make heads or tails of the prospectus. So maybe I've missed out on some random promotional gifts, or the chance to win some prize—many have lotteries that give away cars! I just don't understand it all. Look at all the unoccupied new apartment buildings! If I wait to buy, I'll get to pick and choose. When there's a glut of unsold housing, the prices will come down.

MAO-XIONG: This woman sure knows how to make money. She never tells me anything.

QIU-YUN: Not really. I've saved up one penny at a time. If I had told you, we would be penniless by now.

LITTLE QI: But you still prefer to live nearby.

QIU-YUN: Because it's convenient to everything. I'm used to the neighborhood. I can still run into some old acquaintances here. People help each other out, whatever they can do. Too bad you live so far away now.

MAO-XIONG: All my old buddies are gone. They all moved far away. There was one who used to go to Poker Zhang's to chat. He kicked the bucket right after he moved away. My kids don't like coming back, they say their classmates aren't around anymore. Classmates, my ass! How come you can't come back to visit your old man?

LITTLE QI: Here you go again.

MAO-XIONG: You've seen my eldest, he's very tall now. He used to talk back to me ...

QIU-YUN: Not anymore.

MAO-XIONG: Now he lectures me ... My daughter also works in Taipei. She never tells me how much she makes a month. She dresses really well, and the clothes she buys me are good quality. But she's just like her mother, she won't tell me how much money she has. And the little one, he's in graduate school. It's so expensive. He needs his old mother to send money each month. He's another one who only talks to his mother. Money, I don't have any, sad to say. I often wonder, after all that education, where's he going and what's he going to do? I've no idea. He's definitely not coming back. I tell you, no one talks to me anymore. A-qi, you're all grown up now, and your manners have improved. You used to give me the cold shoulder. The young people in this neighborhood, I don't know any of them. When they pass by, they won't even look me in the eye. What are they scared of? I'm very upset, I can't stand it, but I just keep it to myself. It's not as if I was going to ask them to push my wheelchair. What are they sacred of? When they look at old folks, why the scared look ...

LITTLE QI: You used to be such a smooth talker. You can tell them, I can push the chair myself and, hey, I can walk. Hasn't the physical therapy helped you a lot? Come on, show me how you can walk.

MAO-XIONG: Nah.

LITTLE QI: Give it a try, "Come on, you can make it ..."[6]

---

[6] "Come on, you can make it," appears in English in the original text.

MAO-XIONG: *(Drawing away from Little Qi, moving toward Qiu-yun.)* Qiu-yun, see what she's doing ...

HARUKO: I am much older than he is. My knees act up now and then. That's why I've given up high heels. We need regular exercise. *(Knocking on the wheelchair with her parasol.)*

MAO-XIONG: I don't want to, I'm tired now. *(Turns his face and wheels the chair away himself.)*

The rest of the group, behind him, aimlessly looks around in all directions. Wen-tai turns toward the audience.

WEN-TAI: I'm not quite sure how A-lian feels about coming back to this place, but I know how I'm feeling ... how should I put it ... hesitant, kind of scared, coming so close to the old home. It's awkward, almost regretful, like I've let her down, as if I didn't protect this old place in the alley for her.

YU-ZHEN: *(Turning toward the audience.)* I urged A-lian not to come back ...

XIANG-LIAN: *(Also turning around toward the audience.)* Why are you all telling me it's all gone, and there aren't any new buildings either? What can that mean, "all" gone? I don't believe it.

YU-ZHEN: I didn't believe it either at first. I took a drive there, a special trip, just for you. The street was so much wider—my goodness—excavation was going on everywhere. Really, there's no need to come down here.

XIANG-LIAN: But I want to. I insist on coming back.

YU-ZHEN: It isn't worth the effort.

XIANG-LIAN: *(Turns toward Yu-zhen and bares her soul.)* I'm more than willing. My heart is here. I've spent too much time working for other people, in their companies, in their countries. I was patient. I worked hard. I held nothing back. I helped them go down so many new roads.

YU-ZHEN: *(Takes a step toward her old friend.)* You could have continued down those roads yourself. So many people would love to go abroad, but can't. You could exhibit your products and create your own brands. Those famous designers in Taipei, they all go abroad to refresh and recharge!

XIANG-LIAN: That's only half true. *(Turns to face the audience again.)* There's no lack of local talent here. Only people don't realize it themselves. I've always admired the *joie de vivre* of the people in Tainan. That's what makes me want to come back. I want to clothe these soft-spoken and courteous folks who hold your eyes and smile when they speak to you. I've also met the younger generation from Tainan. They are creative and enterprising. The times are changing. There are bound to be even more girls who are fascinated by fashion design.

YU-ZHEN: You just won't give up on people. I got worried when you said you were going to come back here and open up all different kinds of ladies' dress boutiques, six or seven of them on the same street, each with its own character and tailored to a different clientele. I got worried that you would lose money. I went to go ask A-qi, who's more up on the trends than we are. She's now ...

LITTLE QI: *(Turns and strolls forward.)* Yeah, I also went overseas. For three months the first time. Then just one month the second and third time. That was long enough. *(Takes another step and then says with skepticism.)* I found those foreigners really dull, kind of dumb. *(Walks toward A-lian.)* Sister A-lian, I've got to hand it to you that you stuck it out over there for all those years. Of course, people over here are more into capitalizing on the strengths of others. I know what businesses bring in the most profit.

XIANG-LIAN: I am not aiming for profit.

LITTLE QI: I know. You're here to discover talent. Sister A-lian, *(Taking a small step backwards.)* on behalf of all of Tainan City and Tainan County —I have a branch in Tainan County now—I welcome you back. When you come back to do business here in Taiwan, it's *very* hard not to make a profit.[7]

YU-ZHEN: A-lian, brace yourself for the shock.

WEN-TAI: I'll go first. Yu-zhen, you can pick her up and bring her over.

Lighting and music change. The scenery becomes more clearly discernible.

XIANG-LIAN: I've finally come back to Hai-an Road. Granny Haruko, you haven't changed a bit. *(Slowly turning her head.)* Sister Qiu-yun, how have you been? *(She looks behind Qiu-yun. Mao-xiong, sitting in his wheelchair, extends his right hand toward Xiang-lian, who shakes it. Surveying the*

---

[7] Little Qi says the word for "very" in an intentionally strong local Taiwanese accent here.

Figure 3.5 Xiang-lian (center of group at right), returning to Hai-an Road after many years away, views the devastation, supported by her beloved Wen-tai and her best friend Yu-zhen. Little Qi (far left) and her grandmother Haruko join their former tenant Xiang-lian on her return visit.

wasteland before her eyes, she slowly comes to Wen-tai's side. Wen-tai puts his arm on her shoulder. A-lian says to Wen-tai and Yu-zhen.) Why have I never heard about this? What is this?

WEN-TAI: It was in the papers. I even sent you the press clippings.

YU-ZHEN: It's called the underground mall.

XIANG-LIAN: When did this happen?

YU-ZHEN: Quite some years ago.

XIANG-LIAN: And now?

YU-ZHEN: The project is now in limbo. In the beginning, the underground mall was considered a "super idea."[8]

XIANG-LIAN: And what happened?

YU-ZHEN: There were problems with the project. Underground water seepage. The contractor went out of business. Now some people oppose the project and want the excavations refilled ... Others propose redesigning the project ... So the whole thing just keeps getting put off.

XIANG-LIAN: Why?

YU-ZHEN: *(Sighs.)* Well ...

XIANG-LIAN: Why don't I know anything about this? Are you sure you sent me clippings? Was I in mainland China at the time? Or still in Germany? How come I can't recall anything?

WEN-TAI: You were in Taipei.

XIANG-LIAN: What? Then I just forgot about it? And now? What's going to happen?

LITTLE QI: Don't know. Now they're doing another assessment. They are discussing the BOT option—financing is probably the biggest problem.[9]

XIANG-LIAN: How come I don't recall anything about this? There was no talk of this in Taipei.

WEN-TAI: Taipei has never paid much attention to things that happen in the south.

---

[8] "Super idea" appears in English in the original text.

[9] BOT stands for "build-operate-transfer," an approach to financing infrastructure projects used in Taiwan among other places. A private investor initially funds the project in return for a time-limited concession that enables the investor to recoup the investment. In time, the project transfers to government operation.

LITTLE QI: We moved away. Grandma sensed things were smelling fishy around here. Urban development was leaving us behind and moving to the eastern districts. Mao-xiong is right—people like me don't have too much attachment to this place. But I'm not cold-hearted, I just don't write letters much.

QIU-YUN: This place has seen big changes. Our lives have changed a lot, too. It's just so hard to describe how I feel.

YU-ZHEN: *(To Xiang-lian.)* Don't say we didn't warn you.

WEN-TAI: You didn't believe us even after we told you.

XIANG-LIAN: It's not that I didn't believe you. I just failed to understand. Even as I stand here, I still find it beyond belief. All I can see is the old Hai-an Road.

Music and lighting change.

QIU-YUN: Hey, it's raining now. We need umbrellas. I'll bring some from home.

YU-ZHEN: Showers in the south pass very quickly.

LITTLE QI: Grandma has her parasol. Don't worry. Don't bother, it's only a drizzle.

QIU-YUN: I'll just be a minute. *(Exits hurriedly.)*

YU-ZHEN: I have my foldable umbrella. *(Opens the umbrella to shield A-lian from the rain. A-lian indicates that Mao-xiong needs an umbrella. He stands up and declines Little Qi's offer to help him. He walks about with dignity.)*

LITTLE QI: A-lian, why don't you take a look at our place, how about it? Grandma says you can live together with her on the second floor. The floor space is fifty *ping*.

HARUKO: You can teach English next door. The place is built like a magnificent castle. It's a lot of fun. Many kids come in the afternoon and evening. Do you know how to teach? *(A-lian shakes her head.)* But you speak fluent English, right? Of course, I don't understand the language. Besides, I'm half deaf now. You succeed at everything you do. Just take your time opening your new shop. It'll be a success, no doubt.

YU-ZHEN: Or, instead, you can come with me to Taichung. Or I can go with you to Taipei. I'm fine, either way.

XIANG-LIAN: I was determined to come home, but I never thought I'd feel so empty inside. I'm at a loss.

WEN-TAI: For you, this is all too sudden. Of course it came as a shock. But don't feel so bad. Take it easy. You'll figure out what to do, where to go.

XIANG-LIAN: I don't know. I don't seem to know anything anymore. I feel like crying, but the tears won't come.

MAO-XIONG: There's no need to cry. My tears dried up long ago. These houses have been passed down through generations. I don't know what to feel. The houses aren't big, but our ancestors must have worked so hard, for so long, to get them built. My heart feels empty, I feel so bad. Now they're tearing down the houses, we can't do anything about it. Everyone says there's no development without demolishing old houses and widening the streets.

Qiu-yun returns with two or three umbrellas and passes them out.

QIU-YUN: There are many others who are still waiting. They've waited six or seven years, getting ever more disheartened. But they are still dreaming of the day when the stores in the underground mall will light up, one after the other, and this whole street will be prosperous, and full of life, all the way down.

MAO-XIONG: That's way off in the future. *(To A-lian.)* Don't you agree? The return of the good old days, it's far, far away.

He walks away slowly on his own, with Qiu-yun at his side. Little Qi and Haruko also start leaving. Yu-zhen looks around, then starts walking away, but stays mindful of Xiang-lian and Wen-tai in conversation.

The movements of those leaving gradually turn into slow motion.

WEN-TAI: Do you still remember what I said to you, on the eve of your departure, ten years ago?

XIANG-LIAN: *(Nods.)* You are more optimistic than I am. You don't believe there's winter in this world.

WEN-TAI: I believe in your passion and your ability more than you do. How can it be that you don't understand yourself?

XIANG-LIAN: I've now lost my confidence.

WEN-TAI: Didn't you say that there's no point in just talking about confidence? That what really counts is hard work?

XIANG-LIAN: Yes, I did. But I never thought I'd have to start again from scratch, to truly start from zero.

WEN-TAI: Hasn't it always been this way?

XIANG-LIAN: It has always been this way ... and will always be this way ...

Xiang-lian stands in front of the construction fence. She gazes into the distance, not saying a word. Wen-tai stands behind her, still holding the umbrella over her head.

Music continues. Lighting changes. The scene dims and darkens.

They may choose to walk in slow motion, moving together upstage.

Conversion Charts: Names and Terms

Table 3.1   Title and author

How it appears in this volume's translation	Chinese characters	Mandarin romanization in *pinyin*	Taiwanese romanization in *Tai-lo*
One Year, Three Seasons	一年三季	Yīnián sānjì	Tsít-nî-sann-kuì
Wang Chi-Mei	汪其楣	Wāng Qíméi	Ong Kî-bâi

Table 3.2   Names of characters that appear in the play

How it appears in this volume's translation	Chinese characters	Mandarin romanization in *pinyin*	Taiwanese romanization in *Tai-lo*	Japanese romanization in *romaji*
Haruko	春子	Chūnzi	Tshiu-tsú	Haruko
Little Qi (A-qi)	小琪 (阿琪)	Xiǎo Qí (Aqí)	Sió Kî (A-kî)	
Mao-xiong	茂雄	Màoxióng	Böo-hiông	
Qiu-yun	秋雲	Qiūyún	Tshiu-hûn	
Wen-tai (A-wen)	文泰 (阿文)	Wéntài (Āwén)	Bûn-thài (A-bûn)	
Xiang-lian (A-lian)	香蓮 (阿蓮)	Xiānglián (Ālián)	Hiong-liân (A-liân)	
Yu-zhen	玉珍	Yùzhēn	Giók-tin	

Table 3.3 Names of characters and historical figures mentioned in the play

How it appears in this volume's translation	Chinese characters	Mandarin romanization in *pinyin*	Taiwanese romanization in *Tai-lo*	Frequent English renderings
A-cai	阿彩	Ācǎi	A-tshái	
A-feng	阿峰	Āfēng	A-hong	
A-gou	阿狗	Āgǒu	A-káu	
A-gui	阿桂	Āguì	A-kuì	
Chen	陳	Chén	Tân	
Chiung Yao*	瓊瑤	Qióng Yáo		Chiung Yao
Fong Fei Fei*	鳳飛飛	Fèng Fēifēi		Fong Fei Fei
Hui-qin	惠琴	Huìqín	Huī-khîm	
Jody Chiang*	江蕙	Jiāng Huì	Kang Huī	Jody Chiang, Jiang Hui
Li Shangyin	李商隱	Lǐ Shāngyǐn	Lí Siong-ún	Li Shangyin
Poker Zhang	羅宋張	Luósòng Zhāng	Lôsòng Tiunn	
Sun Yat-sen	孫中山	Sūn Zhōngshān	Sun Tiong-san	Sun Yat-sen

Table 3.4 Names of places mentioned in the play

How it appears in this volume's translation	Chinese characters	Mandarin romanization in *pinyin*	Taiwanese romanization in *Tai-lo*	Frequent English renderings
Dawan	大灣	Dàwān	Tuā-uan	Da Wan
Hai-an Road	海安路	Hǎi'ān lù	Hái-an lōo	Hai-an Road
Kaohsiung	高雄	Gāoxióng	Ko-hiòng	Kaohsiung
Kenting	墾丁	Kěntīng	Khún-ting	Kenting
Minzu Road	民族路	Mínzú lù	Bîn-tsók lōo	
Sakariba	沙卡里巴	Shākǎlǐbā	Sa-khah-lí-pa	Sakariba
Taichung	台中	Táizhōng	Tâi-tiong	Taichung
Tainan	台南	Táinán	Tâi-lâm	Tainan
Taipei	台北	Táiběi	Tâi-pak	Taipei
Yongkang	永康	Yǒngkāng	Íng-khong	Yong Kang

Table 3.5 Names of foods, songs, and other items mentioned in the play

How it appears in this volume's translation	Chinese characters	Mandarin romanization in *pinyin*	Taiwanese romanization in *Tai-lo*	Frequent English renderings
"bathing in the river of eternal love"	愛河永浴	ài hé yǒng yù	ài-hô-íng-iók	
"Coral Love"	珊瑚戀	Shānhú liàn		
"I Am Just a Cloud"	我是一片雲	Wǒ shì yīpiàn yún		"Cloud of Romance"
"lady of good fortune"	全福太太	quánfú tàitai	tsuân-hok-thài-thài	
"Mama, mama, yah, listen to my guitar!"	媽媽媽媽呀, 送我一個吉他	Māma māma ya, sòng wǒ yīge jítā		
"Parting at the Shore"	惜別的海岸	Xībié de hǎi'àn	Sioh-piàt ê hái-huānn	
"Wild Goose on the Wing"	雁兒在林梢	Yàn'ér zài línshāo		"The Wild Goose on the Wing"
Duma tune	都馬調	Dūmǎ diào	Too-má-tiāu	
eel noodle soup	鱔魚意麵	shànyúyìmiàn	siān-hî-ì-mī	
feng shui	風水	fēngshuǐ	hong-suí	feng shui
iron fan	鐵扇	tiěshàn	thih-sìnn	iron fan
ping	坪	píng	pênn	
porridge; *miancha*	麵茶	miànchá	mī-tê	
Romance of the Western Chamber	西廂記	Xīxiāng jì	Se-siunn kì	*Romance of the Western Chamber*
steamed bun	割包 (刈包)	gēbāo (guàbāo)	kuah-pau	
Taiwanese opera	歌仔戲	gēzǐxì	kua-á-hì	Taiwanese opera, gezaixi
traditional facials; *wanmian**	挽面	wǎnmiàn	bán-bīn	

Table 3.5   Continued

How it appears in this volume's translation	Chinese characters	Mandarin romanization in *pinyin*	Taiwanese romanization in *Tai-lo*	Frequent English renderings
waidan kung fu	外丹功	wàidānˈgōng	guā-tan-kang	wai dan kung fu, wai dan gongfu
women who have no luck with marriages	失婚婦女	shīhūn fùnǚ	sit-hun-hū-lú	
yuan	元	yuán	koh	yuan

*Appears in Dramaturgical Notes only.

Contributors

Hsu Rey-Fang received her BA in Chinese Literature from Tamkang University and her MFA. in Theatre Playwriting from Taipei National University of the Arts. She is Assistant Professor in the Department of Drama Creation and Application at National University of Tainan. She was Artistic Director of Tainaner Ensemble from 1994 to 2002 and built the Apollo Ensemble with her students in 2014. A key promoter and developer of modern theater in southern Taiwan, she has published five of her scripts: *Non-Citizen, Take Me to See the Fish, The Phoenix Trees Are in Blossom, Opening the Gate in 1895,* and *Bridge of the Ancestors.* In the past decade Rey-Fang has devoted herself to promoting Theatre-in-Education (T-I-E), creating works of interactive theater including *The Completion of the Mansion, Opening the Gate in 1895, Bridge of the Ancestors, The Nilala Village,* and *La! When Flying Back.* She has published two books on T-I-E: *The Encounter Between Theatre in Education and History: Directorial Explanations for* Opening the Gate in 1895 *&* Bridge of the Ancestors and (with Tsai Chi-Chang) *Echoes of the Surging Tide: Theory and Practice of TIE.* She has produced plays in cooperation with the National Museum of Taiwan History and is currently developing docent theater for the Museum's permanent exhibition.

Yawtsong Lee received his BS in Mathematics from Fu Jen Catholic University and his MS in Mathematics from University of Michigan, Ann Arbor. He worked as a simultaneous interpreter at the United Nations from 1973 to 2005. Lee's literary translations from English to Chinese include Saul Bellow's *More Die of Heartbreak,* William Owens' *The Lifting the Fog of* War, and David Wise's *Cassidy Run.* Literary translations from Chinese to English include Wang Xiaoying's *Behind the Singing Masks,* Zou Zou's *She She,* Peng Ruigao's *Calling Back the Spirit of the Dead,* Xue Shu's

The Most Beautiful Face in the World: Two Novellas, Zhu Lin's *Paradise on Earth*, and short stories by Zhao Changtian, Ye Xin, Chen Cun, and Wang Anyi. Lee has also translated numerous works on Chinese culture into English, including three works in the "Discovering China" series: *Chinese Calligraphy*, *Chinese Painting*, and *Bamboo in China: Arts, Crafts and a Culture History*. Additional cultural translations include *Chinese Kites: An Illustrated Step-by-Step Guide*, *Chinese Style: Interiors, Furniture, Details*, *The Art of Chinese Calligraphy*, and *An Afternoon Tea of Beijing Opera Tidbits*. He also translated the bilingual publication *Shanghai—Our Stories 1978–2008*, compiled by the Information Office of the Shanghai Municipality.

Peng Ya-Ling started her theater career in 1981, as part of the first generation of experimental theater in Taiwan, teaching acting with the Lan-Ling Theatre Workshop, and also acting in the Square-Round Theatre Group. In 1987, when Taiwan's National Theatre was inaugurated, she was invited to do the first show in the National Experimental Theatre, *Oedipus the Rex*. From 1988 to 1991 she studied physical theater in the London School of Mime & Movement, and she joined the Tragic Carpet Theatre Group, performing in *Nosferatu* in the Edinburgh Festival in August 1991. Upon her 1991 return to Taiwan, Peng found that her generation had learned nothing about Taiwanese culture under the KMT's martial law, so she started her Oral History Project. She visited old master of Taiwanese Opera Lady Black Cat Cloud, Taiwanese folk song singer Wu Tien Lo, and blind Nakashi singer Lee Bien Hwei. She invited these long neglected artists to Taipei, living and rehearsing together for her project *Echoes of Taiwan*. Since that time, Peng has visited more than fifty villages to interview villagers for her project, and she has studied the Taiwanese language for four years and the Hakka language for six years. *Echoes of Taiwan* has now had more than thirteen productions.

Wang Chi-Mei is a senior Taiwanese playwright, director, actress, and professor. With a BA in Chinese from National Taiwan University and an MA in theater from University of Oregon, Wang has been teaching and promoting traditional as well as modern theater in Taiwan for more than thirty years. She has also compiled and edited several volumes of plays from contemporary Taiwan theater. Plays written and directed by Wang include *The Orphan of the World, Children of the Good Earth, Tales of the Mountains and the Seas, Paradise Found, Remember Hong Kong, The Bride and Her Double, One Year, Three Seasons, Living History of Wong Marry-King by Her Female Witch Friend, Good XL Good,* and the Bangzi Opera *The Pavilion of Praying to the Moon.* She also founded a theater of the deaf and produced plays with sign language: *Flying Fingers, The Legend of Sculpting Dragons,* and *First Moon, Full Moon* in addition to *A Voyage with Mom* with deaf and blind actors together. She also acted the leading roles in her own plays about outstanding female figures in *Dancer A-Yueh, The Song Is Young,* and *Snow Red.* Other publications include the play *Youth Sorrow—Taiwan AIDS Front* and the prose piece *An Ocean of Tenderness—Literary Memo of AIDS.*

Wang Wan-Jung received two MAs in Dramatic Arts from Indiana University and Chinese Culture University, her MFA in Directing from the New School for Social Research, and her PhD in Applied Drama and Theatre Studies from Royal Holloway, University of London. She is currently Associate Professor in the Department of Drama Creation and Application at National University of Tainan. She is an active director, playwright, teacher, writer, and researcher in the field of applied drama and theater. She has written seven books in Chinese on theater studies: *Peter Brook, Light and Sight on Stage, On Wings We Fly across the Darkness, Country Farmer Enters into the City of God, The Legend of King Da Du, The Public Is No Longer Silent: Local Innovation and Experimentation in Applied Drama,* and *Collected Articles on the Aesthetics of Applied Drama: Everlasting Avant-garde, Glocalization, and Nostalgia.* Her academic articles have been published widely in international and local journals in both English and Chinese, including *Research in Drama Education: The Journal of Applied Theatre and Performance.* She has also regularly devised and directed performances of oral history theater, community theater, and museum theater with her undergraduate students and various community members as her social intervention through applied theater.

John B. Weinstein received his BA in East Asian Studies from Harvard University; MA, MPhil and PhD degrees in East Asian Languages and Cultures from Columbia University; and MA in Educational Leadership from Montclair State University. He is Associate Professor of Chinese and

Asian Studies at Bard College at Simon's Rock and Principal and Dean of the Early College at Bard High School Early College–Newark. From 2006 to 2011, he served as President of the Association for Asian Performance. As a scholar, his primary area of research is modern Chinese and Taiwanese theater, with articles in the journals *Asian Theatre Journal* and *Modern Chinese Literature and Culture*, as well as numerous book chapters in English and Chinese. He has directed plays in both Chinese and English, including plays by Chen Baichen, Ding Xilin, Wang Chi-Mei, and Yang Jiang. His published translations include Ding Xilin's "A Wasp," "Oppression," and "Flushed with Wine" (all with Carsey Yee), and (with Brenda Austin) the model opera *The Red Lantern*, some of which are included in Xiaomei Chen's *Columbia Anthology of Modern Chinese Drama*. He adapted (with Yee) and directed Pai Hsien-yung's *Crystal Boys* at Harvard University. Weinstein first visited Taiwan on a Fulbright grant in 1997–1998.

CORNELL EAST ASIA SERIES

CORNELL
East Asia Series

eap.einaudi.cornell.edu/publications